INTRODUCTION
TO
LEGAL PRACTICE

VOLUME 2

AUSTRALIA
The Law Book Company
Brisbane ● Sydney ● Melbourne ● Perth

CANADA
Carswell
Ottawa ● Toronto ● Calgary ● Montreal ● Vancouver

Agents:
Steimatzky's Agency Ltd., Tel Aviv;
N.M. Tripathi (Private) Ltd., Bombay;
Eastern Law House (Private) Ltd., Calcutta;
M.P.P. House, Bangalore;
Universal Book Traders, Delhi;
Aditya Books, Delhi;
MacMillan Shuppan KK, Tokyo;
Pakistan Law House, Karachi, Lahore

INTRODUCTION TO LEGAL PRACTICE

VOLUME 2

Fourth Edition

Edited by

CRAIG OSBORNE, B.A., M.A. (Econ.)
Solicitor,
Senior Lecturer in Law, Manchester Metropolitan University

Published in Association with
The Institute of Legal Executives

LONDON
SWEET & MAXWELL
1993

First Edition 1983
Second Impression 1984
Second Edition 1987
Second Impression 1988
Third Edition 1991
Fourth Edition 1993

Published in 1993 by
Sweet & Maxwell Limited of
South Quay Plaza, 183 Marsh Wall, London E14 9FT
Computerset by Promenade Graphics Ltd., Cheltenham
and printed in England by Clays Ltd., St Ives plc.

A CIP catalogue record
for this book is available
from the British Library

ISBN: 0–421–50190–1

PREFACE TO FOURTH EDITION

The need to keep up to date with changes in the Law and Practice has led to the need to prepare a fourth edition for publication.

I am accordingly most grateful to my colleagues, all senior lecturers at Manchester Metropolitan University who assisted by updating and substantially re-writing four of the chapters. The chapter on Succession and Probate, and that on Businesses were completely re-written by David Tarrant LL.B., Solicitor; the chapter on Tribunals Administrative Proceedings and Arbitration was re-written by Timothy Grout LL.B., Barrister; and that on Family Practice by Lyn Jones LL.B., Solicitor. I re-wrote the chapter on High Court Proceedings.

The text was largely re-written in January/February 1993 but it has been possible to include some very minor amendments at the stage of galley proof. The text is believed to be up to date as at May 1993. As is inevitable now by the time the book comes out it will be slightly out of date, particularly in the section on Family Practice. Lyn Jones has tried admirably to deal with the many uncertainties surrounding the practice and procedures to be followed under the Child Support Act 1991 and to give sufficient detail in the text to provide a useful commentary on the Act without becoming snowed under with the precise details of computations to be made under it which in any event are subject to formulae which are far from definite at the time of writing.

I would like to thank the Education Secretary of the Institute, Ian Watson for his invaluable assistance throughout the preparation of this edition for publication and of the editorial staff of Sweet & Maxwell Ltd.

May 1993

Craig Osborne

PREFACE TO FIRST EDITION

This is the second edited volume in a set of books published jointly by the Institute of Legal Executives and Sweet & Maxwell Ltd. It is prescribed reading for the second year of study for the Institute's Part 1 examination.

The aim of this work is the same as that of the first volume: "to introduce readers to the legal profession and to describe and explain much of the day-to-day work of a solicitor's office." For a further note on the form of the work readers are referred to the preface to Volume 1. We hope that the book will be read with interest and profit by those who have not yet begun a formal course of study for the Institute's examinations but who, by their reading, may be stimulated to do so. Those entirely outside the law may find something of value here in explaining the mysteries of legal practice.

Many people have helped in the production of this book. In particular we wish to mention the assistance of the members and staff of the Institute of Legal Executives, notably the Chairman of the Education Committee, Peter Stevens, F. Inst. L. Ex., the Secretary-General, Dennis Hill, LL.M., and the Education Officer, Ian Watson, B.A. (Hons.) Law. The joint publishers Sweet & Maxwell Ltd. have been of inestimable service to us. The Editorial Staff have come to expect our arrival at any hour and have efficiently arranged for a complex production process (given the quantity of forms reproduced) to be completed smoothly. They have also been responsible for the preparation of the Index.

April 1983

Charles Blake
Grenfell Huddy

ACKNOWLEDGEMENTS

The editor and publishers wish to thank the following for granting kind permission to reproduce forms included in this volume:

The Controller of H.M.S.O. (for forms which are Crown Copyright)
The Law Society
The Legal Aid Board
The Lord Chancellor's Department
The Solicitors' Law Stationery Society Ltd.

CONTENTS

TABLE OF CASES

TABLE OF RULES OF THE SUPREME COURT

TABLE OF STATUTES

TABLE OF STATUTORY INSTRUMENTS

CHAPTER 1

SUCCESSION

THE law of succession is concerned with the way in which a person's property passes on his death to those thereafter entitled to it. The deceased may have expressed his own wishes in this respect—for example, in his will. Normally to be valid a will must be in writing and comply with certain formalities required by the Wills Act 1837. If a person dies without leaving a valid will, the rules of intestate succession govern the devolution of the deceased's property. Sometimes a partial intestacy arises—*i.e.* where the deceased has effectively disposed by will of some, but not all, of the beneficial interests in his property. In such a case the intestacy rules will take effect subject to the provisions of the will.

In any event, certain procedural steps will be necessary in practice to enable the deceased's property to be transmitted. It is the purpose of this chapter to explore in outline these procedures by reference to two cases dealt with by the Probate Department in the firm of Messrs. Makepiece and Streiff. Mr. Amity is the partner who oversees the work of this Department, the day-to-day running of which is entrusted to an experienced Legal Executive, Mr. Oliver De'Ath with the assistance of a trainee Legal Executive, William. The two cases to be considered are fairly typical of many dealt with in solicitors' offices: no attempt is made to deal with all the possible complications or variations which might be encountered, though some of the more common of these may be mentioned in passing.

Inheritance Tax is an important matter to be considered in relation to an estate. The completion of the two main accounts to be lodged with the Revenue in this connection (IHT FORMS 200 and 202) will be explained. An explanation of the provisions of Inheritance Tax will not be given save to the extent necessary for understanding the completion of the necessary Inland Revenue Accounts.

One of the case studies to be examined later in the chapter is concerned with obtaining a grant of probate of the will of Mr. Willmade. The first section, however, considers some of the issues involved in the drafting of wills, illustrated by Mr. Amity's approach to Mr. Willmade's case.

PREPARING A WILL

The preparation of wills is a matter involving considerable skill and not something to be lightly undertaken by those lacking the necessary experience and expertise. The will draftsman can turn to numerous precedents to help him with the precise wording of the various clauses to be included in the will; but the exercise involves much more than the slavish copying of various formulae—indeed that would be a recipe for disaster, sooner or later.

The solicitor preparing a will for a client has a duty to ensure two things. First, that the will is valid and secondly, that it accurately expresses the testator's wishes.

Validity

There are essentially three issues involved in relation to the first matter:

1. The testator must have the necessary capacity. Normally, this means that he must be aged 18 or over, and must understand the nature of his act and its effects; the extent of his property; and any moral claims he ought to consider. In practice, in the vast majority of cases, this fundamental requirement is not likely to be seriously in issue. Where there is a doubt as to the testator's mental capacity—*e.g.* where the testator is seriously ill or there is a history of mental ill-health—it is desirable that a medical practitioner examine the testator and also be asked to witness the will. If he/she is unwilling to act as a witness the medical practitioner should be asked to make a declaration as to the mental capacity of the testator.

2. The testator must have the necessary intention to make the will. This involves the intention not only to make a will but also the particular will he executes. He must, therefore, know and approve its contents. In practice this will normally be presumed from the fact that the testator had capacity and has executed the will—though special care will be necessary if the testator is blind or illiterate to show the necessary knowledge and approval: this is usually done by adapting the attestation clause to evidence the fact that the will was read over to the testator in the presence of witnesses and that he signified his approval. The presumption referred to above, however, will not be made where there are "suspicious circumstances," *e.g.* where the will substantially benefits the person who prepared it. Here, the person seeking to prove the will must remove the suspicion if the will is to be admitted to probate.

3. The formalities in the Wills Act 1837 must be observed. There are two matters to be considered here:

(a) *Section 9*. This section, in effect, requires that a will (to be valid under English law) must normally be in writing; be signed by the testator (or by someone else in his presence and at his direction) and have such signature made or acknowledged in the presence of two or more witnesses present at the same time. It must appear that the testator intended by his signature to give effect to the will. The witnesses must then attest and sign the will (or acknowledge their signatures) in the testator's presence, though not necessarily in the presence of each other.

The section specifically provides that no form of attestation is necessary. However, it is usual, and highly desirable, to include an attestation clause purporting to show compliance with the requirements of section 9, so that a presumption of due execution is raised. In the absence of such a clause, an affidavit of due execution, sworn by the witnesses, will normally be required to enable the will to be admitted to probate; this may present particular difficulties, for example, where the witnesses are dead or cannot be traced.

(b) *Witnesses and Section 15*. Witnesses must possess the capacity to act as such. Because an attesting witness must be capable of physical and mental presence when the testator signs the will (or acknowledges his signature) blind persons and persons of unsound mind cannot be competent witnesses.

In principle a beneficiary or executor is a competent witness. However Section 15, Wills Act 1837 deprives an attesting witness or his/her spouse of any benefit under the will, albeit that the attestation remains valid; therefore a beneficiary or his/her spouse should not witness a will. "Benefit" includes the benefit of a charging clause given to an executor: it is normal to include such a clause in a will appointing a professional executor, for example, a solicitor. In such a case, the solicitor/executor should not act as a witness (though strictly competent to do so); nor should any of his partners. The effect of section 15 has been modified by the Wills Act 1968, so that now a witness/beneficiary will not be deprived of his/her gift provided there are at least two other non-beneficiary witnesses signing as such under section 9.

Testator's intention

It is the responsibility of the solicitor preparing the will to ensure that it accurately expresses the testator's wishes. This can only be done by taking full instructions from the client himself (and not, *e.g.* from the bank manager introducing his customer as a client) and giving guidance and advice on a number of matters.

Reasons for making a will

It is almost always sound advice to a client that he/she should make a will for the following general reasons:

1. The testator can control the disposition of his property on death rather than relying upon the intestacy rules, the effect of which are arbitrary.
2. A will may be drawn to minimise the charge to tax on the testator's death and/or on the subsequent death of his spouse.
3. The testator may select his own personal representatives and trustees.
4. Additional administrative powers for personal representatives and trustees may be included to facilitate administration of the estate.
5. Guardians may be appointed for the testator's infant children.
6. A will allows the testator to demonstrate his generosity.

Instructions for the preparation of the will

Almost invariably, obtaining the client's instructions for the preparation of a will involves an interview with the client—even if the client has set out his wishes in apparently clear terms in a letter to his solicitor. There may be, for example, implications in what he proposes which the client does not appreciate; he may not realise that there are alternative and possibly more advantageous ways of achieving what he has in mind; and there may be other important issues which the client should be invited to consider. At the end of the day the will prepared must, of course, be the client's will, but in practice he will often rely considerably upon his solicitor's advice and guidance to achieve the most appropriate will to suit his particular circumstances.

It would be inappropriate here to attempt to do more than outline some of the issues and considerations involved in the drafting of a will. This will be done by reference to the case of a client of Messrs. Makepiece and Streiff, who asks Mr. Amity to prepare for him a will under which the principal beneficiaries are to be his wife and children—a common enough situation met with in any solicitor's practice.

THE MAKING OF A WILL

Mr. Willmade is an existing client of the firm and Mr. Amity acted for him when he and his wife purchased their present home some five years ago. Like many firms, Messrs. Makepiece have a simple pro forma upon which those members of the firm involved in will drafting (mainly Mr. Amity and Mr. De'Ath) may summarise the instructions upon which the draft will is to be based. The use of a form such as this can also serve as a reminder to those less experienced than, say, Mr. Amity of the main considerations upon which instructions and advice may be required; and it may also double as a "diary note" for the purpose of recording the time spent on the matter.

The Instruction Sheet completed by Mr. Amity in this case is set out below.

INSTRUCTIONS FOR WILL

Taken by: CA   **Date:** 8/11/93   **Engaged:** 30 mins.

CLIENT: IVAN WILLMADE   **Existing will?** None
1 Cherry Close
Barchester BR2 7AX

Age: 45   **Occupation:** Computer Salesman

Family & Dependants: Wife: Sylvia Willmade (40)
Children: Brenda Joy Willmade (19) Medical
Student
Christopher Robin Willmade (16) still
at school
Other Dependants: none

Present Estate (A):   House: Jointly with SW worth
(net of mortgage) £80,000
IW's share   £ 40,000
Shares: XYZ PLC   £ 5,000

	Personal Effects:		
	Incl. grandfather clock (£2,000)		
	Car (£5,000)	£	9,000
	Premium savings bonds	£	1,000
	Building Society A/c		
	(jointly with SW		
	£20,000)	IW's share	£ 10,000
	Insurance Policies		£ 50,000

Lifetime Gifts (B): None made or contemplated

Expectations (C): None

Total (A+B+C) £115,000

Spouse's Estate:

Share of net value of house	£40,000
Other assets	£ 5,000
	£45,000

Executors: C. Amity—charging clause
S. Willmade—if predeceases, Brenda Joy Willmade

SPECIFIC GIFTS: B. J. Willmade—XYZ Shares
(free of tax/expenses) C. R. Willmade—grandfather clock
yes   yes

PECUNIARY LEGACIES:
(free of tax) Barset Dogs Home   —£1,000
yes C. R. Willmade   —£2,000

RESIDUE: Sylvia Willmade provided she survives for 30 days otherwise to surviving children at 18 equally.
Substitutional gift to grandchildren.

ADMINISTRATIVE PROVISIONS: Extend powers of maintenance, advancement, investment, insurance Include Appropriation clause Authority to accept receipt from infant's parent or guardian or infant himself if 16.

OTHER MATTERS: None (guardianship discussed, but no appointment required).

Form of instructions for will

The first noteworthy point is Mr. Amity's confirmation that Mr. Willmade does not already have a will. Had this been the case, it might have been possible to give effect to his instructions by a codicil to his existing will. To be valid a codicil must be executed in the same manner as a will.

Mr. Amity has then noted brief details of Mr. Willmade's family, whose needs and resources will doubtless be an important factor influencing Mr. Willmade's ultimate instructions. Apart from his wife and children, there are no other dependants. This is important to establish since there might otherwise be a possibility of a claim under the Inheritance (Provision for Family and Dependants) Act 1975. It will also be important to consider this possibility in the event of a testator giving "unusual" instructions—for instance, omitting his wife and/or children from the benefits conferred by his will.

A most important matter is to obtain some idea of the present constitution and value of the testator's estate. Obviously, both in value and content, it may have significantly altered by the time of the client's death, but at least some indication of the potential Inheritance Tax liability can be obtained—and, where appropriate, consideration be given to some tax planning measures (*e.g.* lifetime gifts) in an attempt to mitigate the impact of that tax.

Taxation aspects

For tax purposes, it is also important to ascertain whether there have been any lifetime gifts, or whether any may be contemplated or advised. In the main, lifetime gifts are not subject to Inheritance Tax: however, they may become chargeable if the donor dies within seven years of the gift. Generally, the consideration of the contents of a client's will affords a good opportunity to consider various financial and tax planning matters.

Clearly, in all this, the size of a client's estate is a critical factor. The advice given—both generally and in drafting the will—to the client worth £500,000 will be very different from that given to one whose estate is £50,000. And to obtain the fullest possible picture, it is obviously helpful to have in mind any expected increases in the present estate. Thus, for example, the client may stand to inherit a sizeable fortune on the death of his father. Also—and especially since transfers between spouses are normally wholly exempt from Inheritance Tax—it will be helpful to have some idea of the size of the estate of the client's spouse. He or she should perhaps also be advised to make a will if this has not already been done.

Drafting the will

Turning to the contents of the will itself, Mr. Amity has discussed with his client the choice of executors, and has established that he wishes Mr. Amity and Sylvia Willmade to act, with the substitution of his daughter Brenda in the event of Mrs. Willmade predeceasing him. Mr. Amity, as a professional man, wants to be able to charge for his services and so has secured Mr. Willmade's instructions to include a charging clause; without this, Mr. Amity could not charge a fee for the work undertaken as executor.

Choice of executors

The client may well have settled views on the question, but the choice of executors is a matter upon which frequently a solicitor's advice will be sought. The ultimate choice is, of course, the client's and will depend upon a number of factors such as the size and nature of the estate and the dispositions of it contemplated; the availability and suitability of relations and/or friends who might be willing to act. Generally it is sensible to consider appointing at least two individuals, especially where the will envisages a trust arising, when it will be convenient—and the usual practice—to appoint the same persons both executors and trustees. Normally any professional appointee will wish to charge for his services; so too will a trust corporation or a bank, which will require appointment upon its standard terms and conditions. It is worth noting in this respect that such an institution will employ a solicitor to obtain the grant, whose charges will have to be met in addition to the bank's own fees. There is no reason why a beneficiary should not act—indeed frequently a sole beneficiary is also appointed sole executor. However, it would normally be unwise to appoint one of several beneficiaries to act alone because of the danger that a conflict of interest would arise.

Specific gifts

Mr. Willmade has decided to make a number of specific and pecuniary legacies. An important preliminary matter to be determined is whether or not these are to be "free of Inheritance Tax." Unless the will otherwise provides, the tax will in most cases be borne by the estate (usually by the residue) rather than by the beneficiary. In all cases, however, it is good practice to establish the testator's wishes and provide accordingly. A similar issue arises in relation to specific legacies. Normally, the expenses incurred in the upkeep and preservation of the subject-matter of a specific gift, and of transfer to the legatee must, in the absence of provision in the will, be borne by the beneficiary entitled. Again, instructions should be sought and the appropriate action taken.

The specific gift of the shares proposed by Mr. Willmade will be *adeemed* (*i.e.* will fail) if he does not own any such shares on his death. It will normally be appropriate to draft the clause giving effect to such a gift to deal with possible amalgamations, takeovers, etc., so as to avoid difficulties that might otherwise arise. The doctrine of ademption will, of course, also apply to the other specific gift—of the grandfather clock—if this no longer forms part of Mr. Willmade's estate on his death.

As regards the gift to the charity—the Barset Dogs Home—a number of points arise. It is important to check that the institution concerned does indeed exist and is correctly named. Secondly, it is prudent to include provision for possible changes—*e.g.* change of name, amalgamation, dissolution. Thirdly, the clause should specify the manner in which the executors may obtain a valid receipt. Finally, its charitable status must be confirmed by reference to the Register of Charities.

Providing for the family

Where, as here, the testator has a wife and children it is likely that he will wish the bulk of his estate to pass to one or more of them. There are a variety of possibilities, and it is a question of establishing the testator's priorities. It is important to remember that property passing under the will from one spouse to the other will be exempt from Inheritance Tax. Thus property passing from, say, husband to wife will not suffer tax on the husband's death; but that property is now part of the wife's estate and taxable as such on her death. This could cause problems if she has a considerable estate of her own; because of the exemptions and reliefs available to individual transferors and the availability of nil rate bands, two estates of £100,000 each will bear less tax that one estate of £200,000. This problem could be aggravated if, for instance, the wife were to die very shortly after the husband. Hence it is usual to include "survivorship clauses" to prevent this "bunching" of estates.

Basically, the sort of provisions normally considered in these cases fall into the following categories:

(a) An absolute gift to the surviving spouse with a substitutional gift to the children in the event of the spouse predeceasing or not surviving for the survivorship period. As already explained, there will be no Inheritance Tax payable on the death of the testator, but control of the ultimate destination of the testator's estate is transferred to the spouse if he/she survives. This is the choice of most testators because it ensures maximum provision for the surviving spouse.

(b) A life interest to the surviving spouse with remainder to the children. Here the surviving spouse will be treated for tax purposes as (in effect) owning the property and so the spouse exemption will apply and no Inheritance Tax will be payable on the death of the first spouse. However, in reality, the remaining spouse is only entitled to the income from the property and it may well be that such a course does not provide adequately for the needs of *that* spouse. But the testator does have control over the ultimate destination of the estate.

(c) Legacy to children with residue to surviving spouse. This "compromise" position can have certain tax advantages. However, this course of action should only be seriously contemplated where the testator is satisfied that there is adequate provision for the spouse.

It will perhaps now be beginning to be apparent why it is important to consider the overall estates of both spouses—and, indeed, in practice desirable for both spouses to make wills. However, it is important to stress that the desirability of saving some tax should not be the only concern; nor indeed necessarily even the main concern in most cases. The overall needs and resources of the various members of his family and the testator's priorities in relation thereto are of paramount importance.

A number of questions arise when considering gifts to children. For example:

(a) *Is the gift to be vested or contingent?*

If the gift is absolute (in effect, without precondition) then it will vest on the testator's death and (unless there is some prior interest, *e.g.* a life interest to the spouse) the child can claim the property on attaining the age of 18. Before that time, the child cannot normally give a valid receipt; but as the gift is vested, the property could pass as part of the child's estate in the event of his death under the age of 18. This, however, is not the case with a contingent gift (*e.g.* to A provided he attains the age of 18). Here the gift will not vest until the contingency is fulfilled. It may well be that a testator will wish to postpone a child's enjoyment of a gift until he attains, say, 21 or perhaps even 25. In such cases the gift will be expressed to be contingent upon attaining the required age; problems can, however, arise if the testator wishes to delay vesting of the beneficiary's interest for too long.

(b) *The possibility of the testator having more children*

If the testator names his children individually as beneficiaries, any children born after the date of the will are excluded from benefit. The best way to overcome this problem is to make a "class gift"—"to my children" without actually naming them.

(c) *The position if any children predecease the testator*

Normally, if a beneficiary predeceases the testator, the gift lapses. However, a gift to a child or remoter issue (*e.g.* a grandchild) of the testator may be saved from lapse under section 33 of the Wills Act 1837 if the child or issue concerned is survived in turn by issue who survive the testator, in which case the gift takes effect to the surviving issue. The section applies unless there is a contrary intention in the will, and can apply to class gifts. However, it is important to ascertain the client's wishes on this point, and it is good practice to include a specific substitution clause where required rather than rely upon the statute.

Other matters

Having dealt with the various dispositions of the testator's estate, the will should then deal with a number of administrative matters, not all of which will necessarily be appropriate to all cases. In particular, these may include:

(a) *Investment*

Under the general law, trustees are under a duty to invest capital, but only in authorised investments. Such authority may derive from statute (in particular the Trustee Investments Act 1961) or from the will itself. The statutory powers are in practice restrictive. It is usually considered expedient to widen the statutory powers by express provision in the will; a type of clause in common use (the so-called "beneficial owner" clause) seeks to confer the widest possible discretion upon trustees. If it is desired that estate funds could be made available to purchase a home for any beneficiary, this should be specifically provided for: the purchase of a residence for a beneficiary is not an investment as such.

(b) *Insurance*

Strange as it may seem, trustees and personal representatives are not generally under any duty to insure the trust or estate property. Section 19 of the Trustee Act 1925 gives them a power to insure, but only against loss or damage by fire, and only up to an amount not exceeding three-quarters of the value of the property. However, this does not apply where the beneficiaries are of full age and capacity and are absolutely entitled to the property. Further, it would nowadays generally be accepted that it would be more appropriate to have comprehensive cover for the full value of the property. Provision to this effect should therefore be incorporated into the will.

(c) *Appropriation*

Section 41 of the Administration of Estates Act 1925 allows personal representatives to appropriate assets in or towards satisfaction of any legacy or any share or interest in an estate—so long as no specific gift is thereby prejudiced and the consent required by the section is given. Commonly a will includes a provision for appropriation without consent, to facilitate the administration of the estate. (Since the Finance Act 1985, the inclusion of such a clause no longer effects any significant stamp duty saving).

(d) *Business*

On the death of the proprietor of a business his personal representatives generally do not have authority to carry on the business except with a view to the proper realisation of his estate—*e.g.* to enable the business to be sold as a going concern. Normally, where the deceased's assets include a business it will be advantageous for his will to contain a provision directing or empowering his personal representatives to carry on the business for as long as they see fit. Ideally, the clause should also specify what other assets in the estate may be used for this purpose—otherwise only those in such use at the date of death can be employed. There should also be included a provision conferring indemnity on the personal representatives in respect of liabilities incurred in carrying on the business and the power to employ a manager and staff to run the business.

(e) *Maintenance*

Section 31 of the Trustee Act 1925 enables trustees holding property for a minor, whether he has a vested or contingent interest, to use income from the property (unless someone else is in the meantime entitled to it) for his maintenance, education and benefit.

Any income not so used must be accumulated—*i.e.* invested to produce income which can, in turn, be used for maintenance in future years.

It will, in practice, normally be expedient to consider extending the statutory power to give a much wider discretion.

These extensions can be effected by drafting in full a "maintenance clause" to suit the particular requirements of the case. In practice, however, this may be more succinctly and conveniently achieved by reference to the terms of the section itself—*e.g.* by directing that "the terms 'infant' and 'infancy' used in the section shall be construed and take effect as if the Family Law Reform Act 1969 had not been enacted." (This Act substituted 18 for 21 as the age of majority).

(f) *Advancement*

Section 32 of the Trustee Act 1925 allows trustees to advance capital (as opposed to income, the concern of section 31) to a beneficiary before the time at which he may become entitled to the trust fund. The section confers a discretion to apply capital for the "advancement or benefit" of a beneficiary up to one-half of his vested or presumptive share. If, having been advanced, the beneficiary in due course becomes absolutely entitled to the property, he must bring into account the advance payment to him.

In practice, the statutory power is often extended to permit advancement of the whole of the beneficiary's share.

(g) *Receipts*

Whenever a will contemplates the possibility of a payment of income or capital to an infant, it will usually assist the administration of the estate in due course to permit such payment to be made to the infant's parent or guardian, and to provide that their receipt shall operate as a complete discharge to the trustees. Usually, the clause will also authorise payment direct to the infant personally if of the age of (say) 16.

(h) *Guardians*

A testator often wishes to specify in his will his choice of guardian for his infant children after his death, especially in the event of his spouse having predeceased him. The court has an overriding jurisdiction on this issue, but in practice will only become involved in the event of some unusual circumstance. It is as well—as with the choice of executor—to check that the person nominated is, in fact, willing to act.

The above "catalogue" does not purport by any means to contain an exhaustive list of administrative provisions which might be appropriately considered in a given case. However, it does illustrate some of the more important matters which frequently arise in practice. Due consideration of these issues and the careful drafting of appropriate provisions can greatly facilitate the efficient administration of the estate in due course.

Having discussed and considered with his client all the appropriate matters, Mr. Amity is now able to draft Mr. Willmade's will for his approval. He sends a copy of the draft to Mr. Willmade for this purpose, and on receipt of his client's confirmation that it meets his wishes, Mr. Amity arranges for a copy to be engrossed ready for signature.

WILL

I IVAN WILLMADE of 1 Cherry Close Barchester BR2 7AX, Computer Salesman hereby revoke all wills and testamentary dispositions at any time heretofore made by me and declare this to be my last will.

Executors
and
Trustees

1. I APPOINT CLEMENT AMITY of Bank Chambers Barchester BR1 2YZ, Solicitor and my wife SYLVIA WILLMADE of 1 Cherry Close Barchester aforesaid (but if my said wife shall have predeceased me then and only then my daughter BRENDA JOY WILLMADE of the same address) to be the Executors and Trustees of this my Will and they or the survivor of them or other the Executors and Trustees for the time being of this my Will or any Codicil hereto are hereinafter called "my Trustees" AND I DECLARE that the said

Charging
Clause

Clement Amity or any of my Trustees being a Solicitor or other person engaged in any profession or business shall be entitled to charge and be paid all usual professional or other charges for business done services rendered or time spent by him or his firm in the administration of my estate or the trusts hereof including acts which a trustee not engaged in any profession or business could have done personally.

2. I GIVE the following specific legacies free of tax and costs of transfer

Specific
Legacies

(a) my ordinary shares in XYZ PLC to my said daughter Brenda Joy Willmade absolutely AND I DECLARE that any charge or lien which may be subsisting upon the said shares at my death shall be satisfied out of my residuary estate AND I FURTHER DECLARE that if at my death those shares shall by virtue of any amalgamation reconstruction or rearrangement of capital of the company or sale of the company's business be represented by a different capital holding whether in the same company or in any other company to which at my death I am entitled then this gift shall take effect as if it had been a gift of the capital holding or capital holdings resulting from such amalgamation reconstruction or rearrangement of capital or sale

(b) my grandfather clock to my son Christopher Robin Willmade of 1 Cherry Close Barchester aforesaid absolutely.

3. I GIVE the following pecuniary legacies free of tax

Pecuniary
Legacies

(a) to the Barset Dogs Home of 35 Conduit Road Barchester aforesaid the sum of £1000 absolutely AND I DECLARE that the receipt of the person who professes to be the Secretary Treasurer or other proper officer for the time being of the said charity shall be a sufficient discharge to my Trustees who shall not be obliged to see as to the application thereof AND I FURTHER DECLARE that if the said charity has changed its name or amalgamated with or transferred its assets to any other body then my Trustees shall give effect to the gift as if it had been made (as the case might be) to the body in its changed name or the body which results from such amalgamation or to which the transfer has been made

(b) to my said son Christopher Robin Willmade the sum of £2000 absolutely.

4. <u>I DEVISE AND BEQUEATH</u> the residue of my estate both real and personal wheresoever and whatsoever of which I shall be possessed or entitled at the date of my death or over which I shall have any power of appointment or disposition by will <u>UNTO</u> my Trustees upon trust to sell call in and convert the same into money (with power to postpone such sale calling in and conversion as my Trustees shall in their absolute discretion think fit without being responsible for any consequent loss) and after payment thereout of my debts funeral and testamentary expenses and any Inheritance Tax payable on my death <u>UPON TRUST</u> for my said wife Sylvia Willmade provided she shall survive me for a period of 30 days absolutely <u>PROVIDED THAT</u> if my said wife shall have predeceased me or fail to survive me for the period aforesaid or for any other reason the gift to her shall fail then <u>UPON TRUST</u> for such of my children who shall survive me and attain the age of 18 years and if more than one in equal shares absolutely <u>PROVIDED ALWAYS</u> that if any child of mine shall die in my lifetime or having survived me fail to attain a vested interest hereunder leaving a child or children who survive me and attain the age of 18 years such grandchild of mine shall take by substitution and if more than one in equal shares the share of my residuary estate which his her or their parent would have taken if he or she had survived me and attained a vested interest hereunder.

5. <u>MONIES</u> requiring to be invested under the trusts hereof may at the discretion of my Trustees be applied or invested in the purchase of or at interest upon the security of such stocks funds shares securities or other investments or property of whatsoever nature and wheresoever situate and whether producing income or not (including the purchase or improvement of landed property anywhere in the world for use as a residence) and whether involving liability or not or upon such personal credit with or without security as my Trustees may in their absolute discretion think fit to the intent that my Trustees shall have the same full and unrestricted powers of investing and varying investments in all respects as if they were absolutely and beneficially entitled thereto.

6. <u>SECTION 31</u> of the Trustee Act 1925 (relating to maintenance) shall apply to the income of my residuary estate as if
(a) the words "as the Trustees shall in their absolute discretion think fit" were substituted for the words "as may in all the circumstances be reasonable" in paragraph (i) of subsection (1) thereof
(b) the proviso to subsection (1) thereof had been omitted therefrom and
(c) Trustees were empowered at any time during the minority of any of the beneficiaries on whose account income may have been accumulated under that section to apply such accumulations as if they were income arising in the then current year and as if they were applicable for the benefit of any of the others or other of the beneficiaries and not only for the benefit of the beneficiary on whose account they were made.

Margin notes:

Trust for Sale of Residue

Substitutional Gifts

Investment

Maintenance

Advancement	7. <u>SECTION</u> 32 of the Trustee Act 1925 (relating to advancement) shall apply to the capital of my residuary estate as if the words "one half of" had been omitted from proviso (a) to subsection (1) thereof and shall apply to any trust property whatsoever including land and monies or securities or proceeds of sale by statute or in equity considered as land or applicable as capital money for the purpose of the Settled Land Act 1925.
Appropriation	8. <u>MY</u> Trustees shall have the power to exercise the power of appropriation conferred by section 41 of the Administration of Estates Act 1925 without obtaining any of the consents required by that section.
Insurance	9. <u>MY</u> Trustees shall have power to insure against loss or damage by fire or from any other risk any property for the time being comprised in my residuary estate to any amount and even though a person is absolutely entitled to the property and to pay all premiums for any such insurance at their discretion out of the income or capital of my residuary estate or the property itself and so that any money received under any such insurance shall be applicable as if it were proceeds of sale of the property insured.
Receipts	10. <u>IN</u> any case where they have an obligation or discretion under the provisions of this my will or under the general law to pay income or capital to or for the benefit of any infant my Trustees may discharge that obligation or exercise that discretion if they think fit by making payment either to a parent or guardian of the infant or to the infant personally if of the age of 16 at least and so that their respective receipts shall be a full discharge to my Trustees who shall not be required to see to the application of any income or capital so paid.
Attestation Clause	<u>IN WITNESS</u> whereof I have hereunto set my hand this 25th day of November 1993 　　　SIGNED by the said <u>IVAN WILLMADE</u> as his last will in our joint presence and then by us jointly in his presence.

O. De'Ath
Legal Executive with
Messrs. Makepiece & Streiff
Solicitors
Bank Chambers
Barchester

William Doom
Trainee Legal Executive with
Messrs. Makepiece & Streiff
Solicitors
Bank Chambers
Barchester

Mr. Willmade is then asked to call at the offices of Messrs. Makepiece & Streiff to sign his will; Mr. Amity asks Mr. De'Ath and William to act as witnesses, and they all sign in the presence of each other as indicated in the copy will.

Mr. Willmade asks Mr. Amity to hold the original of his will in the firm's strongroom, and Mr. Amity completes two copies of the will—one for his file (this may prove valuable should the original be lost—hopefully an unlikely event here!) and one for Mr. Willmade to keep. Mr. Amity's parting advice to his client is to keep his will "under review" over the years as his circumstances and those of his family change.

Intestacy

A total intestacy arises where the deceased dies without having disposed of any of his property by a valid will. A partial intestacy arises where the deceased has left a valid will but it fails to dispose of all his estate. This occurs, *e.g.* where the will contains no residuary gift or the gift of residue has failed wholly or in part because a residuary beneficiary has died before the testator and there is no effective substitutional gift in the will.

The deceased's property which is not disposed of by a will, *i.e.* that "passing on intestacy," is held on statutory trusts and devolves according to the intestacy rules which lay down an arbitrary order of entitlement as follows:

(a) *The Surviving spouse*

If the deceased leaves one then the spouse's entitlement depends upon whether and if so which relevant relatives also survive the intestate.

If there is/are also surviving *issue* of the deceased then the spouse is entitled to:

(i) Personal Chattels as defined by section 55(1)(x) of the Administration of Estates Act 1925.
(ii) A so-called statutory legacy of £75,000.
(iii) A life interest, *i.e.* the right to income for life, in one half of residue.

The spouse also has, subject to conditions, special rights to capitalise the life interest and to take the matrimonial home in total or partial satisfaction of his/her entitlement under the intestacy rules.
The rest of the estate is held on trust for the intestate's issue.

Where there is no issue surviving the deceased but there are surviving parent(s) or brothers or sisters of the whole blood or their issue then the spouse's entitlement is as follows:–

(i) Personal Chattels, as before.
(ii) A statutory legacy of £125,000.
(iii) One half or residue *absolutely* (not merely for life).

The parent(s) take the rest in equal shares, or if none, the brothers and sisters or their issue take it equally.

If there are no issue, parents or brothers or sisters of the whole blood or their issue then the surviving spouse takes *all* the property passing under the intestacy absolutely.

(b) *Other Relatives*

Where the deceased left no spouse surviving him then the property passing under the intestacy devolves according to the following order of entitlement:

(i) Children and issue of any child who predeceased the intestate, if none

(ii) Parents, if none
(iii) Brothers and sisters of the whole blood and issue of any who predeceased the intestate, if none
(iv) Brothers and sisters of the half blood and issue of any who
predeceased the intestate, if none
(v) Grandparents, if none
(vi) Uncles and Aunts of the whole blood and issue of any who predeceased the intestate, if none
(vii) Uncles and Aunts of the half blood and issue of any who predeceased the intestate, if none
(viii) The Crown.

The above arbitrary order of entitlement demonstrates a very good
general reason why it is always in a client's interest to make a will and
thereby exercise control over the ultimate destination of his estate.

PROBATE PRACTICE

Probate jurisdiction

The word "probate" is used by lawyers in a wide and a narrow sense. In
the former (such as in the expressions "probate jurisdiction" or "probate practice") it refers to the whole jurisdiction or practice concerned
with obtaining grants of representation to deal with the estates of
deceased persons; in the latter (as in the expression "Grant of Probate")
it is used to denote a particular type of grant, issued only to the executors duly appointed by a will or codicil.

Probate jurisdiction is largely vested in the High Court, and is traditionally divided into two categories:

(a) *Contentious business—sometimes termed "solemn form" business*

In the High Court, such business is assigned to the Chancery Division,
where action is commenced by the issue of a writ. In the main, actions
will be concerned with one or more of the following issues:

(i) the validity of an alleged will. If the court pronounces for its validity the will is said to be proved "in solemn form."
(ii) the validity of a claimant's entitlement to a grant (*e.g.* a dispute as
to whether or not he or she is the child of a deceased intestate).
(iii) the revocation of previous grants (*e.g.* because a will or a later
will is found).

The judge of a county court may exercise the jurisdiction of the High
Court in respect of a contentious probate matter, provided he has jurisdiction in the deceased's place of abode and the deceased's estate (after
deducting funeral expenses, debts and incumbrances) does not exceed
the prescribed monetary limit of jurisdiction of the county court—
currently £30,000.

(b) *Non-contentious business—sometimes referred to as "common form" business*

The majority of grants are issued in this form without there being any dispute, and the jurisdiction is vested in the Family Division of the High Court. In fact, all grants are issued by this division, since once contentious business has been "terminated" by an order of the Chancery Division (or County Court) any consequent grant is a matter of non-contentious business. Most non-contentious business is dealt with in the Principal Registry of the Family Division in London or in one of the District Probate Registries around the country. The District Registries originally had a geographically limited jurisdiction, but this is no longer so. It is therefore normally possible to apply for a grant at either the Principal Registry or any District Registry, irrespective of where the deceased lived. Applications for grants may be made through solicitors who may attend at the Registry concerned for the purpose or (in most cases) apply by post. It is also possible for personal applications to be made by executors or intending administrators; such applications normally involve the applicant in at least two attendances at the Registry. Procedure in non-contentious cases is largely governed by the Non-Contentious Probate Rules 1987 as amended (hereinafter referred to as "NCPR" or "the Rules").

Necessity for grant

A grant of probate or letters of administration is generally necessary to establish the right to recover or receive any part of the deceased's estate in the United Kingdom. There are, however, a number of statutory provisions under which payment of certain sums due may be made without production of a grant; for example, sums in a Trustee Savings Bank Account, National Savings Bank Account, National Savings Certificates or Building Society Account. By virtue of the Administration of Estates (Small Payments) Act 1965 as amended the sum payable under these various provisions is in almost every case restricted to a maximum of £5,000. It should be noted also that these provisions, whilst authorising payment up to the limit, do not compel the payer to make payment without production of a grant. The provisions do not apply to banks or insurance companies, but in practice if there are few (if any) other assets, and they are satisfied that there are unlikely to be any complications, such bodies will sometimes pay out small sums, as a matter within their discretion, without production of a grant. Indeed, some banks and building societies may occasionally be persuaded, provided they are satisfied as to entitlement, to pay out sums in excess of even the normal £5,000 limit. It should perhaps be stressed that although payment may be made without a grant, Inheritance Tax liability (if any) is not also "waived," and it may well be that the payer will wish to see a certificate from the Revenue before he makes payment, indicating that either no tax is payable or that any liability has been discharged.

Quite apart from the above cases, the production of a grant may not be necessary to enable certain types of property to be dealt with. For example:

(a) *Section 11 of the Married Women's Property Act policies*

Such policies effected by the deceased are held on trust for his spouse and/or issue and therefore the policy moneys do not form part of his estate. Payment will usually be made to the trustees of the policy on production of a death certificate.

(b) *Nominated property*

A number of statutes allow the disposal of certain types of investments—*e.g.* deposits in certain Friendly Societies and Industrial and Provident Societies—by a nomination, usually in writing signed by the nominator, and delivered to the appropriate body in which the investment is made. Sometimes, but not always, the nominator's signature must be made in the presence of an attesting witness, and a statutory nomination may be made by anyone aged 16 or over. The nominee takes no interest in the nominated funds until the death of the nominator, so that the latter remains free to deal with them during his lifetime as he pleases: and if the nominee predeceases the nominator, the nomination fails. A valid nomination is unaffected by any subsequent will or codicil; however, property which is capable of being nominated may be (and in practice usually is) disposed of by will instead of using a statutory nomination. And even if the property is the subject of a nomination, it is still part of the deceased's estate for the purposes of Inheritance Tax.

(c) *Joint property*

Any property owned by the deceased and another (or others) as beneficial joint tenants passes to the joint tenant(s) by survivorship and does not devolve upon the deceased's personal representatives. No grant is, therefore, necessary to enable title to be made to such property (though the value of the deceased's share or interest therein forms part of his estate for tax purposes).

Types of grant

There are in fact three basic grants of representation which may be general or limited (*e.g.* as to the property to which the grant extends or as to its duration).
These are:

(i) Probate—granted where an executor proves a will
(ii) Letters of Administration with the will annexed—granted where some person other than an executor proves a will
(iii) Letters of Administration—granted when the deceased died wholly intestate.

Grant of probate

Entitlement to grant

A grant of probate issues only to an executor or executors who prove the deceased's will. Executors may claim entitlement as being appointed expressly in the will (*i.e.* by name or by description—*e.g.* the partners in Messrs. Makepiece & Streiff my Solicitors) or by implication (*i.e.* "according to the tenor of the will," the testator having indicated an intention that that person should act without expressly nominating him as executor—*e.g.* "I wish AB to pay all my debts"). Sometimes a testator nominates someone to appoint executors of his will after his death.

By his will a testator may appoint any number of executors, but a grant of probate cannot issue to more than four. If more than four are appointed, the grant normally is issued to the first four named with power reserved to the others to apply should a vacancy subsequently occur. Probate may be granted to a sole executor, even if a minority or life interest arises.

An infant appointed an executor cannot obtain a grant until he attains his majority, and a person who is incapable of managing his affairs by reason of mental or physical incapacity may not act or take a grant of probate whilst such incapacity continues. Executors who may be insolvent or have a criminal record are not thereby automatically disqualified, but in practice the court has power to pass over an executor and appoint someone else to act if this appears to be necessary or expedient where "special circumstances" exist.

Normally, no grant of probate will be issued within seven days of the deceased's death, though in practice it will rarely be the case that all the necessary papers could be prepared within anything like that time! There is no maximum time limit within which a grant must be obtained.

Effect of grant

An executor (whether appointed expressly or by implication) derives his authority and title from the will. The grant merely confirms his title and, indeed, is the only acceptable means of proving his right to act in a court of law. Provided the executor is of full age and capacity, the deceased's property will have vested in him on the death, and prior to the grant an executor has considerable powers enabling him to deal with the deceased's property. For instance, he may commence a court action and pay debts and legacies; he can even sell and transfer assets to the purchaser, though in some cases (*e.g.* land) he will need a grant to be able to complete the sale. In spite of this authority, however, in most cases the executor will in practice await the issue of the grant unless there is some pressing need for earlier action on his part.

Application for grant of probate

An application for a grant must be supported by:

1. An oath in the form of an affidavit sworn or affirmed by the applicant(s).
2. The will duly "marked" by the executors (*i.e.*) in practice signed by them and the Commissioner or solicitor administering the oath. Usually the original will must be lodged (sometimes with a typed copy); but if this is not available (*e.g.* because the original has been lost) it may be possible to have a copy or completed draft admitted to probate.

3. Such other affidavit evidence as the Registrar may require. In most cases this will not be necessary; where required it will often take the form of:

(a) Affidavit of due execution. If the will contains no attestation clause or a clause which appears to be deficient, or if it appears to the Registrar that there is some doubt about the execution of the will, he will require an affidavit of due execution before admitting the will to probate. This should, if possible, be from one of the attesting witnesses, or (at second best) from anyone else present when the will was executed. If no such affidavit evidence can be obtained, the Registrar may accept evidence as to the deceased's handwriting (*i.e.* that the signature on the will is in his handwriting) or of any other matter which may raise a presumption in favour of due execution. Often he will also ask for the consents of those persons who would be prejudiced if the will were admitted to probate (*i.e.* those who would be entitled on an intestacy).

(b) Affidavit of "plight and condition". Such an affidavit may be required, for instance, in the following situations:

(i) If there are marks on the will (*e.g.* pinholes or the marks left by a paper clip), the Registrar will want to be satisfied that whatever was at some time fastened was not another testamentary document (*e.g.* a codicil or a later will). However, he may not require this evidence in affidavit form if, for instance, the solicitor filing the application is able to state (in a letter filed with the application) from his own knowledge what was fastened to the will—*e.g.* other relevant papers handed to him by the executor on instructing him to act.

(ii) If there are material alterations (the Registrar has power to disregard alterations which appear to him to be of no practical importance) evidence will be required to rebut the presumption that an unattested alteration was made after the execution of the will and is, therefore, invalid. If it can be shown to have been present when the will was executed, the will as altered can be admitted to probate. Otherwise, the will is admitted to probate in its unaltered form, or with a blank if a word or words have been so obliterated as to be indecipherable by any natural means, with the intent to revoke that part of the will. If the alteration is attested, it is valid; it is good practice therefore to take pains to ensure (on execution of the will) that any alterations are initialled (full signatures are not essential) in the margin by the testator and the attesting witnesses.

(iii) If the will is torn or bears burn marks or, indeed, bears any other signs of a possible attempted revocation, the Registrar will require affidavit evidence (usually from the person finding the will) to satisfactorily account for the will's condition.

4. An Inland Revenue Account, if required, for the purposes of Inheritance Tax. No Inland Revenue Account will normally be required (unless the Revenue serve written notice requiring one within 35 days after the issue of the grant) where the following conditions are satisfied:

(a) the total gross value of the estate for tax purposes does not exceed £125,000;

(b) the estate comprises only property passing under the deceased's will or intestacy, or by nomination, or beneficially by survivorship;

(c) not more than £15,000 consists of property situated outside the United Kingdom; and

(d) the deceased died domiciled in the United Kingdom and had made no lifetime gifts chargeable to Inheritance Tax.

For the purpose of deciding whether the £125,000 limit in (a) has been exceeded, the gross value of the deceased's interest in any joint property must be taken into account.

If a grant has been obtained without delivery of an account, and it is subsequently discovered that the estate does not satisfy all these conditions, an Inland Revenue Account must then be delivered.

5. Fees. Where the net estate is sworn as not exceeding £10,000 no fee is payable; (exceeding £10,000) but not exceeding £25,000, a fixed fee of £40; (exceeding £25,000 but) not exceeding £40,000 a fixed fee of £80; (exceeding £40,000 but) not exceeding £70,000, a fixed fee of £150; (exceeding £70,000 but) not exceeding £100,000, a fixed fee of £215; (exceeding £100,000 but) not exceeding £200,000, a fixed fee of £300. Thereafter, for every additional £100,000 or fraction thereof by which the net estate exceeds £200,000, there is a further and additional fee of £50.

(In the case of personal applications, the fees are calculated differently).

It will usually in practice be helpful to have, in addition to the original grant, some office copies (which essentially have the same evidential effect as the original grant). How many will be required will depend on the nature and composition of the estate; the copies are ordered and paid for when the application for the grant is lodged.

Instructions for probate

In order to prepare the papers to lead to a grant of probate, a considerable amount of information is required, and a number of steps have to be taken. It is proposed to consider these matters in relation to the estate of Mr. Willmade, who has now—quite unexpectedly—died after a heart attack. Mr. Amity has been informed of the death by telephone, and arranges to call to see Mrs. Willmade to obtain her instructions and details of the estate. It will be recalled that the firm is holding Mr. Willmade's will in its strongroom, and Mr. Amity asks for this to be brought to him so that he may take it along with him when he goes to see Mrs. Willmade. It is not often these days that a will is actually formally "read" to the assembled relatives and (hopeful) beneficiaries, but clearly it will be necessary to have the will at hand, or at least a copy, at the initial interview.

INSTRUCTIONS FOR PROBATE

Taken by:	CA	**Date:** 4/4/94	**Engaged:** 45 mins.
DECEASED:	IVAN WILLMADE	**Date of BIRTH:** 1/12/40	
	1 Cherry Close	**Date of DEATH:** 1/4/94	
	Barchester BA2 7AX	**Occupation:** Computer Salesman	

Marital Status: M / S̶ / D̶ / W̶   **Surviving Relatives:** H̶W
                                                                    Child(ren)
                                                                    P̶a̶r̶e̶n̶t̶(s̶)

Tax District & Reference: Barchester 2. BCM / 515 / F.

Domicile: E&W / S̶ / N̶I̶ /

WILL: Dated 25/11/93—drawn by us
                       No obvious problems

EXECUTORS: CA (charging clause)
                       Sylvia Willmade (widow) (Telephone B 6789)

BENEFICIARIES:
  Specific: B. J. Willmade (daughter—over 18)   XYZ shares
                                   C. R. Willmade (son—16)   grandfather clock

  Pecuniary: Barset Dogs Home   £1,000
                                   C. R. Willmade   £2,000

  Residuary: S. W. Provided she survives 30 days, otherwise
                                   children (BJW & CRW) at 18

IHT: Lifetime Gifts   NIL

SPECIAL INSTRUCTIONS:
  1. NB Clause 10 of will re: CRW
  2. No lifetime gifts, settled property or nominations
  3. Joint property: (a) House—purchased January 1984 in joint names IW & SW. Both contributed capital, balance from mortgage. Matrimonial Home.
                        (b) Building Society A/C—opened May 1973 in joint names IW & SW. Both contributed capital and shared income.
  4. Firm's pension scheme—lump sum payment due, but under trust deed, does not form part of estate? Check.
  5. No pressing financial needs, but consider interim distribution later.

ESTATE
Assets   £

House – 1 Cherry Close, Barchester – Freehold – Jointly owned
           by IW & SW Value £120,000   IW's share   60,000
Barset Building Society – Share A/c No. 456789 –   IW & SW
Capital & interest to date of death £20,500   IW's share   10,250
XYZ Ordinary Shares (1000) SE value per share £5.50   5,500

Personal Effects: Car	£5,000	
Grandfather clock	£2,000	
Others	£2,000	9,000
Premium Savings Bonds		1,000
Insurance Policies: Eternal Life Assurance Co. Policy No. 654321		
Sum Assured £30,000 Bonus £7,750		37,750
Long Life Assurance Co. Policy No. 12345		
Sum Assured £20,000 Bonus £4,000		24,000
Barset Bank PLC – Current A/c		1,000
Salary to date of death		500
		£148,000

Liabilities		
Mortgage – Barset Building Society A/c 987654		
owing at date of death £40,000	IW's share	20,000
ACE Garages, Barchester – work done		150
Paylater Credit Card Co. – Balance due		450
Funeral A/c – E. N. Tomb & Co. Barchester		400
		£21,000

Mr. Amity takes with him an instruction sheet which he has devised upon which to record the basic information required, and which it is the firm's practice to staple to the inside of the cover of the estate's file as a "check list" to ensure that nothing is overlooked. The sheet is in two pages, on the first of which are recorded various formal details regarding the deceased, necessary for the completion of the various forms. It also records details of the will, the executors and beneficiaries and the testator's total of chargeable lifetime gifts for Inheritance Tax purposes. Under the heading "Special Instructions" Mr. Amity records any other important matters: for example, points 3 and 4 will help the firm to draft the appropriate replies to the questions on page 4 of the form IHT 202. He ascertains (and notes) that a lump sum benefit is due under Mr. Willmade's firm's pension scheme but suspects that (as in many such cases) the terms of the trust deed regulating the scheme will confer a discretion on the scheme's trustees so that this sum will not form part of the estate. He makes a note to confirm that this is indeed the case here.

On the second page, he lists the various assets and liabilities of the estate. It will be necessary to establish the respective values of these as at the date of death to enable the various forms (particularly the Inland Revenue Account) to be completed. At this stage, Mr. Amity merely lists the items involved, and the figures are added later as they are confirmed. He collects from Mrs. Willmade the share certificate, premium savings bonds, insurance policies and building society pass book, and also the copies of the death certificate which Mrs. Willmade has obtained from the Registrar of Births, Marriages and Deaths. He also takes from her the various accounts relating to the estate's liabilities, and arranges with her to let him have the funeral account when it arrives. Reasonable expenses in this connection are deductible (including those of mourning and the cost of a tombstone).

Finally, he discusses her financial position and immediate financial and practical needs. Mrs. Willmade has a part-time job and her own bank account: she also has access to the funds in the Building Society Account and so, happily, has no immediately pressing requirements. However, Mr. Amity makes a note to consider making an interim distribution at a later stage.

On his return to the office, Mr. Amity passes all the papers to Oliver De'Ath and asks him to prepare the various papers to lead the grant on the assumption that Mrs. Willmade will survive for the necessary 30 days as stipulated in the will, and to let him know when they are ready for signature. Mr. De'Ath in turn asks William to open a file, and to draft standard letters registering the death with the various institutions and asking for confirmation of the various amounts due to the estate. Some (depending on the number of death certificates available) can be sent off immediately, others being dispatched as these are returned to the office. As the information is received, the figures are noted on the instruction sheet attached to the front file cover: in this way, when completed, the figures to be included in the Inland Revenue Account and the other information necessary to complete the forms will be conveniently to hand. William is also asked to draft letters to the various creditors, indicating that the respective accounts have been handed to the firm with instructions to settle in due course as funds become available.

In the meantime, Mr. De'Ath drafts a letter informing the Barset Dogs Home of the legacy left by Mr. Willmade and that, subject to the will being admitted to probate, the executors will endeavour to send a cheque in settlement as soon as there are funds available. He decides that similar letters are not necessary in the case of the other legatees (the deceased's children). It will be necessary to obtain a valuation of the house and Mr. Willmade's personal effects, and Mr. De'Ath asks Messrs. Sellars, Wright, Quick to provide this. A valuation of the shares is also needed; as there is only one holding, Mr. De'Ath decides not to instruct stockbrokers to do this for him, but to check himself the valuation for the date of death from the stock exchange list. Again, as all this information is obtained, it is entered on the instruction sheet. At a fairly early stage Mr. De'Ath also organises the insertion in the *London Gazette* and the local Barset newspaper of the "statutory advertisements" for creditors and claimants, giving the necessary minimum notice of two months in which particulars should be delivered as laid down in section 27 of the Trustee Act 1925. The purpose of these advertisements is to obtain for the executors the protection afforded by compliance with the provisions of that section—namely that (provided the distribution of the estate is not made until after the time limit has expired) the executors will be protected against any claims of creditors or beneficiaries of which they had no notice.

In due course, all the information required to enable the papers to be completed is available. In this case, there being no problems requiring affidavit evidence of any description it will be necessary to complete an oath of executors and an Inland Revenue Form IHT 202. The latter is necessary because Mr. Willmade's gross estate exceeds the limit of £125,000 prescribed by the excepted estate provisions.

Oath for executors

This is, in one sense, the most important of the papers to be prepared, in that it contains the evidence required to establish the executors' title to the grant. In practice, it must be carefully prepared, and any erasures avoided if possible! All alterations and deletions should be initialled by the Commissioner or solicitor administering the oath. If the executors are to affirm (rather than swear) then the appropriate amendments must be made in the body of the form (marginal note 3) and to the jurat at the bottom of the page.

In most cases the completion of the oath will not present many problems. In the event of any difficulty, the Probate Registry will be prepared to settle the terms of the oath on payment of the prescribed fee. More informally, the Registry staff are usually very happy to tender advice if asked. The following points should perhaps be stressed:

1. "*In the estate of . . .* " Here should be inserted the full correct name of the deceased. If the deceased had an alias, there should be added "otherwise (alias)" and at a later stage in the oath, it should be asserted which is the correct name and the reason for requiring the alias (*e.g.* that the deceased held property in his "other name"). This addition is usually made at the end of the oath, continuing over the page if necessary.

2. *Marginal notes (1) and (2).* Here, the full correct names of each of the proving executors should be given, explaining any discrepancy with that appearing in the will (*e.g.* "John Smith . . . in the will called Jon Smith"). Each executor's full permanent postal address should be given (an executor applying in a professional capacity may give his business address) followed by his occupation or description. If the address in the will is not the executor's present address, add "formerly of . . . "

3. The full correct name of the deceased with his last residential address should be inserted next (again referring, if appropriate, to any alias). If the address shown differs from that in the will add "formerly of . . . " otherwise these words should be deleted.

4. *Date of death.* Insert the date of death stated in the death certificate: it is normally not required that the certificate itself be produced.

5. *Marginal note (6).* It is most important to swear correctly the domicile of the deceased, particularly where the deceased was domiciled in some part of the United Kingdom. Where the deceased died domiciled in England and Wales, an English grant of representation is automatically recognised in Scotland and Northern Ireland, so that a separate grant is not required there if there are assets located within those jurisdictions. (Similarly Scottish confirmations and Northern Irish grants will be directly recognised in England and Wales where the deceased was domiciled in Scotland or Northern Ireland respectively.) The Family Division also has power to reseal grants issued in most Commonwealth countries, whereafter they have the same effect as English grants. (In other cases

where there are assets in this country a separate grant will be required here to deal with them.)

6. *Marginal notes (9) and (10)*. The will and any codocil(s) must be "marked" by the signatures of the executors and the person administering the oath.

7. *Settled property*. This paragraph must be completed as appropriate. It should not be deleted under any circumstances.

8. *Marginal notes (14) and (15)*. At this point the oath seeks to establish directly the executor's right to the grant by reference to his appointment in the will, and this section must be carefully completed. It is not necessary to state a relationship to the deceased unless necessary to prove title. For example, if Mr. Willmade had appointed his wife by referring to her as "my wife" without naming her it would have been necessary to complete this section along the following lines: "I the said Sylvia Willmade am the lawful widow and was at the time that the said will was executed lawfully married to the said deceased and we are the executors named in the said will . . . " If not all of the executors are proving the will, then the wording of this section will indicate this (*e.g.* "the surviving"; "one (two) of the . . . ") and if power is to be reserved to the other(s) the non-acting executor's name should be noted in the margin. If an executor has renounced, this need not be specified in the oath, but the document of renunciation should be lodged with the other documents to lead to the grant. An executor who has not accepted office may renounce probate, and (except with the leave of the court) this cannot be retracted. The renunciation must be in writing and becomes effective only when it is filed. Renunciation cannot normally be partial; and unless it expressly otherwise provides it does not affect the rights which the executor might have to a grant of letters of administration in some other capacity (*e.g.* as a beneficiary or creditor).

9. *Marginal notes (19) and (22)*. One of these paragraphs must be completed and the other deleted. In this case, the former will be deleted and the latter completed, the figures being taken from page 4 of IHT Form 202 (totals 7 & 8).

10. *Jurat*. Separate jurats should be prepared (over the page) for each deponent. The oath must be sworn before a Commissioner/solicitor who is *not* a member of the firm preparing the papers.

Inland Revenue Account—IHT Form 202

In those cases where an Inland Revenue Account is required (see p. 20) this form should be used whenever possible (otherwise IHT 200 should be completed where the deceased died domiciled in some part of the United Kingdom, IHT 201 if not). These Inland Revenue Account Forms are used whether the grant sought is probate or letters of administration (with or without a will), the declaration on page 2 being completed to indicate the type of grant being sought in a particular case.

OATH FOR EXECUTORS/EXECUTRIXES

Extracted by Makepiece and Streiff
Solicitor of Bank Chambers
.Barchester, BR1 2YZ
Solicitor's Reference O FeA/W

IN THE HIGH COURT OF JUSTICE

FAMILY DIVISION

THE DISTRICT **PROBATE REGISTRY (AT)** BARCHESTER

In the Estate of(4)   IVAN WILLMADE   deceased

(1)(2) We CLEMENT AMITY of Bank Chambers Barchester BR1 2YZ
Solicitor and Mrs SYLVIA WILLMADE of 1 Cherry Close
Barchester BR2 7AX

make OATH and say (3)

(4)   IVAN WILLMADE   that
of   1 Cherry Close Barchester BR2 7AX
(his   only and permanent address)
(5) (formerly of

died on the   1st   day of   April   19 94
domiciled in England and Wales (6)

aged (7)   53 years
and (1)   we   believe the paper writing now produced to and marked by
(8) us to contain the true and original last Will and Testament (9)(10)
of the deceased and that to the best of (11)our knowledge information and belief
there was (no) (12) land vested in the deceased which was settled previously to the
death (and not by the said Will (9)   )
and which remained settled land notwithstanding the said death (13)

And (1) we further make Oath and say (3)
that (14)   we are   the (15)

Executors named in the said Will and that (1)   will:-
(i)   collect, get in and administer according to the law the real and personal estate
(16)   of the said deceased(17)

(ii)   when required to do so by the Court, exhibit on oath in the Court a full
inventory of the said estate (16)
and when so required render an account of the administration of the said
estate to the Court; and

(iii)   when required to do so by the High Court, deliver up the Grant of Probate of
the Will to that Court
AND THAT to the best of (11)   our   knowledge, information and belief:-
(19) [the Gross estate passing under the Grant does not exceed £ xxxxxxxxxxxxx
and the Net estate does not exceed £ xxxxxxxxxxxxxx and that this is not a case
in which an Inland Revenue Account is required to be delivered]x

(22) [the Gross estate (18)   passing under the Grant amounts
to £ 78,750   and the Net estate (18)   amounts
to £ 77,750   ]
And xxxxxx further make oath and say xxxx
that notice of this application has been given to the other executx x xto whom powerxx
is being reserved.

(23)

(24)

continued overleaf

Marginal notes (left column):

(1) "I" or "We"

(2) Insert full names, places of residence and occupation of each of the deponents. A female deponent should add "Mrs." or "Miss" as the case may be if she wishes.

(3) or "do solemnly and sincerely affirm".

(4) insert full names and address of the deceased and any alias required

(5) insert address shown in the Will here if different from above otherwise delete.

(6) or as the case may be.

(7) give approximate age if exact age is unknown.

(8) "me" or "us"

(9) "with one/two Codicil(s)", if any

(10) each testamentary paper must be marked by each deponent **And** by the person administering the oath preferably the back of each document.

"my" or "our".

(12) Delete if there are settled land vested in the deceased which remained settled notwithstanding the death. If the applicants are not also entitled to a grant in respect of the settled land a separate grant must be obtained.

(13) Include details of the settlement if appropriate. The 'Special Executors' must establish their title.

(14) "I am" or "We are"

(15) Insert (if necessary) the relationship to the deceased and the nature of the Executorship e.g. "the sole", "the sole surviving" etc. as the case may be. If power is to be reserved the marginal note below must be completed.

(16) Insert "save and except settled land" or "including settled land" as the case may be and if appropriate.

Add any necessary limitation here when proving a Copy Will or as the case may be.

(18) If the deceased died outside England and Wales insert here "in England and Wales".

(19) Complete this paragraph only if the deceased died on or after April 1st 1981 domiciled in England and Wales AND an Inland Revenue Account is NOT required. The paragraph below should be deleted if this paragraph is completed.

(20) Insert £100,000 in respect of a death on or after April 1st 1989, or £70,000 in respect of a death on or after April 1st 1987, but before April 1st 1989, or £40,000 in respect of a death on or after April 1st 1983 but before April 1st 1987, or £25,000 in respect of a death before April 1st 1983. But see (19) above.

(21) Insert £100,000, £70,000, £40,000, £25,000 or £10,000 as the case may be.

(22) Complete this paragraph only if an Inland Revenue Account is required. The paragraph above should be deleted if this paragraph is completed.

(23) If appropriate the names of all executors to whom power is being reserved but notice cannot be given should be shown here preceded by "Save for".

(24) If an alias has been sworn show here the true name of the deceased and the reason for alias.

SWORN by   CLEMENT AMITY
the above named deponent at   Guildhall Chambers Barchester

this   13th   day of   May   19 94   *Clement Amity*

Before me,   *Finbar Horton*
                        A Commissioner for Oaths/Solicitor

SWORN by   SYLVIA WILLMADE
the above named deponent at   Guildhall Chambers Barchester

this   13th   day of   May   19 94   *S. Willmade*

Before me,   *Finbar Horton*
                        A Commissioner for Oaths/Solicitor

PROB. 1   OYEZ|WELBOURN

Page 2

Paragraph 1 of the declaration should be completed to indicate the type of grant being sought. Note that no alterations are permitted to paragraphs 2, 3, 4, 5, 6, 7 or 8: in particular, observe that if any of the statements in paragraphs 3, 7 or 8 do not apply the form cannot be used even if no tax will be payable. The form is signed (not sworn or affirmed) by the executor(s) or intending administrators.

Account A (pages 2 & 3) lists and values all the property comprised in the estate at the date of death in respect of which the grant is to be made. The Account groups such property under two headings—"Property without the Instalment Option" and "Instalment option property". Where IHT is payable, the amount attributable to certain types of property can be paid by instalments (see further IHT 200 *infra*), and although where IHT 202 is appropriate no question of any payment of tax arises the distinction is nonetheless maintained.

In completing IHT forms, pence are ignored when valuing the assets and liabilities. (Traditionally, assets are shown to the £ below and liabilities to the £ above.) The assets and liabilities should be listed under the appropriate headings: no entry of any kind is required if the estate does not include a particular item listed. If there is insufficient room to give the information required, free use of schedules should be made (*e.g.* as in the case of Mr. Willmade's insurance policies), the totals being carried to the body of the form. Where schedules are used, it is essential that they are headed with the full name and date of death of the deceased.

Reference is made in IHT 202 to IHT 40 and IHT 37B. These are, in effect, printed schedules for use where the estate includes stocks and shares, etc. and land respectively. They are not in fact supplied with prints of IHT 202 but are with IHT 200: we will examine them later when discussing that form.

The various totals (1, 2, 3 and 4) are carried to the summary on page 4.

Page 4

Account B requires details of nominated property, and joint property accruing by survivorship—in relation to the latter, the questions at the top of the page should also be completed.

The summary (headed "Value for probate purposes") yields at "Total 7" the gross estate and at "Total 8" the net estate figures respectively for use in completing the oath. For tax purposes, the nominated and joint property net total (Total 6) must also be taken into account. Finally, any available exemptions and reliefs are claimed against "Total 9" to leave the "Net estate for tax purposes," which figure must be within the Nil Rate Band for IHT current at the date of death, currently £150,000. A statement should be annexed showing the details of exemptions and reliefs claimed.

**Inland Revenue
Inheritance Tax**

Inland Revenue Account

For use for an original full grant where

- the deceased died on or after 18 March 1986 domiciled in the United Kingdom; and
- the estate comprises only property which has passed under the deceased's Will or intestacy or by nomination or beneficially by survivorship, and all that property was situate in the United Kingdom; and
- the total net value of the estate, after deducting any Exemptions and Reliefs claimed, does not exceed the threshold above which Inheritance Tax is payable at the date of death.

If the above conditions are met, save only that the deceased died on a date between 27 March 1981 and 17 March 1986 inclusive, the appropriate form is Cap 202. In all other cases form IHT 200 or 201 or Cap 200 or 201 as appropriate must be used unless the estate is an excepted estate under the IHT (Delivery of Accounts) Regulations. For an excepted estate no account need be completed, although exceptionally one may be required.

Name and address of person to whom any communication should be sent.	For Official use
MESSRS MAKEPIECE & STREIFF SOLICITORS BANK CHAMBERS BARCHESTER Postcode BR1 2YZ	Date of Grant FCS _____ Review S _____ Reader _____ Stats _____

Reference CA/ODeA/W	Telephone No. Barchester 4321

In the High Court of Justice Family Division (Probate)

The (a) _____ BARCHESTER DISTRICT _____ **Registry**

(a) Insert "Principal" or "District" as required; in the latter case please add the name of the district

In the estate of _____ IVAN WILLMADE _____
please use CAPITAL letters

Surname in CAPITAL letters	WILLMADE		
Title and first names in full	MR IVAN		

Date of birth (eg 9 September 1988 = 09 SEP 1988)	0 1 D E C 1 9 4 0	Date of death	0 1 A P R 1 9 9 4

Last usual address		Marital status	*Tick as appropriate*
	1 Cherry Close BARCHESTER	married ☑ divorced ☐ single ☐ widowed ☐	
		Surviving relatives	Husband ☐ Child(ren) ☐ Wife ☑ Parent(s) ☐
	Postcode BR2 7AX	Occupation	Computer Salesman

Country of domicile *Tick as appropriate* England and Wales ☑	Scotland ☐	N. Ireland ☐

Names and addresses of executors or intending administrators:

CLEMENT AMITY Bank Chambers BARCHESTER Postcode BR1 2YZ	SYLVIA WILLMADE 1 Cherry Close BARCHESTER Postcode BR2 7AX
Postcode	Postcode

IHT 202   1

Declaration

1   I/we desire to obtain a grant of (b)   Probate of the Will   *(b) insert kind of grant*

No alteration is permitted to paragraphs 2-8

2   To the best of my/our knowledge and belief all the statements and particulars furnished in this account and its accompanying schedules are true and complete.

3   The deceased made no transfers of value or potentially exempt transfers chargeable with Inheritance Tax (ie no transfers of value that were not covered by the IHT exemptions) within 7 years of the death.

4   The deceased made no gifts, subject to a reservation to the donor, on or after 18 March 1986 and within 7 years of the death.

5   Account "A" is a complete and true account of all the property in the estate at the death in respect of which the grant is to be made and of its value at that time.

6   Account "B" is a complete and true account of any nominated property, and of any property held jointly with any other person(s) the beneficial interest in which passed by survivorship, and of its value at the date of death.

7   No property situate outside the United Kingdom was comprised in the estate at the death.

8   The deceased did not have an interest in settled property at his death nor had he within 7 years of his death an interest in settled property or settled any property.

Signed by the above named *Clement Amity* Date 13th May 1994	Signed by the above named *S. Willmade .* Date 13th May 1994
Signed by the above named Date	Signed by the above named Date

Warning: An executor or intending administrator who fails to make full enquiries and personally verify that the statements in this account are true may make himself liable for prosecution or penalties.

Account A — property of the deceased in respect of which the grant is to be made

Property without the instalment option

	Gross value at date of death (before deduction of exemption(s) or relief(s)) £
1 British Savings Bonds and other Government Securities, Savings Certificates and Premium Bonds. *Give description and state amount of each security held, attaching a schedule if necessary.* In the case of Savings Certificates please attach a letter from the Savings Certificates Division or a list giving details of purchase and value of each certificate at date of death. Premium Savings Bonds	1,000
2 Other Stocks, Shares or Investments including Unit Trusts. (Give details on form Cap 40 or similar schedule attached and state in adjoining box the total value of all investments). 1000 XYZ plc Ordinary Shares @ £5.50	5,500
3 Cash and Cash at Bank, Savings Banks or in Building, Co-operative or Friendly Societies, including interest to date of death (state each separately and attach a schedule if necessary). Barset Bank plc Current A/c	1,000
4 Policies of Insurance a on the life of the deceased, including any bonuses thereon (state each item separately, giving names of companies). Statement A annexed b on the life of any other person (enter surrender value and attach letter from the Company).	61,750

5 Household and Personal Goods (furniture, jewellery, clothes, car, etc).

Unsold – estimated
(Includes car £5,000: Grandfather clock £2,000)

| | 9,000 |

6 Other assets not included above or as instalment option property. (If space is insufficient please give details on schedule attached and state in adjoining column total value of these assets).

Salary to date of death

| | 500 |

| **Total 1** | 78,750 |

Debts due from the deceased | **Amount** |
| | £ |

1 Debts (other than mortgage and business debts)

Name and address of creditor	Description of debt	
Ace Garages, Barchester	Work done	150
Paylater Credit Card Co	Balance due	450

If there is insufficient space to list all debts a schedule should be attached

2 Funeral expenses

| | 400 |

| E N Tomb & Co., Barchester | **Total 2** | 1,000 |

Instalment option property | **Gross value at date of death (before deduction of exemption(s) or relief(s)** |
| | £ |

1 Freehold and leasehold property *(form Cap 37 should also be completed)* situated at

2 Business interests *state nature of business*
  a Net value of deceased's interest in business, as statement or balance sheet annexed.

  b Net value of deceased's interest as a partner in a firm of

as statement annexed.

| | **Total 3** | |

Debts due in respect of instalment option property | **Amount** |
| | £ |

1 Mortgages on freehold and leasehold property (amount outstanding at date of death)
  Date of mortgage
  Property on which mortgage charged
  To whom owed

2 Other debts. If space is insufficient please attach a schedule

Name and address of creditor	Description of debt	

| | **Total 4** | |

Joint Property – Questions

Was the deceased joint owner of any property of any description or did he hold any money on a joint account (apart from property or money of which he was merely a trustee)?

Tick as appropriate

Yes [✓]   No [ ]

If so, please give full particulars including

See Account B, Items 1 & 2

a   the date when the joint ownership began (or the date of opening the joint account)

b   the name(s) of the other owner(s)

c   by whom and from what source the joint property was provided and, if it or its purchase price was contributed by one or more of the joint owners, the extent of the contribution made by each

d   how the income (if any) was dealt with and enjoyed

e   what is considered to be the extent of the deceased's share of interest

(a) Item 1 – Jan 1984 Item 2 May 1973

(b) Items 1 & 2 – Sylvia Willmade

(c) Both contributed equally

(d) Shared equally

(e) One half

Account B – Nominated and joint property

Gross value at date of death (before deduction of exemption(s) and relief(s))

Full description of property, real and personal, being nominated property and property held jointly with any other person(s) the beneficial interest in which passed by survivorship. *Show gross value at date of death of the proportion chargeable to tax before deduction of exemption(s) and relief(s). If space is insufficient, please attach a schedule.*

£

Item 1   1 Cherry Close Barchester. Freehold. Deceased's ½ share:
£60,000   **Total 5**

70,250

Item 2   Barset Bldg. Society. Share A/C 456789 with interest to date of death. Deceased's ½ share: £10,250

Less appropriate share of debts or incumbrances thereon. *Give details. If space is insufficient please attach a schedule.*   Barset Building Society A/C 987654
Mortgage on 1, Cherry Close: Deceased's ½ share.

20,000

Total 6

50,250

Value for probate purposes

£

Gross estate	as total 1 as total 3	78,750	**Total 7**	78,750
Less debts	as total 2 as total 4	1,000		

Net estate for probate purposes Total 8

77,750

Value of estate for tax purposes

£

Nominated and joint property (net)

as **Total 6**

50,250

Net estate for probate purposes

as **Total 8**

77,750

Deduct Exemptions and Reliefs claimed

Total 9

128,000

1   Agricultural relief: Schedule annexed
2   Business relief: Schedule annexed
3   Spouse exemption: Schedule annexed   )
4   Other (please specify)   Charity   )   STATEMENT B
                 (Schedule annexed)

118,500

Net estate for tax purposes

9,500

Prints of this form and of the instructions (IHT 210) can be obtained from the Capital Taxes Office, Inland Revenue, Rockley Road, London W14 0DF and on personal application only at the Stamps Office, Room G3, South West Wing, Bush House, Strand, WC2B 4QN, the London Chief Post Office, King Edward Street, EC1A 1AA, The Branch Post Offices at 24 Throgmorton Street, EC2N 2JE; 40 Fleet Street, EC4Y 1BT; 181 High Holborn, WC1 1AA; 2-4 Bishops Court, Chancery Lane, WC2A 1EA, and from other large branch post offices in major towns and cities outside the Metropolitan Postal District as listed in form Cap 18 (which can be obtained from the Capital Taxes Office).

A0186/1844L Dd 0400005 150M 10/90 TP Gp649

IVAN WILLMADE, deceased

Date of death: April 1, 1994

Statement "A". Life Policies

Eternal Life Assurance Co.

Policy No. 654321

		£
Sum assured	£30,000	
Bonus	£7,750	
		37,750

Long Life Assurance Co.

Policy No. 12345

Sum assured	£20,000	
Bonus	£4,000	
		24,000
		61,750

IVAN WILLMADE, deceased

Date of death: April 1, 1994

Statement "B"

EXEMPTIONS CLAIMED ON PAGE 4, IHT 202

Charity Exemption   £

Legacy to Barset Dogs Home (payable from
ACCOUNT A property)   1,000

Spouse Exemption

The remainder of the estate (as part residue under the will
or accruing by survivorship) save and except specific and pecuniary legacies to children totalling £9,500 (payable from
ACCOUNT A property)

i.e. – ACCOUNT A   67,250
– ACCOUNT B   50,250

Total Exemptions 118,500

The grant

The Registrar satisfies himself that everything is in order (if not the documents may be returned with a note of any error or omission) and in due course (usually between one and two weeks after the papers have been lodged) the original and office copies of the grant issued are posted to the extracting solicitor. The original grant has bound into it a copy of the will, whereas the office copies are simply of the grant itself.

In the HIGH COURT of JUSTICE

The District Probate Registry at Barchester

BE IT KNOWN THAT IVAN WILLMADE of 1 Cherry Close Barchester BR2 7AX died on the 1st day of April 1994 domiciled in England and Wales

AND BE IT FURTHER KNOWN that at the date hereunder written the last Will and Testament (a copy whereof hereunto annexed) of the said deceased was proved and registered in the said Registry of the High Court of Justice and Administration of all the estate which by law devolves to and vests in the personal representative of the said deceased was granted by the aforesaid Court to

CLEMENT AMITY of Bank Chambers Barchester BR1 2YZ and Mrs. SYLVIA WILLMADE of 1 Cherry Close Barchester BR2 7AX the executors named in the said will

And it is hereby certified that an Inland Revenue account has been delivered wherein it is shown that the value of the said estate in the United Kingdom (exclusive of what the said deceased may have been possessed of or entitled to as a trustee and not beneficiary) amounts to £60,750 and that the net value of the estate amounts to £59,750

Dated the 28th day of May 1994.

P.R.O. Bates

District Registrar

Extracted by Makepiece & Streiff, Bank Chambers, Barchester BR1 2YZ (Ref. CA/ODe'A/W)

ADMINISTRATION

Grant of letters of administration with will annexed

When issued

Such a grant issues to a person, other than an executor, who proves the will not earlier than seven days after the death. The following are some of the circumstances which might necessitate a grant in this form.

1. Where there is no executor appointed by the will, or a purported appointment is void for uncertainty.

2. Where the executor appointed cannot prove the will because he is a minor, or is mentally or physically incapable of managing his affairs.

3. Where the executor appointed by the will has renounced his right to prove the will, or has been cited to accept or refuse probate and has not entered an appearance to the citation. As we have already seen, an executor is generally free to accept the office or renounce as he pleases. A citation is the means by which an executor may be compelled to "make up his mind" whether to take out a grant or not, and is issued by the court on the application of an interested party who wishes to apply for a grant of letters of administration. The citation requires the executor to enter an appearance and accept or refuse probate of the will. If he fails to appear (or renounces), his rights as executor are at an end. (A citation may also be issued requiring an executor who has accepted office to take out a grant if he has not done so within six months of the death; this is often the prelude to an application to the court to "pass over" an executor even though he has intermeddled in the estate in favour of someone else entitled to a grant of administration.)

4. Where the executor appointed by the will has predeceased the testator or has survived the testator but died before proving the will.

To whom issued

The order of priority is governed by *NCPR, rule 20*.

1. Residuary legatee or devisee on trust, *i.e.* trustees of residue.

2. Any other residuary legatee or devisee, whether entitled absolutely or for life, or, in the case of partial intestacy, any person entitled to share in undisposed-of residue.

3. PRs of any residuary legatee or devisee (but not life tenant or trustee), or PRs of person entitled on partial intestacy.

4. Any other legatee or devisee (including one for life or one holding as trustee), or any creditor.

5. PRs of any other legatee or devisee (but not life tenant or trustee), or of any creditor.

Entitlement

Entitlement to a grant must be established in the oath to lead to the grant. Those with a higher entitlement must be "disposed of" (*e.g.* by renunciation or citation) and the manner of the "disposal" stated in the oath. A maximum of four persons may apply for the grant, and if a minority or life interest arises under the will, there must normally be at least two applicants. The authority of the administrator (with the will) derives from the grant itself.

Grant of letters of administration

Entitlement to grant

A grant of "simple administration" only issues (normally not earlier than 14 days from the date of death) where the deceased died wholly intestate (on a partial intestacy, the executor or administrator with the will applies the intestacy rules in so far as the will does not dispose of the testator's estate). A person entitled to apply for a grant cannot be compelled to do so, though a citation may be issued requiring him to accept or refuse a grant on the application of a person having an inferior right to the grant: if there is no appearance to the citation the citor may apply for the grant himself. Like an executor, an administrator may renounce his right; this should be done in writing and be filed with the other papers to lead the grant.

The maximum number of applicants if four: if as a result of the intestacy a minority or life interest arises, there must normally be at least two grantees. However, where the net value of the estate does not exceed the statutory sums to which a surviving spouse is entitled (*infra*) and where no minority or life interest arises a surviving spouse may apply for a grant alone. If the gross value of the estate exceeds the so-called "statutory legacy" applicable to the case, a number of deductions are made to discover whether the spouse is entitled to apply alone as the only person entitled to the estate and should be set out in the oath to lead to the grant. They are:

(a) the value of the personal chattels as defined by section $55(1)(x)$ of the Administration of Estates Act 1925.
(b) the debts and funeral expenses.
(c) costs of obtaining the grant and administering the estate.
(d) Inheritance Tax.
(e) Probate Court fees.

Effect of grant

An administrator actually derives his title from the grant, so that this is rather more than simply the means of proving his title. Pending the grant, the intestate's property vests in the President of the Family Division. An administrator cannot commence an action prior to the issue of the grant, nor does he have any authority to do anything as administrator in this period.

Application for grant

Those who may apply for a grant are essentially those who have an interest in the intestate's residuary estate, and the order of priority is governed by *NCPR, rule 22*. As indicated previously, at least two applicants will normally be required where (under the intestacy rules) a minority or life interest arises. The Rules also provide that the grant may be made to any person entitled without prior notice being given to others of equal entitlement. Where a person has died after the intestate, that person's personal representatives have the like right to a grant. However, normally a living beneficiary is preferred to the personal representative of a deceased person who would have been entitled in the same degree: similarly a person not under a disability is preferred to an infant in the same degree. Any living beneficiary is preferred to the personal representative of a spouse, unless the spouse was entitled to the whole estate under the intestacy rules.

Of those persons entitled under the intestacy rules to a beneficial interest in the estate the order of priority is:

1. Surviving spouse—but not where the deceased's marriage had been dissolved or annulled prior to death, nor where a decree of judicial separation was then in force and the separation continuing at the date of death. A magistrates' court order containing a non-cohabitation clause does not, however, prevent the separated spouse from applying for the grant.

2. Children and issue of any child who predeceased the intestate.

3. Parents.

4. Brothers and sisters of the whole blood and issue of any who predeceased the intestate.

5. Brothers and sisters of the half blood and issue of any who predeceased the intestate.

6. Grandparents.

7. Uncles and aunts of the whole blood and issue of any who predeceased the intestate.

8. Uncles and aunts of the half blood and issue of any who predeceased the intestate.

In default of any of the above.

9. Treasury Solicitor claiming *bona vacantia* on behalf of the Crown.

10. A creditor.

Documents in support

An application for a grant must be supported by

1. An oath in the form of an affidavit sworn or affirmed by the applicant(s), clearing off any applicants having a prior entitlement

2. An Inland Revenue Account, duly receipted, if required (see *supra*, p. 20)

3. Fees (see *supra*, p. 21)

Sureties

At one time, an administrator was normally required to enter into an administration bond (usually with one or more sureties) for the due performance of his duties. This is no longer the case, though the court may still require a guarantee from one or more sureties in certain specified cases—*e.g.* where the grant is to be made to a creditor or to a person residing outside the United Kingdom—or where the Registrar considers that there are "special circumstances" which make it desirable.

Instructions for administration

In order to prepare the papers to lead to a grant of letters of administration, much of the information and action required is similar to that discussed earlier in relation to the proof of Mr. Willmade's will (*supra*, pp. 21 *et seq*.). It is essentially necessary to establish who is entitled to the estate (in this case by applying the intestacy rules) and who will apply for the grant. The various assets and liabilities must be ascertained and valued so that the appropriate Inland Revenue Account (if required) can be prepared. Again, advertisements under section 27 of the Trustee Act 1925 should be made so that the administrators may be protected from claims of which they have no notice. In this case, however, the advertisements cannot strictly be made until the grant is issued.

INTESTACY—A CASE STUDY

The day following that on which Mr. Amity went to see Mrs. Willmade to obtain instructions to obtain the grant in respect of Mr. Willmade's estate, Oliver De'Ath has an appointment with a Mr. Smith, who had telephoned the previous day to say that his widowed sister had recently died, and that as he (Mr. Smith) was her nearest relative he assumed there must be something he would be required to do in order to wind up her affairs. Mr. De'Ath asked Mr. Smith to come to the office, bringing with him any relevant papers, etc., which he could find. At the interview with Mr. Smith, Mr. De'Ath completes the firm's pro forma "Instructions for Administration" devised by Mr. Amity.

All the inquiries having been completed, Mr. De'Ath then asks William to draft the probate papers.

<u>INSTRUCTIONS FOR ADMINISTRATION</u>

<u>Taken by:</u> O De'A   <u>Date:</u> 5/4/94   <u>Engaged:</u> 30 mins.

<u>DECEASED:</u>   IONA NOWILL   <u>Date of BIRTH:</u> 10/5/1914
            21 Almond Avenue   <u>Date of DEATH:</u> 29/3/1994
            Barchester BR3 8MN <u>Occupation:</u> Retired Schoolteacher
<u>Marital Status:</u>   M/S/D/W   <u>Surviving Relatives:</u> ~~H/W Child(ren)~~
                                            ~~Parent(s)~~

<u>Tax District & Reference:</u> Barchester 2. CO/45/f

<u>Domicile:</u> E + ~~W/S/NL~~
<u>BENEFICIARIES ENTITLED TO ESTATE:</u>
            No spouse, issue, parents
            Nearest relative her
            ONLY BROTHER   —   JOHN EDWIN SMITH
                                         32 Hazel Grove
                                         Barchester BR3 1AZ
                                         Company Director
                        (Telephone B 5678)

<u>ADMINISTRATOR(S):</u> John Edwin Smith
<u>IHT:</u> Lifetime gifts – NIL
<u>SPECIAL INSTRUCTIONS:</u> JES has applied for Death Grant

<u>ESTATE ASSETS:</u>
   House   21 Almond Avenue, Barchester
           Freehold   £
           (inherited on death of husband 1975)   140,000

DHSS Retirement Pension – balance due	50
Cash in house	25
Barset Bank C/A	300
(Barchester Branch) D/A with interest to date of death	12,400
Paymaster General – Balance of teacher's pension	225
National Savings Certificates	1,000
Effects (unsold)	1,700
	155,700

LIABILITIES:	
British Gas – gas bill	£ 25
Buyitnow Limited – goods supplied	£ 75
Funeral A/c – E N Tomb & Co.	£600
	£700

The Oath

Again this is in a sense the most important of the papers in that its purpose is to establish the applicant(s) title to the grant. Especial care is necessary in relation to "clearing off" and the description of the applicant(s) to show title; these and some other important matters are summarised below.

1. *Alias.* Any alias of the intestate should be dealt with as previously described.

2. *Marginal notes (1) and (2).* Essentially, the same details are required for administrators as executors: their full names and addresses and occupations/descriptions. Where the applicants have different degrees of entitlement they should be listed in order of priority.

3. *Domicile.* As already explained it is important that this be correctly stated.

4. *Marginal note (7).* At this point it is essential to show the status of the deceased (*e.g.* a married man/woman; a bachelor/spinster; a widow(er)), and where necessary clear off (*i.e.* (in effect) account for) all applicants who would have a prior right to those seeking the grant. In the present case the applicant is the deceased's brother, so it is necessary to clear off any surviving spouse, issue and parents of the intestate. If the applicant had been (say) an uncle of the whole blood, then the statement at this point would read:
"a widow without issue parent brothers or sisters of the whole or half blood or their issue or grandparent."
If the intestate's marriage had been dissolved or annulled and he/she had not remarried, the proper description of the deceased is "single man/woman" and the oath should give details of the decree of dissolu-

tion or annulment, an office copy of which should be lodged with the papers.

5. *Marginal note (8)*. The words following (8) down to and including "enactment" are intended to clear illegitimate, legitimated and adopted children who now have essentially the same rights to a grant as the intestate's lawful children. They should normally be deleted where the application is made by a surviving spouse or a child. In other cases, (as here) they should be left in, otherwise the clearing off will be incomplete.

6. *Marginal note (9)*. Again this section of the oath must be completed as appropriate: it should not be deleted.

7. *Marginal notes (13), (14) and (15)*. Here it is necessary to describe the relationship of the applicant(s) to the deceased and the capacity in which the grant is applied for (*e.g.* "the only person now entitled to the estate" or "one (two) of the persons entitled to share in the estate").

8. *Marginal notes (18) and (21)*. Again, one of these two paragraphs should be completed as appropriate and the other deleted. In this case the second of the two statements is completed by inserting the figures derived from the Inland Revenue Account—in this case IHT 200 (*infra*).

9. *Jurat*. Again, the oath must be sworn or affirmed before a Commissioner or solicitor who is not a member of Messrs. Makepiece & Streiff.

OATH FOR ADMINISTRATORS

Extracted by .... Makepiece & Streiff
Solicitor of .... Bank Chambers
.... Barchester BR1 2YZ
Solicitors Reference ... O DeA/W

IN THE HIGH COURT OF JUSTICE

FAMILY DIVISION

(1) "I" or "We".

(2) Insert full names, places of residence and occupation of each of the deponents. A female deponent should add "Mrs." or "Miss" as the case may be if she wishes.

(3) or "do solemnly and sincerely affirm".

(4) Insert full names of the deceased and any alias required.

(5) Give approximate age if the exact age is unknown.

(6) or as the case may be.

(7) Where necessary give status and clear off any classes entitled in priority e.g. "a spinster", "widower without issue", "without parent" etc.

Strike out the words to "enactment" if applicants are the surviving spouse child of the deceased.

Complete as appropriate. If such interest does arise, two grantees will usually be required.

(10) "my" or "our".

(11) Delete if there was land which remained settled notwithstanding the death. If the applicants are not also entitled to a grant in respect of the settled land a separate grant must be obtained.

(12) Include details of the settlement if appropriate. All applicants must also show how they are entitled to the settled land.

(13) "I am" or "We are".

THE DISTRICT **PROBATE REGISTRY (AT)** BARCHESTER

In the Estate of(4)   IONA NOWILL   deceased
(1)(2)   I JOHN EDWIN SMITH

of   32 Hazel Grove Barchester BR3 1AZ
          Company Director
(3) **make OATH and say**   that
(4)   IONA NOWILL
of   21 Almond Avenue Barchester BR3 8MN
(her   only and permanent address)
died on the   29th   day of   March   19 94
aged (5)   79 years   domiciled in England and Wales (6)

INTESTATE (7)   a widow without issue or parent

                                                              (8) or any other
person entitled in priority to share the said estate by virtue of any enactment

and that (9)   no   minority (9)   or   life
interest arises under the intestacy; and that to the best of (10)   my
knowledge, information and belief there was [no] (11) land vested in the said
deceased which was settled previously to the death of the deceased and which
remained settled land notwithstanding the said death (12)

(14) Give applicants relationship to deceased e.g. "sister of the whole blood" etc as the case may be.

(15) Show applicant as being the only person entitled or one of the persons entitled or as the case may be. In the case of nephews, nieces or cousins derivation of title may be required.

..) Insert "save and except settled l' or "including settled land" as the .e may be and if appropriate.

(17) Add any required limitation · in respect of attorney, mental incapacity or as the case may be.

(18) Complete this paragraph only if the deceased died on or after April 1st 1981 domiciled in England and Wales AND an Inland Revenue Account is NOT required. The paragraph below should be deleted if this paragraph is completed.

(19) Insert £100,000 in respect of a death on or after April 1st 1989, or £70,000 in respect of a death on or after April 1st 1987, but before April 1st 1989, or £40,000 in respect of a death on or after April 1st 1983 but before April 1st 1987, or £25,000 in respect of a death before April 1st 1983. But see (18) above.

(20) Insert £100,000, £70,000, £40,000, £25,000 or £10,000 as the case may be.

(21) Complete this paragraph only if an Inland Revenue Account is required. The paragraph above should be deleted if this paragraph is completed.

(22) If the deceased died domiciled outside England and Wales insert "In England and Wales".

(23) If an akas has been sworn show here the true name of the deceased and the reason for akas.

AND (1)　　I　　further make OATH and say (3)

　　　　　　that (13) I am　　the (14) (15)　　lawful brother of the whole blood and the only person now　　　　　entitled to　　　　the estate

of the said intestate and that (1)　I　will:-

(i)　collect, get in and administer according to the law the real and personal estate (16)　　　　　　　　　　　　　　of the said deceased (17)

(ii)　when required to do so by the Court, exhibit on oath in the Court a full inventory of the said estate (16) and when so required render an account of the administration of the said estate to the Court; and

(iii)　when required to do so by the High Court, deliver up the Grant of Letters of Administration to that Court

AND THAT to the best of (10)　my　　knowledge, information and belief:-

(18) [the Gross estate passing under the Grant does not exceed £ xx xx and the Net estate does not exceed £ xx xxxxxxxxxxxxxx and that this is not a case in which an Inland Revenue Account is required to be delivered] xxx

(21) [the Gross estate (22)　　　　　　　　　　　passing under the Grant amounts to £ 155,700　　　　　and the Net estate (22)　　　　　　　amounts to £ 155,000　　　　　　]

(23)

continued overleaf

SWORN by　　　　　　　　　JOHN EDWIN SMITH
the above named deponent at

this　　　14th day of　　MAY　　19　94　　*JE Smith*

Before me, ...*Findar Horton*........................
　　　　　　　　A Commissioner for Oaths/Solicitor

SWORN by
the above named deponent at

this　　　　　day of　　　　　19　　　................................

Before me, ...
　　　　　　　A Commissioner for Oaths/Solicitor

Inland Revenue Account IHT Form 200

This form should be used where the deceased died domiciled anywhere in the United Kingdom (if not use IHT 201) in cases where an Inland Revenue Account is required but IHT 202 is not appropriate.

The printed form comprises some 12 pages, with two printed inserts (CAP 40 and CAP 37B) which should be completed or discarded as appropriate. As before, no entry of any kind need be made where an item listed does not feature in the estate.

Pages 1 and 2

Largely formal matters which should, in practice, cause little difficulty. On page 2, paragraph 1 of the declaration should be completed as appropriate, and paragraph 3 either completed or deleted. Where IHT may be paid by instalments, paragraph 4 should be completed to indicate whether or not the option is being exercised.

Page 3

Replies must be given to all the questions on this page and, where in the affirmative, the necessary additional information supplied.

Pages 4 and 5

In section 1 of the Accounts which follow, the value of the property belonging to the deceased beneficially and in respect of which the grant is to be made must be stated. Section 1A asks for details of such property in respect of which there is no option to pay IHT by instalments. (Section 1B—page 7—is where details of the property enjoying that option should be given.) Again, pence are ignored in showing the value of assets and liabilities; and schedules should be used where there is insufficient room to give the information required.

CAP Form 40 is used to list all stocks, shares and other securities: alternatively where there are a number of such assets, a separate valuation may be enclosed to which reference is made on Form 40. Where (as in Mrs. Nowill's case) National Savings Certificates are held, a letter giving the value of the total holding at the date of death can be obtained and enclosed with the account: this is in practice particularly useful where the deceased held a number of these, since otherwise they will have to be listed giving full details of the Issue, date of purchase, etc.

In the case of personal effects (top of page 5) the Revenue prefers a valuation to be supplied, identifying separate items valued at £500 or more. In practice, however, it will normally accept the completion of the account as in Mrs. Nowill's case (with any particularly valuable items identified in a manner similar to that done in Mr. Willmade's case when completing IHT 202).

At the bottom of page 5, instructions are given to carry the total to pages 6 and 12.

Page 6

Here should be set out (to the nearest £ above) the liabilities of the deceased as at the date of death, with the funeral expenses separately stated. It is important not to show here liabilities which should be included elsewhere (*e.g.* a mortgage on land which the deceased held in his sole name would be a deduction in section 1B (page 7) because the value of the land would be included in that part of the Account.

At the bottom of the page is a summary which should be completed and the net total carried to page 11, section 1A.

Page 7

Section 1B contains details of other items of property in the deceased's estate in respect of which the grant is to be made, but in respect of which IHT may be paid by 10 equal annual instalments—the first being payable six months after the end of the month in which the death occurred (the date upon which the tax is otherwise payable in full). If this option is not exercised, the tax is payable in full as on other property: and if the property concerned is sold during the instalment period, any outstanding tax must then be paid in full. Interest on the outstanding tax (running from the date upon which the tax would normally be payable in full) must be added to each instalment where the property concerned is land. In other cases, the instalment option is in effect "interest free" so long as the instalments are not paid late—and even then, interest is only payable on the late instalment.

The questions at the top of the page must be answered as appropriate. The values are totalled and carried as instructed to page 12. Details should then be given of any incumbrances (such as mortgages) charged upon any of the property included in this section. After these have been deducted in the summary, the net total is carried to page 11, section 1B.

Page 8

Section 2 of the Account deals with all other property for which the personal representatives are liable to pay tax—including foreign property, nominated property and (most commonly) jointly-held property which passes by survivorship. Again, distinction is to be made between property not enjoying the instalment option (*e.g.* joint bank or building society accounts) which belongs in section 2A; and property in respect of which tax can be paid by instalments (*e.g.* jointly-held land) which should be detailed in section 2B. The net values (*e.g.* after deducting the deceased's share of any mortgage from his share of the value of land jointly held) should be carried to page 11 as instructed. Note that the gross values (unlike section 1 property) do not feature on page 12 because the grant is not issued in respect of property in this part of the Account.

Page 9

Here, in section 3, should be listed any other property treated as part of the deceased's estate for tax purposes, such as the value of any settled property in which he enjoyed a life interest. In section 4, which relates to the deduction of debts and liabilities, the appropriate box must be ticked. The answer will usually be "No."

Page 10

On this page any claims for exemption from tax (*e.g.* because the property passes to a surviving spouse or charity) or relief from tax (*e.g.* because the property qualifies for business property or agricultural property relief) should be made. The totals of the exemptions, etc. claimed are carried to the appropriate places on page 11.

Page 11

The Assessment of Tax. In some cases this must be done by the Capital Taxes Office, to whom any case of exceptional difficulty may also be referred for assessment. In most cases, however, a system of self-assessment operates, the solicitors submitting the form calculating the tax (and any interest) payable as directed in the various parts of the assessment.

The "Summary for determining chargeable rates" comprises the net value of the property transferred on the death—basically the net values brought forward as directed from the various sections of the Account and the exemptions and reliefs claimed on page 10—and then at "A" gives the total value of property potentially chargeable to tax on death. To this figure must be added (at "B") the cumulative total of chargeable lifetime transfers—broadly gifts made within the seven years prior to the death. This gives at "C" the aggregate chargeable transfers upon which IHT is payable.

Under "Calculation of tax" the IHT is then calculated by reference to the table of rates applicable at the date of death (currently a flat rate of 40 per cent. applies to the extent that the chargeable transfers exceed the nil rate band). Tax attributable to the lifetime chargeable transfers is then deducted, *i.e.* tax on the figure at "B"—this is not primarily the responsibility of the personal representatives. This gives the tax payable on the property passing on death at "D."

That part headed "Value on which tax is now being paid" is concerned with identifying the property on which IHT is "*now*" (*i.e.* on the submission of the Account) to be paid. No mention would therefore be made here of any instalment option property where the option is being exercised and the time for the first instalment to be paid has not yet arisen.

Under "Amount payable on this account" an apportionment of the tax payable is made as between the non-instalment and instalment option property respectively. The tax (and any interest due) is calculated as directed—in practice, only in respect of the property on which tax is being paid on delivery of the Account—and carried as directed to the summary at the middle of page 12.

Page 12

At the top of the page, the Probate Summary details the gross and net value of the estate in respect of which the grant is to be made, and these figures are carried to the oath—and ultimately to the grant itself.

The rest of the page is concerned with any tax payable. The solicitors submitting the form may send the completed IHT 200 with a cheque for the tax (and any interest) to the Capital Taxes Office. (In practice, the personal representatives will probably have to borrow the money (from, *e.g.* a bank and/or a beneficiary) to pay the tax since they will not be in a position to realise sufficient (if any) of the assets). The Capital Taxes Office will briefly examine the Account, and if prima facie in order it will be receipted and returned to the solicitors submitting it. The grant cannot be issued until the tax payable on the delivery of the Account has been paid. In the usual case the *receipted* Account together with the other papers to lead to a grant must be submitted to the District or Principal Registry by the solicitor applying for the grant.

If subsequently amendments are necessary, these are usually dealt with by way of a corrective account (Form D-3).

Inland Revenue
Inheritance Tax *

Inland Revenue Account

- For use where the deceased died on or after 18 March 1986 domiciled in the United Kingdom
- Please see IHT 210 for instructions on how to complete this form

* *Capital Transfer Tax in the case of a death before 25 July 1986*

For Official Use	
Status O	
C	
Review S	
D	
Allcn	
Reader	
Stats	

Your reference

O De A/W

Your telephone number

Barchester 4321

Name and address of solicitors ∅

Makepiece and Streiff
Bank Chambers
BARCHESTER

DX   Postcode BR1 2YZ

∅ All communications concerning Inheritance Tax will be sent to the Solicitors unless the executors or administrators request otherwise.

In the High Court of Justice Family Division (Probate)

The DISTRICT Registry AT BARCHESTER

In the estate of   IONA NOWILL

Please use CAPITAL letters

| Surname | NOWILL | Date of birth | 1 0 M A Y 1 9 1 4 |

| Title and Forenames | MRS IONA | Date of death | 2 9 M A R 1 9 9 4 |

Marital Status   *Please tick as appropriate*

Married ☐   Single ☐   Divorced ☐   Widowed ☑

Surviving Relatives

Husband ☐   Wife ☐   Child(ren) ☐   Parent(s) ☐

Domicile

England and Wales ☑   Scotland ☐   N.Ireland ☐

Last usual address

21, Almond Avenue, Barchester

Postcode BR3 8MN

Occupation   Retired Schoolteacher

Please state the Tax District at which the tax affairs of the deceased were handled   Barchester 2.

Tax District Reference   CO/45/F.

Please give the names and permanent addresses of the executors or intending administrators:

JOHN EDWIN SMITH
32, HAZEL GROVE,
BARCHESTER. Postcode BR3 1AZ.

Postcode

Postcode

Postcode

Date of Grant

IHT200

1

Declaration

1. I/We desire to obtain a grant of ~~Letters of Administration~~ of the Estate   of the aforenamed deceased.

2. To the best of my/our knowledge and belief all the statements and particulars furnished in this account and its accompanying schedules are true and complete.

3. ~~I/We have made the fullest enquiries that are reasonably practicable in the circumstances but have~~ not been able to ascertain the exact value of the property referred to in Exhibit   to section   So far as the value can now be estimated, it is stated in section   . I/We undertake, as soon as the value is ascertained, to deliver a further account, and to pay both any additional tax payable for which I/We may be liable, and any further tax payable, for which I/We may be liable on ~~the other property mentioned in this account.~~

4. So far as the tax on the property disclosed in sections 1B, 2B and 3 may be paid by instalments, I/We elect to pay/~~not to pay~~ by instalments as indicated in these sections.

Signed by the above-named JOHN EDWIN SMITH *J. E. Smith* date 14th May 1994
Signed by the above-named   date
Signed by the above-named   date
Signed by the above-named   date

Warning

An executor or intending administrator who fails to make the fullest enquiries that are reasonably practicable in the circumstances may be liable to penalties.

He or she may be liable to penalties or prosecution if he or she fails to disclose in Section 1A, 1B, 2A, 2B and 3 (as appropriate) and in his or her answers to the questions on page 3 and at the foot of page 9 all the property to the best of his or her knowledge and belief in respect of which tax may be payable on the death of the deceased.

Transfers of value which need not be reported are

a. gifts or other transfers of value made to the deceased's spouse unless at the time of transfer the deceased was domiciled in the United Kingdom and the spouse was not

b. gifts of money not exceeding £3,000 in any one year, where the executors or intending administrators are satisfied that they are wholly exempt as normal gifts out of income

c. outright gifts to one individual which are clearly exempt as not exceeding £250 in any one year (to 5 April): (for gifts before 6 April 1980 the exemption is restricted to £100 in any one year)

d. other gifts of money, or of shares or securities quoted on the Stock Exchange, where these, together with any other gifts not within (b) or (c) above, do not in total exceed the exemption for gifts of £3,000 in any one year (to 5 April)

- Any property mentioned on this page which is subject to Inheritance Tax, whether or nor tax is actually payable, must also be included in sections 1A, 1B, 2A, 2B, or 3 of this account as appropriate. If it is claimed that the property is not subject to Inheritance Tax, reasons should be given.
- Even if a full report has been made or any other information relevant to the answers to any of the questions below has been given to an Inland Revenue Office, affirmative answers must nonetheless be given to the appropriate questions. Please also identify the office and quote any relevant official reference.
- Where necessary schedules may be attached.

1. Gifts etc.

For official use only

Did the deceased, within 7 years of his/her death

Please tick yes or no
yes · no

- make any gift, settlement or other transfer of value other than a transfer mentioned in the notes on page 2. ☐ ☑

- make any disposition for the maintenance of a relative ☐ ☑

- pay any premium on a policy of life assurance not included in Section 1 of this form? ☐ ☑

Did the deceased at any time on or after 18 March 1986 dispose of any property by way of gift where either

- possession and enjoyment of the property was not bona fide assumed by the donee, or ☐ ☑

- the property was not enjoyed to the entire exclusion of the donor and of any benefit to him/her by contract or otherwise? ☐ ☑

If the reply to any of the questions above is "yes", please give full particulars including dates, details of any property affected and the names and addresses of the other parties concerned, on a separate sheet of paper.

2. Settled property

- Was the deceased, at the time of his/her death, entitled to a life interest, annuity or other interest in possession in settled property whether as beneficiary under the settlement or otherwise? ☐ ☑

- Did the deceased cease to be entitled to any such interest in settled property within 7 years of his/her death? ☐ ☑

If the reply to either question is "yes", please give full particulars of the title (including, in the case of a Will/intestacy, the name and date of death of the testator/intestate and date and place of grant). Where the interest was under a settlement and no previous report has been made, kindly forward a copy of the settlement.

3. Nominations

Did the deceased in his lifetime nominate any Savings Bank Account, Savings Certificates or other assets in favour of any person? ☐ ☑

If you have answered "yes", please give full particulars in section 2 on page 8.

4. Joint property

Was the deceased joint owner of any property of any description or did he/she hold any money on a joint account (apart from property or money of which he/she was merely a trustee)? ☐ ☑

If you have answered "yes" please give the following details on a separate sheet of paper

- the date when the joint ownership began (or the date of opening the joint account)

- The name(s) of the other joint owner(s)

- By whom and from what source the joint property was provided and, if it or its purchase price was contributed by one or more of the joint owners, the extent of the contribution made by each

- how the income (if any) was dealt with and enjoyed

- whether the deceased's interest passed under his/her will or intestacy or by survivorship.

Section 1

A schedule of all the property of the deceased within the United Kingdom to which the deceased was beneficially entitled and **in respect of which the grant is made,** excluding property over which the deceased had and exercised by will a general power of appointment. The appointed property should be included in Section 3. Property gifted by the deceased subject to a reservation retained by the deceased should also be included in Section 3 rather than here.

Section 1A Property without the Instalment Option	Gross value at date of death*	For official use only
Stocks, shares, debentures and other securities as set out in CAP 40:		
• **Quoted** in the Stock Exchange daily official list except so far as included in Section 1B		
• **Others,** except so far as included in Section 1B		
National Savings Certificates and interest to the date of death	1000	
Uncashed dividends and **interest received, dividends declared,** and **interest accrued due,** in respect of the above investments, to the date of death, as statement annexed		
Cash at the bank:		
• On current account and interest (if any) to the date of death at		
Basset Bank, Barchester	300	
• On deposit and interest to the date of death at		
Basset Bank, Barchester	12400	
	25	
Cash (other than cash at banks)		
Money at a National or Trustee Savings Bank and **interest** to the date of death, as statement annexed		
Money out on Mortgage, and **interest** to the date of death, as statement annexed		
Money with a building society, co-operative or friendly society, and **interest** to the date of death, as statement annexed		
Money out on promissory notes, bonds and other securities, and **interest** to the date of death, as statement annexed		
Other debts due to the deceased and **interest** to the date of death, except book debts included in Section 1B, as statement annexed		
Unpaid purchase money of real and leasehold property contracted in the lifetime of the deceased to be sold, as statement annexed		
Rents of the deceased's own real and leasehold property to the date of death		
Apportionment of the rents of the deceased's real and leasehold property to the date of death		
Income accrued due, but not received before the death, arising from real and personal property, in which the deceased had a life or other limited interest, viz:-		
Apportionment of Income from that source to the date of death		
Any other income, apportioned where necessary, to which the deceased was entitled at his death (eg pensions, annuities, director's fees, etc) as statement annexed ✱ *Balance of Retirement Pension — DSS.* ✱✱ *Balance of Teachers Pension — H.M.Paymaster General.*	✱ 50 ✱✱ 225	
Policies of insurance and bonuses (if any) thereon, on the life of the deceased, as statement annexed		
Saleable value of policies of insurance and bonuses (if any) not payable on the death of the deceased, as statement annexed		

* All claims for exemptions or reliefs should be made in the Summary on page 10

To be carried forward | 14000

4

Inland Revenue
Capital Taxes Office

CTO Reference

Name of Deceased, Transferor or Settlement

IONA   NOWILL

Date of Death or Transfer
29/3/1994

Schedule of stocks and shares etc

- Securities quoted on the Stock Exchange should be listed first in the order in which they appear in the Official Lists followed by those quoted on any other recognised Stock Exchanges. Other items should be grouped together at the end of the list and their values carried separately into the appropriate parts of the Account.

- If the source of the market price is other than the Stock Exchange List for the date of valuation details should be given in column 3, or if space is insufficient, in a separate schedule.

- Prices based upon published quotations should normally be taken at ¼ up from the lower to the higher limit of quotation—See instructions for completion of Accounts.

- If the date of valuation is a day for which no quotations are available, prices may be based on the List for either the latest previous date or the earliest subsequent date. The date of the List used must be stated in column 3.

1 Name of Company followed by full description of class of share or stock and unit of quotation. If bearer the fact should be stated.	2 No of Shares or amount of Stock	3 Market Price at date of valuation	4 Principal value at date of valuation £ p	For official use only
National Savings Certificates (See letter attached) *			1000 . 00	
* A letter from the Director of Savings valuing the holding should be obtained and attached to the form.				
	Total carried overleaf			

Sheet............

Cap 40

Cont'd

1 Name of Company followed by full description of class of share or stock and unit of quotation. If bearer the fact should be stated.	2 No of Shares or amount of Stock	3 Market Price at date of valuation	4 Principal value at date of valuation £	p	For official use only
....					
....					
....					
....					
....					
....					
....					
....					
....					
....					
....					
....					
....					
....					
....					
....					
Total carried to Sheet					

Printed in the UK for HMSO. 3/90 Dd 8173413 269M 29038

		Gross value at date of death*
	Brought forward	14 000

Household and personal goods, including pictures, china, linen, clothes, books plate, jewels, motor cars, boats, etc.

Sold, realised gross	£	
Unsold, estimated	£ 1700	1700

The deceased's interest expectant upon death of

aged   years, under the will/intestacy of

who died on the
or under a settlement dated the
and made between

(setting out the parties to the deed), in the property set out in the statement annexed, of which fund the present trustees are

                                                Tick as appropriate

Was the interest at any time acquired for value whether
by the deceased or a predecessor in title?   Yes ☐   No ☐

Income tax repayable

Other personal property not comprised under the preceding heads
Please give details

Gross property not subject to the instalment option to be carried to page 6 and to the Probate Summary on page 12	15 700

* All claims for exemptions or reliefs should be made in the Summary on page 10

Section 1A   Continued

Section 1A continued

Schedule of liabilities and funeral expenses. Particulars of the funeral expenses of the deceased and the liabilities due and owing from him at the time of his death to persons resident within the United Kingdom or to persons resident out of the United Kingdom but contracted to be paid in the United Kingdom, or charged on property situated within the United Kingdom (other than liabilities deducted in Section 1B or section 2 under footnote (b) on page 8).

Name and address of creditor	Description of liability	Amount	For official use only
British Gas	Gas Bill	25	
Buyitnow Ltd.	Goods supplied	75	

Funeral expenses

E N Tomb + Co.		600	

Total to be carried to the Summary below and to the Probate Summary on page 12 — **700**

Summary

Gross property (from page 5) not subject to the instalment option	15 700
Less total of liabilities and funeral expenses from above	700
Net property in the United Kingdom not subject to the instalment option to be carried to page 11 (Section 1A, net total before relief(s))	15 000

Section 4 on page 9 must be completed in respect of all liabilities listed in the above schedule.

6

Section 1B	Property with the Instalment Option	For official use only

Tick as appropriate

- Is the tax on this property to be paid on delivery of this account?   Yes ☐   No ☑
- Is payment to be made in yearly instalments?   Yes ☑   No ☐

Value at date of death

Land etc. owned by the deceased in the United Kingdom (not being settled land) whether or not subject to a trust for sale as described on Cap 37 annexed.

140 000

Business interests

- Net value of deceased's interest in the business(es), as statement or balance sheet annexed.

- Net value of deceased's interest as partner in the firm of

  [   ]

  as statement or balance sheet annexed

Stocks, shares, debentures and other securities, as set out on Cap 40.

- Shares or securities etc within Section 228(1) (a) Inheritance Tax Act 1984 which gave the deceased control of the company immediately before his death *see Section 269 Inheritance Tax Act 1984.*

- Other unquoted shares or securities etc. within Section 228(1) (b) or (c) or (d) Inheritance Tax Act 1984 (all other unquoted shares to be included in Section 1A).

Value of property within the instalment option to be carried to the Probate Summary on Page 12.

140 000

Liabilities charged at the date of the deceased's death on the property included above other than those already taken into account above

Particulars of liability	Property on which charged	Amount

Total liabilities to be carried to the Probate Summary on page 12.

Value of property with the instalment option less liabilities to be carried to page 11 (Section 1B, net total before reliefs).

140 000

* All claims for exemptions and reliefs should be made in the Summary on page 10.

Section 4 on page 9 must be completed in respect of all liabilities listed above

Section 2

All other property on which the personal representatives are liable to pay the tax (or would be liable if any tax were payable) including:-

- all nominated property and property passing by survivorship

- all property situated outside the UK

Section 2A - Property without the Instalment Option

For official use only

Particulars of the property, local situation and details of disposition if nominated or in joint names	Value at date of death
Gross Value	

Liabilities* in respect of the property above		Amount
Name and Address of Creditor	Description of liability	
	Total liabilities	

Net value to be carried to page 11 (Section 2A, net total before reliefs)

Section 2B - Property with the Instalment Option

Tick as appropriate

- Is the tax on this property to be paid on delivery of this account? ☐ Yes ☐ No
- Is payment to be made by yearly instalments? ☐ Yes ☐ No

Particulars of the property, local situation and details of disposition if nominated or in joint names	Value at date of death
Gross Value	

Liabilities* In respect of the property above		Amount
Name and Address of Creditor	Description of Liability	
	Total liabilities	

Net value to be carried to page 11 (Section 2B, net total before reliefs)

---

* All claims for exemptions or reliefs should be made in the Summary on page 10
+ Liabilities   (a) due from the deceased at the time of his death to persons resident outside the United Kingdom (other than liabilities contracted to be paid in the United Kingdom, or charged on property within the United Kingdom which have been deducted in Sections 1A and 1B) or
(b) (so far as not included in (a) charged upon incurred in connection with or otherwise affecting the property included in this Section

Section 4 on page 9 must be completed in respect of all liabilities listed above.

Inland Revenue

Capital Taxes Office

CTO Reference

Schedule of Real, Leasehold, Heritable and Immovable Property

Name of Deceased, Transferor or Settlement
IONA NOWILL

Date of Death or Transfer
29/3/1994

Name and address of the person to whom the Valuation Office should send any communication	Makepiece & Streiff Solicitors Bank Chambers BARCHESTER Postcode BR1 2YZ

Reference
O De/W

Telephone Number
Barchester 4321

Please read the notes below before completing this form.

Separate forms should be used for properties in England and Wales, Scotland, Northern Ireland and any other country.

The description of the property in column 2 should be sufficient to enable it to be readily identified. Please include the address and any street number and the types of buildings and distinguish between arable, pasture, orchards, gardens, moors, commons, woodland, building and other land. If necessary, please state the area and O.S. Enclosure numbers (and the sheet number and edition) and attach a plan. A map delineating the exact boundary of Northern Irish property should be attached.

In column 3 please state whether the tenure is freehold, leasehold etc or in Scotland is feu, lease tack etc.

For let property in column 4 please state
- the date of the tenancy
- the term of the letting
- the current rent
- the rent review pattern
- who is responsible for outgoings, or in Scotland feu duty.

If the property was occupied by the deceased/transferor or was unoccupied please say so.

In column 5 please state separately the value of
- any agricultural property in respect of which agricultural relief is claimed
- any timber in respect of which relief under the FA 1975 Schedule 9 or the CTTA/IHTA 1984 Sections 125-130 is claimed
and supply sufficient details to enable each area of agricultural and/or timber-bearing land to be identified.

In column 6 please state the value of the property including the value of any agricultural property or timber but ignoring any reliefs or exemptions claimed.

Please also indicate on the form, or if space is insufficient on a separate schedule, whether
- any value has been agreed with the District Valuer
- any property has been sold and, if so, the gross sale price and completion date
- any property is on the market for sale or is intended to be sold.

1 Item No	2 Description	3 Tenure	4 Lettings	5 Agricultural/ Timber element £	6 Gross Value £
1.	21, Almond Avenue BARCHESTER	Freehold	—	—	140 000
	Note : There are no plans at present that the property be sold. The value given has not been agreed with the District Valuer.				
	Sheet......1.........	Total(s) carried overleaf			140 000

Cap 37

CTO Reference

1 Item No	2 Description	3 Tenure	4 Lettings	5 Agricultural/ Timber element £	6 Gross Value £
		Total(s) carried to Sheet................			

Note: Further copies of this form may be obtained where the Account or Inventory was supplied, or from The Capital Taxes Office, Rockley Road, London, W14 0DF, or in Scotland, 16 Picardy Place, Edinburgh, EH1 3NB; or in Northern Ireland, Law Courts Building, Chichester Street, Belfast. BT1 3NU.

Printed in the UK for HMSO. 3/90 Dd 8173413 258M 25038

Section 3

Any other property in the UK and elsewhere in which the deceased had or is treated as having had a beneficial interest in possession immediately before his death including:-

- property over which the deceased had and exercised by will a general power of appointment.

- property outside the UK comprised in a settlement made by a UK domiciled person.

- property gifted by the deceased subject to a reservation retained by the deceased.

Part 1 Property on which tax is elected to be paid on delivery of this account should be listed below and headed "Part 1"

- Is the tax on any property with the Instalment Option to be paid by yearly   *Tick as appropriate* instalments?

  ☐ Yes   ☐ No

- Separate net totals for Part 1 (property without the instalment option) and Part 1 (property with the instalment option) should be carried to page 11 (Sections 1a (non-instalment option property) and 1b (instalment option property) net totals before reliefs).

Part 2 Property on which tax is not to be paid on delivery of this account should be listed below and headed "Part 2" and its net value carried to page 11 (Section 1c, net total before reliefs).

Separate consecutive numbering for part 1 and part 2	Particulars of the property	Net value at date of death *		For official use only
		Property without the instalment option £	Property with the instalment option £	

* *All claims for exemptions or reliefs should be made in the Summary on page 10*

Section 4

Deductions of liabilities listed in this account

Tick as appropriate

Yes   No

In the case of any liability for which a deduction has been taken in either section 1A, 1B, 2A, 2B or 3 of this account did the consideration for any such debt or incumbrance incurred or created on or after 18 March 1986 consist of property derived from the deceased or was the consideration given by any person who was at any time entitled to, or amongst whose resources there was at any time included any property derived from the deceased?

☐   ☑

If "Yes", please give full particulars, including the liabilities in question, the consideration given and the derivation of that consideration from the deceased.

Please attach schedules as necessary.

Summary of exemptions and reliefs against capital

- please see instruction booklet IHT 210 as to how this page should be completed
- Schedules should be attached as necessary

Property in respect of which exemption or relief is claimed. The description should not be more detailed than is necessary to identify the property	Nature of exemption or relief claimed	Net value of property £	Amounts exemption or relief claimed £	For official use only
Property included in Section 1A				
Total of exemptions and reliefs Section 1A to be carried to page 11 (reliefs column)				
Property included in Section 1B				
Total of exemptions and reliefs Section 1B to be carried to page 11 (reliefs column)				
Property included in other sections - state and show separately which section (sections 2A and B and 3 (Part 1) and 3 (Part 2) A separate total of exemptions and reliefs for each of these sections should be carried to page 11 (reliefs column)				

Assessment of Inheritance Tax

Summary for determining chargeable rates

Section of accounts	Net total £	Reliefs £	Value of property after reliefs £
1(a) Property without the instalment option			
1A	15000		15000
2A			
3, Part 1			
Total 1(a)	15000		15000
1(b) Property with the instalment option			
1B	140 000		140 000
2B			
3, Part 1			
Total 1(b)	140 000		140 000
1(c) Other property on which tax is not being paid on this account			
3, Part 2			
Total 1(c)			
Total 1 (a) to (c)	155 000		A 155 000
Cumulative total of chargeable transfers made prior to the deceased's death		B	
Aggregate chargeable transfers (A + B)		C 155 000	

Amount payable on this account

Calculation of tax

	£	p
Tax on **C** on first £ 150000 plus on balance of £ 5000 @40%	NIL 2000	– 00
Total	2000	00
Less tax on **B** at death rate on first £ plus on balance of £ @ %		
Total		
Less QSR (as attached schedule)		
Total tax chargeable on **A**	D 2000	00

Any capital figure multiplied by **D** gives the **A** proportion of tax assessable on that capital

Value on which tax is now being paid

	Value of property	
	non-instalment £	Instalment option £
Total value at 1(a)	15000	
That part of 1(b) on which tax now to be paid		

Amount payable on this account

Non instalment property	£	p
Total value at 1(a) £ 15000 × D/A =	193	55
Less reliefs against tax other than QSR Net tax	193	55
add interest on net tax from 19 to 19 (years days at %)		
Total tax and interest on non-instalment property (carried to page 12)	193	55
Additional tax and interest due under S7 IHTA 1984-as attached schedule (carried to page 12)		

Instalment option property	£	p
That part of 1(b) on which tax now to be paid £ × D/A =		
Less reliefs against tax other than QSR Net tax		
add interest on net tax from 19 to 19 (years days at %)		
Instalments - tenths of net tax		
add interest on instalments now assessed from 19 (date last instalment due) to 19 (days at %)		
†add interest on whole of net tax on instalment property from 19 to 19 (years days at %)		
Total tax and interest on instalment option property (carried to page 12)		

Interest

* Tax becomes due 6 months after the end of the month in which the death occurred. Unpaid tax carries interest from and including the day after the due date, irrespective of the reason for the late payment.

† Only if the due date for the second or subsequent instalment has now passed and interest relief (see IHT 210) is not in point, add here interest on the whole of the net tax on the instalment option property up to the due date of the last instalment.

Interest on overpaid tax, please note that, where tax or interest is paid in excess of the amount found to be due, interest is allowed on the amount overpaid.

11

Probate Summary

		£
Aggregate Gross Value which in law devolves on and vests in the personal representatives of the deceased, for and in respect of which the Grant is to be made	Section 1A	15700
	Section 1B	140 000
	Section 3*	

* absolute power property only

Total to be carried to the probate papers	155700

Deduct

Section 1A, total of liabilities and funeral expenses	700
Section 1B, total of liabilities	
Net value for probate purposes	155 000

For official use only

Total of Tax and Interest from page 11 £

Total Tax and Interest - Non-Instalment Property	193 — 55
Total Tax and Interest - Instalment Option Property	
Additional Tax and Interest due under S7 Inheritance Tax Act 1984	
Total tax and interest payable now on this account	193 — 55

EDP

On the basis of this Account the tax (and interest) payable now is	193 — 55

Makepiece & Streiff .

14th May 19 94

Solicitor(s) for the applicant(s)

This receipt and stamp do not imply that the assessment is not subject to rectification: the account will be fully examined after the issue of the grant.

Prints of this form and of the instructions (IHT 210) can be obtained from the Capital Taxes Office, Inland Revenue, Rockley Road, London W14 0DF (Britdoc: DX90200, Minford House W14) and on personal application only at the Stamps Office, Room G3, South West Wing, Bush House, Strand, WC2B 4QN the London Chief Post Office, King Edward Street, EC1A 1AA, the Branch Post Offices at 24 Throgmorton Street, EC2N 2JE; 40 Fleet Street, EC4Y 1BT; 181 High Holborn, WC1 1AA; 2-4 Bishops Court, Chancery Lane, WC2A 1EA and from other large branch post offices in major towns and cities outside the Metropolitan Postal District as listed in form CAP 18 (which can be obtained from the Capital Taxes Office).

12

Printed in the UK for HMSO. 3/90 Dd 8173413 258M 25038

In the HIGH COURT of JUSTICE

The District Probate Registry at Barchester

BE IT KNOWN THAT IONA NOWILL of 21 Almond Avenue Barchester BR3 8MN died on the 29th day of March 1994 domiciled in England and Wales

intestate

AND BE IT FURTHER KNOWN that at the date hereunder written letters of Administration of all the estate which by law devolves to and rests in the personal representative of the said intestate were granted by the High Court of Justice at the said Registry to

JOHN EDWIN SMITH of 32 Hazel Grove BARCHESTER BR3 1AZ

And it is hereby certified that an Inland Revenue Account has been delivered wherein it is shown that the gross value of the said estate in the United Kingdom (exclusive of what the said intestate may have been possessed of or entitled to as a trustee and not beneficiary) amounts to £155,700 and that the net value of the estate amounts to £155,000.

Dated the 31st day of May 1994.

P.R.O. Bates

Extracted by Makepiece & Streiff, Bank Chambers, Barchester BR1 2YZ (Ref. O De'A/W)

Post-grant practice

The first action to be taken on receipt of a grant (of whatever type) is to check it. There is a simplified process for dealing with some errors on omissions (in practice a rare occurrence) found within 14 days of the grant being sealed by the Registrar. If discovered at a later date, any amendment has to be effected by a Registrar's order.

The precise action necessary will of course vary with the individual case, but broadly the pattern for a solvent estate (*i.e.* one where the assets are sufficient to pay funeral, testamentary and administration expenses, debts and liabilities in full) is broadly as follows:

The first step is to register the grant—*i.e.* to produce it (usually, in practice, an office copy) to the various institutions in which the deceased held investments or accounts for them to record and mark accordingly. At the same time, and in accordance with the instructions of the personal representatives, arrangements will be put in hand to realise the amounts due to the estate: this will usually be achieved by arranging for the withdrawal of the sum due or for the sale of the asset concerned. When funds become available, normally any loan to fund the payment of Inheritance Tax is first discharged, and then the other debts and liabilities discharged provided the time specified in the statutory advertisements (under section 27 of the Trustee Act 1925) for the submission of claims has elapsed. Provided he does not distribute within six months of the date of the grant the personal representative is protected against personal liability in the event of the court permitting an application after the expiry of that period under the Inheritance (Provision for Family and Dependants) Act 1975. Subject to this period having elapsed the personal representative may safely proceed to distribute the estate. First, he will pay and discharge the various legacies bequeathed by the will (if any). The estate's tax position will need to be finalised. There may be a refund of Income Tax due to the estate: this forms part of the estate for Inheritance Tax purposes, whilst an amount of Income or Capital Gains Tax due from the deceased at the date of his death will be a liability which can normally be deducted. In either event (and if other alterations are found to be necessary) a corrective account for Inheritance Tax will have to be submitted (sometimes this is done informally by means of a letter where there are only small differences in value) and any refund due collected or further liability discharged. The estate may well have a liability to Income or Capital Gains Tax for the period since the date of death. Where any Inheritance Tax has been paid, normally the personal representative will apply to the Capital Taxes Office (through his solicitor) for a certificate of discharge (using IHT Form 30) from any further liability (both for himself and the property comprised in the deceased's estate).

Having done all these things, the final accounts can be prepared for the approval of the personal representatives. These will show how the various assets in the estate have been dealt with, the liabilities discharged, and the net estate distributed. Once approved by the executor(s) or administrator(s), they are submitted to the residuary beneficiaries for their agreement, and the residue can then be distributed to those entitled.

As this may be a fairly lengthy process, often interim distributions will be made to residuary beneficiaries, which are then brought into account on the final distribution. If the personal representative is satisfied that an asset is not required for administration purposes (*e.g.* to pay debts or legacies) he may, instead of realising it, transfer it to a beneficiary absolutely entitled by the means appropriate to the type of asset concerned—for example, an assent in the case of land, with a memorandum indorsed on the original grant.

Limited grants

Most grants are general in the sense that the grant is not by its terms limited in any way. This may be so even though the grant is preceded by another in respect of the same estate. For example:

(a) *Double probate.* If an executor to whom power has been reserved on the making of the original grant later applies for probate he will be issued a grant called "double probate." If the original grant was made to four executors, he must await a vacancy before he can apply. The grant of double probate is a general grant which runs concurrently with the original grant.

(b) *Cessate grant.* Where a grant has been issued limited as to its duration, it automatically terminates on the occurrence of the event which limits its duration. When this happens, a further grant called a cessate grant may be made, which may be general.

Some grants, however, are specifically limited grants—either as to duration or as to the property to which the grant extends. The following are some examples:

1. *Settled land grants*

Issued where the deceased had vested in him at his death settled land, *i.e.* settled previously to his death and not by his will and remaining settled notwithstanding his death. Such a grant is made to the deceased's special personal representatives (usually in practice the trustees of the settlement). Normally in these cases the grant made in respect of the deceased's free estate must exclude the settled land.

2. *Limited probate*

An executor's appointment may be qualified as to subject-matter (*e.g.* a literary executor) or as to time (*e.g.* during the minority of my son S). The grant issued to such an executor will be similarly limited.

3. *Grant "de bonis non"*

This is correctly styled a grant of "administration de bonis non administratis," and is made in respect of the unadministered estate of a deceased to enable the administration to be completed. It is only necessary where a sole, or last surviving, personal representative has died without having completed the administration of the deceased's estate, but has obtained a grant. If, for example, an executor begins to act but dies before a grant is issued to him, there will be an original grant of administration with the will annexed and a grant *de bonis non* would be inappropriate. However, even if there has been a previous grant, a grant *de bonis non* will not be necessary if there is an unbroken chain of proving executors. The concept of the so-called "chain of representation" is best illustrated by an example:

Suppose A is the sole (or last surviving executor) of a testator T. A has obtained a grant of probate of T's will but dies, having by his will appointed B to be his (*i.e.* A's) executor, and B proves A's will. The consequence is that B is the executor of A and also the executor by representation of T. If B is not prepared to act in this capacity, he must renounce probate of A's will, he cannot accept that office and renounce office as executor by representation of T.

The chain of representation can in principle extend to any number of estates, since the last executor in an unbroken chain is the executor of every preceding testator. However, the chain is broken by:

(i) an intestacy
(ii) the failure of a testator to appoint an executor
(iii) the failure to obtain probate of a will.

Where a grant *de bonis non* is necessary because the chain of representation has been broken, or where the court has revoked a previous grant for some reason (*e.g.* the mental or physical incapacity of the grantee rendering him unfit to act), the rules of priority (*NCPR, Rules 20 and 22*) regulating original grants equally apply to the *de bonis non* grant.

4. *Administration for the use and benefit of a minor*

A person under the age of 18 cannot take a grant; where such a person is appointed a sole executor a grant of administration with will annexed can be made for the use and benefit of the minor until he attains the age of 18, when it will automatically terminate. (If the grant which would otherwise have been made is simple administration, then the grant for the minor's use and benefit will be of the same kind.) The grant is normally to the infant's parents or guardians under *NCPR, Rule 32* and if a minority or life interest arises under the will or intestacy, the grant must normally be made to at least two persons. If an infant is appointed as one of two or more executors, such a grant is normally unnecessary; a grant of probate can be issued to the other executor(s), power being reserved to the minor.

5. *Administration during mental or physical incapacity*

A grant of probate or letters of administration cannot be taken by a person incapable, by reason of mental or physical incapacity, of managing his affairs. A grant of administration for that person's use or benefit during his incapacity may be made—with will annexed if the deceased left a will. Normally, no such grant will issue unless all persons equally entitled have been cleared off, and (as in the case of an infant executor) power can be reserved to an incapacitated executor on a grant to others appointed by the will. The grant will be made (under *NCPR, Rule 35*) to the person authorised to take the grant by the Court of Protection in the case of mental incapacity. If there is no such authorised person or in the case of physical incapacity, the grantee will according to the circumstances normally be either the person entitled to the deceased's residuary estate or the person who would be entitled to a grant of letters of administration to the estate of the person suffering the incapacity if he had died intestate.

6. *Administration ad colligenda bona*

This grant can be made to any suitable person with a view to preserving the assets of an estate until a general grant can be made. It is always limited until such further grant is issued, and is usually limited to the purpose of collecting, getting in and receiving the estate and doing acts necessary for its preservation. The grant is always one of simple administration; no distribution is authorised by the grant, so annexing any will would be superfluous.

7. *Administration pendente lite*

Such an administrator may be appointed to act under the court's supervision and control where a probate action has been commenced, on the application by any party to such action or any other interested person (*e.g.* a creditor). Usually such a grant is made to someone totally unconnected with the action, who will have authority under the grant to act only during the course of that action. An administrator *pendente lite* has no authority to make any distribution (even interim) of the estate, though he can realise assets and pay debts and discharge other liabilities such as funeral and testamentary expenses.

Caveats

These are governed by *NCPR, Rule 44*. A caveat is a written notice to the Family Division not to seal a grant without notice to the caveator, (the person entering the caveat) and its purpose is to prevent the issue of a grant in respect of the deceased's estate (other than to the caveator himself). The Registrar must not allow a grant to be sealed if he had knowledge of an effective caveat, and to this end the index of caveats maintained at the Principal Registry is always searched on any application for a grant in any Registry.

If an applicant for a grant discovers that a caveat has been entered, he may issue a warning in the form prescribed by the rules to the caveator. This states the applicant's interest (*e.g.* as executor named in the deceased's will) and directs the caveator to do one of two things within eight days:

(a) to enter an appearance to the warning, setting out the caveator's interest (*e.g.* that he is the executor appointed by another will of the deceased). If an appearance is entered, no grant can be issued without an order of the court;

(b) to issue a summons for directions if the caveator has no contrary interest but wishes to show cause against the sealing of a grant to the applicant issuing the warning.

If the caveator does neither of these things, then the caveat ceases to have any effect, and the grant may issue to the applicant. A caveat also ceases to be effective at the end of six months from the date of its entry, though during the last month of this period the caveator may apply for its extension for a further six months; this exercise may be repeated, each time extending the caveat for a further six months.

CHAPTER 2

TRIBUNALS, ADMINISTRATIVE PROCEEDINGS AND ARBITRATION

TRIBUNALS

Introduction

Tribunals, like courts, have the power of adjudication in matters properly brought before them and, subject to any rights of appeal, their decisions are binding on the parties. Whilst there have been tribunals throughout the centuries, their development to cover many matters of intimate personal concern to the citizen has been a feature of the post-war years. Three important influences in this have been (1) the growth of benefits for the underprivileged, (2) measures to protect the employee and (3) the advances in technology, calling for rulings in the public interest on complex scientific or technical matters.

Tribunals are set up by particular statutes, for the special purposes of each. It follows that they vary widely in their composition, powers and procedures. Together they do not form any sort of co-ordinated system, being, as they are, entirely independent of each other. They function parallel with the law courts and the ways in which they inter-relate with the courts will be mentioned as we proceed. Procedurally tribunals contrast with courts in their accessibility, informality and relative speed of decision.

The Council of Tribunals, which exercises a general supervision over their activities, lists over 40 different kinds of tribunal. Some have a single place for sittings, where cases from all over the country are heard. Others are regionalised systems, with local sittings in many towns throughout the United Kingdom. Thus, there are over 400 tribunals of General Commissioners of Income Tax which hear appeals from tax-payers in the localities in which the tax-payers reside or carry on business. Chosen from the local business and professional community, the General Commissioners deal with nearly a million cases a year.

Some indication of the scope and variety of subject matter covered by the whole range of tribunals is given below (p. 89).

Statutory regulation and tribunals are in a sense the two sides of the same coin. Regulations commonly confer a power of adjudication on someone in authority and this in turn calls for a means of seeing that the power is not used unfairly against an individual. The extension of social security and welfare benefits, for instance, has brought into existence a network of local officials of the DSS (Department of Social Security) who have the power to grant or refuse benefits to individuals in need. Persons dissatisfied ("aggrieved" is the term often used) by their decisions can ask for a hearing before a tribunal, which can if it thinks fit reverse the decision of the official.

The legislations passed in the 1960s, 1970s and 1980s for the protection of employees has brought a new class of tribunals in its train: the industrial tribunals, whose decisions are often in the news. Many other tribunals on the other hand, govern the activities of specialist bodies and persons and are little heard of by the public.

Legal representation has not hitherto been common in most kinds of tribunal and the relative simplicity of the procedures makes it possible for the individual to fight his own case. Many do. Disadvantaged persons often have friends, social workers and others to speak for them at hearings. Trade union officials represent their members in employment cases. Legal representation is allowed before most tribunals and solicitors are increasingly called on to represent applicants before industrial tribunals. Legal aid, on the other hand, is not generally available to parties to tribunal applications, except before the Employment Appeals Tribunal, the Lands Tribunal and the Mental Health Review Tribunal. However, advice and assistance can be given in the office under the Green Form Scheme (see Vol. 1, Chap. 4).

To show the way in which the business of one kind of tribunal is conducted, we will take a closer look at the industrial tribunals.

Industrial tribunal practice

The protection of employees at work has been a notable aspect of social reform in the 1960s, 1970s and 1980s and most of the statutory rights enacted in their favour have been made enforceable through the industrial tribunals. Thus, a tribunal may have to deal with such diverse claims against an employer as failure to give equal pay to women; sex or race discrimination; failure to notify terms of employment; failure to pay redundancy compensation; unfair dismissal and so on.

Industrial tribunals sit in over 70 centres in England and Wales. Each sitting normally comprises a legally qualified chairman and two other members, one from a panel nominated by employers' organisations and one from that nominated by the trade unions. Decisions are by majority vote, but if a tribunal has only two members the chairman has a casting vote.

The procedure for making an application and bringing a case to a hearing is laid down by the Industrial Tribunals (Rules of Procedure) Regulations 1985.

There are time limits to be observed, but the tribunal will be prepared to extend the limits if there is a reasonable excuse. Generally an application must be made within three months of the act complained of.

Originating applications, as they are called, are made in writing to the Central Office of Industrial Tribunals, Southgate Street, Bury St. Edmunds, Suffolk IP33 2AQ. If an application is received in a Regional Office, this will comply if the Assistant Secretary there accepts it for forwarding to the Central Office.

It is possible for someone who has been dismissed to ask the employer for a written statement of the reasons for the dismissal. This enables the former employee to see if he or she has any kind of case to take to a Tribunal.

The preparation of a case for hearing is summarised on an adjoining page. Sometimes a pre-hearing assessment is held. This may be called for by a party or may be required by the tribunal itself. A pre-hearing assessment may be held where on the face of the documents one party has no case. Following the pre-hearing, which will usually be heard by a chairman only and at which no witnesses will be called, a party may be notified of the tribunal's view that he does not appear to have a case. If following this the party notified goes on, the hearing will be by different tribunal members. The other consequences are mentioned below.

Hearings are invariably in public. The conduct of a case is in form not unlike a court hearing: witnesses are normally sworn, and are examined in chief, cross-examined and re-examined, as in court. However, strict rules of evidence are not followed and hearsay evidence can be accepted. Members of the tribunal often take an active part in asking questions and in assisting witnesses and unrepresented parties to put their points.

The case may be opened by either party. The general rule is that the party on whom the burden of proof lies opens. Thus, an applicant who alleges discrimination must open by proving it. In a claim arising out of dismissal, the respondent may deny that the applicant was dismissed. If so, the applicant must first prove the dismissal. In most claims for unfair dismissal, however, the employer's case is presented first. In unfair dismissal cases the employer must show what the reason was for the dismissal, *e.g.* poor work, bad timekeeping or dishonesty at work. It is then for the tribunal to decide whether the dismissal was fair or not in accordance with the equity.

When the parties' cases are closed, the tribunal may retire to deliberate. On resuming, the decision may be given with the reasons therefore. However, both the decision and the reasons, or just the reasons, may be reserved. In this event, whatever is reserved is communicated to the parties or their representatives after a lapse, perhaps of several weeks. Detailed reasons need only be given if asked for by either party.

Costs are not normally awarded, but the tribunal has the power to make an award of costs where a party has acted frivolously, vexatiously or unreasonably. Failure to heed a warning given at a pre-hearing assessment (see above) that there is no case to answer may justify an award of costs to the other party. If awarded, costs may be of a sum fixed by the tribunal or for the whole or a part of a party's costs as taxed. In this event, the costs will be taxed in the county court.

In unfair dismissal cases, the tribunal's power extends to ordering the reinstatement or re-engagement of the employee. Reinstatement results in the employee being entitled to be treated in all respects as if he had not been dismissed, so that any pay or other benefits lost by reason of the dismissal should be made good to him. Re-engagement requires the employer to give the employee a new start on terms specified by the tribunal. But the usual remedy is compensation based on loss of earnings, pension and other rights subject to certain maxima which change from time to time.

However, there is no way of forcing an employer to take back an employee he does not want. If the order is not complied with, the employee's remedy is to apply again to the industrial tribunal for compensation. In these circumstances, the tribunal is able to award compensation over and above that normally available for unfair dismissal. The addition may be up to 52 weeks' wages, depending on the circumstances.

The decision of an industrial tribunal may be called in question by one of two methods:

(1) Application may be made by a party at the hearing or within 14 days for a review. If granted, this leads to a rehearing at a further session of the same, or other, members. This is appropriate where it is alleged that there has been some error by tribunal staff, or a party did not receive due notice or was absent or new evidence has become available. Finally, a review may be had if "the interests of justice require such a review."

(2) Appeal lies to the Employment Appeal Tribunal (EAT) on a point of law. This supervisory tribunal is presided over by a High Court judge who is supported by two lay members as in the case of the industrial tribunal. Decisions of the industrial tribunal have no force as precedents, but decisions of EAT are reported and bind industrial tribunals. The EAT, on the other hand, is not bound to follow its own decisions, but normally does so. An appeal lies on a point of law from the EAT (with leave) to the Court of Appeal and on to the House of Lords in the usual way.

Unfair dismissal—outline of procedure

References to A(Applicant) and R(Respondent) include their solicitors.

Pre-hearing

(1) A sends *Form IT1* (or, in case of urgency, letter) to Secretary of Tribunals, Central Office.

(2) Secretary checks application for completeness, etc., allocates case number and assigns case to appropriate Regional Office, to which papers are sent.

(3) Secretary sends acknowledgement to A and a copy to D with *Form IT3* (Notice of Appearance by Respondent) giving 14 days for entry of appearance.

(4) R sends *Form IT3* to Secretary.

(5) Secretary sends copy *IT3* to A and copies of *IT1* and *IT3* to the Advisory, Conciliation and Arbitration Service (ACAS). Its job is to try to promote a pre-hearing settlement.

(6) (Assuming no preliminary hearing required) Secretary fixes hearing date and notifies parties, giving not less than 14 days' notice. Up to seven days before hearing date, a party can make further points on the issues raised in writing to the Secretary, sending a copy to the other party.

Note: If agreement is reached, whether through ACAS or independently, both parties complete and sign *Form CO3* and sen it to the Secretary.

Hearing

(Order where A claims unfair dismissal following notice of dismissal).
(7) Opening statement by R.
(8) Evidence for R.
(9) Evidence for A.

Note: Evidence on oath, as in court: examination in chief—cross-examination—re-examination—questions by tribunal.

(10) Statement by A.
(11) Final statement by R.
(12) (Where they so wish) Tribunal retires and later resumes.
(13) Tribunal announce decision with reasons, or intimate that decision will be communicated to the parties.

An application to an industrial tribunal for unfair dismissal

John Fraser v. *Huco Engineering Ltd.*

Mr. John Fraser consults Messrs. Makepiece & Streiff after receiving a letter from his employers dismissing him. He is seen by Phillip Friendly, the assistant solicitor, who does much of their advocacy work. Mr. Fraser opens the interview by showing Mr. Friendly the letter and recounting the events that led up to it. He wants to know if he can make a case against them. He makes it clear that he disputes what they say in the letter and thinks they are being unfair to him.

Before inquiring further into the background, Mr. Friendly asks the client whether he is able to meet the legal fees that may be involved. He explains that if on examination there appears to be a claim for unfair dismissal, it would be taken to an industrial tribunal, where, unfortunately, legal aid is not available. If he is a member of a trade union the union may be prepared to represent him. He says he is not a member. Mr. Friendly tells him that if his means are limited he may be eligible for advice and assistance under the Green Form Scheme, but this would not extend to representation before the tribunal. Mr. Fraser says he is buying a house on mortgage. Mr. Friendly tells him that this does not have to be taken into account. However, he states that he has about £3,700 in savings and his disposable income (see Vol. 1, Chap. 4, "Legal Aid") whilst in work is more than the limit for making an application under the scheme. He has received six weeks' wages in lieu of notice. He says he will stake part of his savings to "have a go" at his employers.

Mr. Friendly tells his client that even if the claim failed, provided he has acted reasonably, he will not be ordered to pay his opponents' costs. Messrs. Makepiece's costs would depend on how much work was involved. Mr. Fraser says he wishes the matter to proceed. He pays the firm £500 on account of costs.

Mr. Friendly is now ready to take instructions and questions his client to obtain the details he requires. But first he re-reads the letter from the employers:

HUCO ENGINEERING LIMITED

Bessemer Works,
Barset.
Tel. 00765 1112
13th May 1993

Mr J. Fraser,
5 Byron Way,
Barset.

Dear Mr Fraser,

I regret that your continued inability to keep to the firm's rules on timekeeping makes it necessary to give you notice of dismissal.

As you well know, you have been warned repeatedly about lateness. Verbal warnings have been given to you by your supervisor, Mr Seemly and I wrote to you on 8th January last giving you clear warning of the consequences of continued lateness. In spite of this you have been late three times so far this month. Your repeated flouting of the rules is having a detrimental effect on staff discipline generally. It cannot be tolerated and I have, therefore, to terminate your employment and enclose a cheque for six weeks' wages in lieu of notice. Please sign and return the attached receipt.

Yours faithfully,

J. Booth
Personnel Officer

Mr. Friendly now takes Mr. Fraser through the events leading up to the dismissal. He questions his client on these matters, jotting down his answers in short note form:

MAKEPIECE & STREIFF

ATTENDANCE NOTE

NOTE OF: Interview   DATE: 24.5.1993

CLIENT: John Fraser   ADDRESS: 5 Byron Way

MATTER:

TAKEN BY: PF.   TIME 10.30

Has lost job at Huco Engineering Ltd. Design engineer. Age, 45, Born 23.4.1948 With Huco from about 1.10.81. Basic salary £18,000 p.a.

Not eligible under green form.

Letter of dismissal 13.5.93. Denies repeated warnings about lateness. Late on a handful of occasions in last 12 months? 10 times. Son, 8 years, has chronic asthma. Has bad bouts at night. Very distressed. Mr Fraser has had to stay at home to look after the other children (3, 5 yrs) whilst Mrs F. takes son to doctor's morning surgery. Or just to comfort him.

Head of department knows all about it, has expressed sympathy and understanding more than once. F. usually manages to get a message to head of department when he knows he will have to stay to look after the children. Will be able to show that reasons for lateness were accepted and lateness excused.

Firm works flexi-time system. 'Core time' is 0900–noon. Whenever he has been later than 0900 he has put in the extra time at the end of the day. Admits that getting up early is not always easy, particularly after a disturbed night with son. Will send in the warning letter. Also statutory notice with particulars of employment. No staff handbook issued.

Time-keeping of other staff just as bad. Nobody else dismissed: nobody else warned so far as F. knows. Unlikely that colleagues will speak openly on his behalf. No complaints about work or other conduct. Has been in a design team designing a workshop layout. Job was delivered last month. Other members of team are on a new job. No further work allocated to F. Has no information on new work coming in.

Time records: Every employee has a card to put into the time clock. Daily print-out goes to head of department.

Mr. Friendly explains the system of awards for unfair dismissal:

(1) A basic award related to years of employment. This is the same as the compensation payable on redundancy;

(2) A compensatory award, which is at the discretion of the tribunal and has an upper limit that is adjusted from time to time.

They discuss the possibility that the Company are really getting rid of Mr. Fraser because there is no work for him. If this were so, there would be an award under (1). However, the only available evidence to support a claim on these grounds is the fact that no new work has been allocated. Unfortunately, the only persons who would be able to give the true reasons for this are the senior managers of the Company and they could be expected to support the Company, rather than a member of the staff. It is decided, therefore, to bring the claim for unfair dismissal on the ground that Mr. Fraser's conduct was not such as to justify taking this extreme step. Mr. Friendly is, accordingly, to proceed with the application to an industrial tribunal. At the right time he will apply to the Company, as respondents, to produce the record of time-keeping of Mr. Fraser and comparable staff and any record they may have of warnings to such staff.

After the client leaves, Mr. Friendly passes the papers to the legal executive, Mr. W. White, who manages the litigation department, requesting him to deal with the matter. The Application is despatched to the Secretary of the Tribunals at the Central Office for England and Wales. From there it is referred to the appropriate regional centre, in this case, Barchester see pp. 76/77. Several days later Messrs. Makepiece receive formal acknowlegement, as follows on p. 78.

FOR COIT USE ONLY

Received at COIT	Case Number	Code
	Initials	ROIT

Application to an Industrial Tribunal

Please read the notes opposite before filling in this form

1. Say what type of complaint(s) you want the tribunal to decide *(see note opposite)*.

Unfair Dismissal

2. Please give your name and address in CAPITALS

Mr [✓]   Mrs [ ]   Miss [ ]   Ms [ ]

Surname   Fraser

First name(s)   John

Address

5 Byron Way
Barset

Postcode BA20 6CO

Telephone   00765 4444

Date of birth   23 April 1948

3. Please give the name and address of your representative, if you have one.

Name   Makepiece & Streiff

Address

Bank Chambers
Barset
Ref: PF/WW/Fraser

Postcode BA1 7DT

Telephone   00765 4321

4. Please give the details of the employer or body (the respondent) you are complaining about *(see note opposite)*.

Name   Huco Engineering Ltd.

Address

Bessemer Works
Barset

Postcode BA11 1TG

Telephone   00765 1112

Please give the place where you worked or applied for work, if different from above.

Name   As above

Address

Postcode

Telephone

5. Please say what job you did for the employer (or what job you applied for). If this does not apply, please say what your connection was with the employer.

Design Engineer

IT 1 and IT 1(Scot) (Revised Feb 1991) ————————————————— Over ▶

6. Please give the number of normal basic hours you worked per week.

Hours | 35 | per week

7. Basic wage/salary £ 18,000 per year

Average take home pay £ 1,110 per month

Other bonuses or benefits £ Car use per

8. Please give the dates of your employment. *(if applicable)*

Began on October 1981

Ended on 25 June 1993

9. If your complaint is not about dismissal. please give the date when the action you are complaining about took place (or the date when you first knew about it).

Date

10. Please give full details of your complaint *(see notes attached)*:

I have been given notice of termination of my employment on the grounds of bad timekeeping. I claim that I have been unfairly dismissed because:-

(1) My timekeeping was not so bad as to justify dismissal.

(2) The reasons for being late on a number of occasions were made known to my employers and my lateness had been excused by them.

11. Unfair dismissal claimants only *(Please tick a box to show what you would want if you win your case)*

☐ **Reinstatement:** to carry on working in your old job as before. ──────

☐ **Re-engagement:** to start another job. or a new contract, with your old employer. ──────

→ Orders for re-instatement or re-engagement normally include an award of compensation for loss of earnings.

☑ **Compensation only:** to get an award of money.

You can change your change your mind later. The Tribunal will take your preference into account. but will not be bound by it.

12. Have you already sent us a copy of this application by facsimile transmission (fax)?

Yes ☐   No ☑

Signed J. Fraser   Date 31-5-93

1797/13.9.2ᴴᴷˢ

Messrs. Makepiece & Streiff,
Bank Chambers,
Barchester,
BR1 2YZ

Your reference
PF/WW/12/Fraser
Case No
7255/91/18
Date 3rd June 1993

INDUSTRIAL TRIBUNALS (RULES OF PROCEDURE)
REGULATIONS 1985
NOTICE

1. The application for a decision of a tribunal under the above Regulations has been received. It has been entered in the Register and allotted the case number shown above. This number should be quoted in any further communications which should be sent to the address at the foot of this notice.

2. A copy of the application has been sent to the respondent and a copy of any reply will be sent to you.

3. A notice of hearing will be sent to you not less than 14 days before the date fixed for the hearing of the application.

4. In all cases where the Act under which the application is made provides for conciliation the services of a conciliation officer are available to the parties. In such cases a copy of the application is sent to the Advisory Conciliation and Arbitration Service accordingly.

(Signed)
for Assistant Secretary of the Tribunals.

Regional Office of the
Industrial Tribunals
(Barsetshire)
Crown Buildings,
Guildhall Street,
Barchester.

Industrial Tribunals

Case number: 7255/93/18

Notice of Appearance by Respondent

1 Please give the following details

Mr ☐ Mrs ☐ Miss ☐ Ms ☐

Other title _____

(Or give the name of the company or organisation)

Name HUCO ENGINEERING LIMITED

Address BESSEMER WORKS

BARSET

Telephone 00765 1112

5 If a representative is acting for you, please give his/her name and address
(NOTE *All further communications will be sent to him or her, not to you*)

Name Messrs. Rime & Reason, Solicitors

Address Invicta house,

Market Street,

Barset

Telephone 00765 1234

Reference SS/HUCO

2 Do you intend to resist the application made by
John Fraser

YES ☑   NO ☐

3 Was the applicant dismissed?

YES ☑   NO ☐

If YES, what was the reason?

CONDUCT

4 Are the dates of employment given by the applicant correct?

YES ☑   NO ☐

If NO, please give the correct dates

Began on _____

Ended on _____

6 Are the details given by the applicant about wages/salary or other payments or benefits correct?

YES ☑   NO ☐

If 'NO', or if details were not given, please give the correct details:

Basic wage/salary

£ _____ per _____

Average take home pay

£ _____ per _____

Other bonuses/benefits

£ _____ per _____

7 **Maternity rights cases only**

When the applicant's absence began did you have more than five employees?

YES ☐   NO ☐

Please continue overleaf ►

IT 3

8 If you answered YES to question **2**. please give below sufficient details to show the grounds on which you intend to resist the application: *(continue on a separate sheet if there is not enough space for your answer)*

The flexi-time system worked by the office staff at Bessemer Works allows between 0800 and 0900 hrs. for starting work. From 0900 is core time which all members of the design team must work together. The Applicant has a long history of lateness and has been repeatedly warned. On 8th. January he was given written warning of the adverse effect this was having on staff morale and told that making up loss of core time after the others have gone home was not acceptable. In January and February he arrived after 0930 on 8 occasions and on 5 of these he was more than 1 hr. late. In the first week of May he was late on 3 successive occasions and on one of these he arrived at 1223 hrs. On 13th. May, therefore, he was given notice of termination of his employment. It is denied that the Applicant's lateness was excused.

9

Signed *Rim & Reason*

Date 25·6·93

---

10 Please send this form to:

The Assistant Secretary

Regional Office of the Industrial Tribunals (Barsetshire) Crown Buildings Guildhall Street Barchester BA1 5RD

For official use

Date received   Initials

IT 3 (Reverse)

At this time also, Huco Engineering Ltd. receive in the post a copy of the Application. With it is an explanatory form and a form on which to enter an appearance. The explanatory form tells them that to enter an appearance they must within 14 days present to the Secretary of the Tribunals at their Barchester Office a written notice of appearance on the form provided. If they do not, it states, they will not be able to take any part in the proceedings except to apply for an extension of time. They are also notified, as is the Applicant, of the good offices of a conciliation officer offered by ACAS.

On receiving the Application, Huco Engineering Ltd. consult their solicitors, Messrs. Rime & Reason, following which, an appearance is entered and a copy of it is forthwith sent to Messrs. Makepiece. This form is illustrated on pp. 79 and 80.

Shortly after receiving the notice of appearance, Messrs. Makepiece receive from their client the original letter of January 8, which confirms what is stated in the appearance and gives no other information. With the letters Mr. Fraser has sent the notice of particulars of employment which he was given when he took up his post with the Company in 1979. On working hours this states only that they are 35 per week.

Mr. White now writes to Messrs. Rime to request copies of timesheets for all the members of the design team for the period January 4 to May 14, 1993. In reply Messrs. Rime write to say they are preparing for the tribunal a schedule extracted from the time records showing times of arrival of the Applicant over this period. The records are available for inspection and they suggest that after inspection by Messrs. Makepiece the schedule should be agreed. They state that the schedule will substantiate the Applicant's flagrant disregard of his conditions of contract and they do not consider that information relating to the other members of the team is relevant, or will help the tribunal. However, Messrs. Makepiece are free to extract what information they please.

In due course Mr. White attends at the office of Messrs. Rime and examines the timesheets. He is given a copy of the schedule of Mr. Fraser's arrival times and satisfies himself that it is correct. It shows that Mr. Fraser often clocked in 5 to 10 minutes after 0900 hours and that the occasions of more serious lateness were as stated in the appearance. From the end of February, his timekeeping was exemplary until the first week of May. In that week on three successive days his arrival times were 11.26, 12.53 and 10.54 hours. Mr. White was unable to find any entries for the other members of the team which compared with Mr. Fraser's, although arrival times of up to 09.20 were quite common.

Mr. White asks his opposite number to let him see the personal files of all six members of the design team, which, however, he is unwilling to do, saving they are not relevant. He asserts that no comparable warnings were given to any of the others. He produces Mr. Fraser's file, which contains only the file copies of the two letters of warning. There is no reference to verbal warnings or to any knowledge of the son's illness.

If Messrs. Rime's clients had refused to give discovery of documents the Tribunal has power to make an order in a suitable case.

In the course of chatting about the case Mr. White learns that the Company did know about the son's illness, but in the light of Mr. Fraser's long record of slackness in arrival time, they had not taken this seriously.

On returning to the office Mr. White telephones Mr. Fraser to tell him that the time record does not bear out his statement that his colleagues' records were as bad as his. He says the tribunal's decision may turn on showing the genuineness of his domestic problem and that the Company were fully informed of it and expressly or implicitly condoned his lateness. Mr. White asks him to see his doctor and request him to let him have a letter about his asthmatic son. It would be useful if the doctor was able to say that his condition is quite serious. He should be asked to state how often it has been necessary to take him to the surgery and the dates on which this happened this year. It would also help if he was able to indicate, without giving precise times, how long a visit to the surgery is liable to take. Would the doctor perhaps, say that it had been very important to have his father on hand when the boy has an attack? Mr. Fraser says he will do all he can to get a suitable letter. When he has it he is to come in to enable Mr. White to prepare a proof of the evidence he will give to the tribunal. He will be the only witness. A tentative appointment is made for August 12.

The following day Messrs. Makepiece receive an inquiry from the Secretary on the possible length of the hearing:

Regional Office of the
Industrial Tribunals
(Barsetshire)
Crown Building
Guildhall Street,
BARCHESTER
Telephone No. 00765 2345
Ext. 238

THE INDUSTRIAL TRIBUNALS
LENGTH OF HEARING

CASE NO: 7255/93/18
RE: John Fraser v. Huco Engineering Ltd.

The adjourning of a case part-heard usually involves a delay of over a month before the resumed hearing date.

If you consider that the hearing of the above case cannot be completed in one day will you please notify this office in writing of the number of days that you consider necessary. Such notification should be received by this office within 7 days of you receiving this form.

If we do not hear from you as above the case will be set down for one day.

To the Applicant(s) (Ref: PF/22/12/Fraser)
Mr. J. Fraser by his solicitors
Messrs. Makepiece & Streiff
Bank Chambers Barset.

Signed ...T. Powell (Miss)...
for Assistant Secretary of the
Tribunals
Date ...5th August 1993...

and the Respondent(s) (Ref: NW/SM/51)
Huco Engineering Ltd. by their solicitors
Messrs. Rime & Reason,
Invicta House, Market Street,
Barset.

Mr. White is confident that Mr. Friendly will present the Applicant's case in less than half a day and does not have to answer the inquiry. Messrs. Rime will answer for themselves.

This is followed a week later by receipt from the Secretary of Notice of Hearing. With it is a note on the preparation of documents for the hearing:

Preparation of Documents for the Hearing

At an Industrial Tribunal hearing parties frequently wish to refer to certain letters or documents in support of their case.

It will be helpful, and may simplify and shorten the hearing, if each party sends to the other, well in advance of the hearing date, a list of documents which he or she intends to produce at the hearing.

It will then be open to either party to ask to see, or to receive a copy of, particular documents before the hearing. Experience has shown that compliance with such a request may be to the advantage of both parties in avoiding delays or adjournments of hearings to permit documents to be studied.

Would you please send to this office a copy of any list of documents which you send to the other party. The documents themselves or copies of them should *not* be sent to this office.

Note for professional advisers

Professional advisers should prepare a bundle containing all correspondence and other documents on which they intend to rely at the hearing, arranged in correct sequence and numbered consecutively. It is desirable, whenever it is practicable, that there should be an agreed bundle.

Three sets of documents should be made available for the use of the tribunal.

It is Mr. White's normal practice to prepare a list of documents for the Tribunal. In this case the only documents are the agreed schedule of extracts from the time records and the letter of warning. He agrees these documents with Messrs. Rime on the telephone and prepares a list, of which he sends a copy to the Secretary. He also puts in hand the preparation of six bundles of copies so that at the hearing he can hand one to each of the three members of the Tribunal, one to Messrs. Rime's advocate (so that he will know what the Tribunal members have). That leaves two for themselves, one of which will be for Mr. Friendly, who will conduct the application.

Mr. Fraser calls as arranged and brings the doctor's letter. This very effectively supports Mr. Fraser's story: the boy is suffering from chronic asthma which, if not promptly treated, will adversely affect his growth and development. It is vital that the parents should be on hand to attend to him when he is in great distress and the father's presence has a reassuring and beneficial effect. The most telling part of the letter is that in which he sets down the dates on which, according to the boy's medical card, he was brought to the morning surgery. This tallies exactly with those mornings on which Mr. Fraser is recorded as being upwards of one hour late. The doctor comments that he has a busy surgery and patients must be prepared to take their turn. Even with early attendance a patient may have to wait an hour or more to be seen.

With renewed confidence, Mr. White takes the client once more over the events and takes down a full statement. When the interview is over he reports to Mr. Friendly and it is decided to use the surprise value of the doctor's letter. Accordingly, no prior intimation will be given to Messrs. Rime. However, copies are made to be passed round at the hearing.

On September 9, the parties and their respective representatives assemble in the separate rooms provided for applicants and respondents. Mr. Friendly tells his client that the proceedings will be quite informal. Everyone will stay seated. The Tribunal will comprise a qualified chairman—a lawyer—and two other members, one nominated by trade union organisations and the other by employers. In no sense, he says, do these two represent the interest of their respective sides of business life. They are chosen for their personal qualities and experience. Mr. Friendly continues that it will be for the Respondent's advocate to open the case and seek to justify the dismissal. Their witnesses will be called first.

A clerk comes into the waiting room and makes contact with Mr. White. He asks if all the Applicant's witnesses are present and notes that Mr. Friendly is to be his advocate. The case is then called in and when they go into the Tribunal chamber the members are already on the dais. The Respondents are represented by Mr. N. Wisdom of Messrs. Rime. He is invited by the chairman to open the case. He outlines the facts he will seek to prove. He has one witness only, Mr. Seemly, the supervisor. The witness takes his place at the desk in front of the dais and the oath is administered to him by the clerk.

Mr. Wisdom's examination in chief is uneventful: there are no surprises. Emphasis is placed on the Applicant's long record of bad time-keeping, going back long before 1993. The need for the members of the team to be present together for the effective use of core time is stressed. Mr. Wisdom is well aware that Mr. Friendly will try to prove that in some way the Applicant's lateness was excused. He therefore tries to forestall him:

Wisdom: Mr. Seemly, did you at any time discuss with the Applicant the reasons for his lateness?

Seemly: Yes I usually asked him why he was late.
Wisdom: What explanation did he give?
Seemly: It varied. Sometimes he said he had had a bad night. Sometimes he said one or other of the children was ill. Sometimes he just shrugged it off. He was late so regularly that I came to think he did not care.
Wisdom: Did you ever excuse him being late?
Seemly: No.

In cross-examining Mr. Friendly had no need to go over the Applicant's attendance record. However, he must try to shake the supervisor's evidence about the reasons for his lateness:

Friendly: Mr. Seemly, you knew Mr. Fraser has a domestic problem.
Seemly: I thought his problems were brought on by himself.
Friendly: You are not answering my question. You said some of Mr. Fraser's failures to turn up on time were due to the illness of one or other of the children.
Seemly: He gave that excuse.
Friendly: Didn't you believe him?
Seemly: I thought he might be putting it on a bit.
Friendly: But Mr. Fraser told you on several occasions that his son had acute asthma and was liable to alarming attacks at night?
Seemly: He did mention his boy being ill. I did not know it was alarming or how severe it was.
Friendly: Had you accepted his word you would have known how severe it was.
Seemly: —
Friendly   If you had known would it have affected your attitude to his lateness?
Seemly: Possibly.
Friendly: Mr. Seemly will you look at this letter from the family doctor?

Hands a copy to the witness and gives the original to the clerk to hand to the chairman.

Seemly: (Looks at the letter.)
Friendly: You see the boy's illness can be very distressing to the parents.
Seemly: No doubt.
Friendly: And you say you knew nothing of this.
Seemly: I did not know how serious. . . .
Friendly: But you were told exactly that.
Seemly: I thought he was exaggerating.
Friendly: But when Mr. Fraser arrived at the end of the morning on Wednesday in the first week of May and explained what he had gone through with his son did you say "I quite understand."?
Seemly: Possibly.

Friendly: You are not an unsympathetic man?
Seemly: I don't think so.
Friendly: And in fact the conversation you had on that day was much the same as those you had on similar occasions in January and February?
Seemly: No I don't thinks so. There were many occasions when he was late and said nothing about the family.
Friendly: But all the members of the team are late occasionally?
Seemly: Only minutes.
Friendly: 10 to 15 minutes?
Seemly: Possibly.
Friendly: This often happened?
Seemly: No not often.
Friendly: I suggest to you that apart from those occasions when Mr. Fraser reported to you that his son had had an attack his time-keeping was no worse than anybody else's.
Seemly: No that is not so.
Friendly: Mr. Seemly will you look at the dates given in the doctor's letter? Those you will see are the dates when the boy was taken to the surgery. They include do they not all the dates when Mr. Fraser is recorded as arriving more than half an hour late?
Seemly: (Looks at the dates and compares them with the schedule which is before him.) Yes that is so.
Friendly: And there are other dates of surgery visits that coincide with other dates on the schedule.
Seemly: I cannot check them easily.
Friendly: You will accept that is so.

When he sits down Mr. Friendly feels that he has satisfactorily opened the case and the position is not materially altered by Mr. Wisdom's re-examination.

When Mr. Fraser's turn comes to give evidence, he answers well in accordance with his proof and asserts that he left Mr. Seemly in no doubt of his personal difficulties. Mr. Seemly had appeared very sympathetic. Without in express terms excusing his lateness, he had given the impression that it would not be treated as a disciplinary matter. There had been verbal warnings, but no more to him than to the others. They were of the kind of chivvying meted out to all staff for minor infringements of discipline.

His testimony is not shaken by cross-examination. Mr. Friendly does not re-examine.

It is now for Mr. Friendly to summarise his case, picking out the points that tell in his favour and explaining away, so far as he can, those that do not. Mr. Wisdom now puts his final plea on behalf of the Respondents.

The chairman asks for a few moments for consultation with his colleagues. The parties and their representatives leave the chamber and when they are recalled the chairman states that the tribunal will take time to reach their decision and that the parties' solicitors will be notified in due course.

Early in October the two firms of solicitors receive notification of the decision.

RESERVED DECISION   Case Number 7255/93/18

THE INDUSTRIAL TRIBUNALS

BETWEEN

Applicant   *Respondent*
Mr John Fraser   **AND**   Huco Engineering Ltd.

DECISION OF THE INDUSTRIAL TRIBUNAL

HELD AT Barchester   ON 9th September 1993

CHAIRMAN: Mr B. Sharp   MEMBERS: Mr T. E. Bright
                                                            Mr R. P. Fairbother

DECISION

The unanimous decision of the Tribunal is that the applicant was unfairly dismissed.

REASONS

1. The applicant was dismissed for indiscipline (bad time-keeping) on 13th May 1993 with six weeks' wages in lieu of notice. He was then 45 years of age. The defence is that the dismissal was fair and was on the ground of persistent breaches of discipline.
2. The applicant worked for 12 years and 8 months for the respondent as a design engineer.
3. The respondent is a small engineering firm which advises on and plans systems for machine tool manufacturers. The applicant has throughout been a member of a design team which, including the applicant, comprises six persons.
4. The firm works a flexi-time system which allows the staff to start work at any time between 0800 and 0900 hrs. From 0900 hrs. is core time to be worked by all staff. This is intended to ensure the proper degree of co-ordination between the members of the team whilst working on a single project.
5. The respondents make no complaint about the standard of the applicant's work, which, they agree, has been entirely satisfactory.
6. There is no doubt about the facts of the applicant's time-keeping. The dates and times are clearly set out in the daily record. There was, however, a dispute about the reasons for the applicant's lateness. The respondent had come to the conclusion that the applicant was slack and lacking in self-discipline. The respondent discounted the reason given by the applicant to his supervisor on several occasions when he was seriously late.
7. We are satisfied that the reason for the applicant's bad timekeeping was the serious illness of his son and that this was reported by him to his supervisor.
8. It is unfortunate that there was a lack of liaison within the organisation and no knowledge of the applicant's difficulties appears to have reached the Personnel Officer who was generally responsible for staff discipline. The letter of warning of 8th January takes no account of the son's illness or of the discussions the applicant had had with his supervisor about it.

9. In face of the explanations given by the applicant on subsequent occasions of lateness and the absence of any clear warning in respect of those infringements they must be assumed to have been excused.

10. In these circumstances we find that the treatment of the applicant by the respondents was unfair.

B. Sharp ....

CHAIRMAN

RESERVED DECISION

DATE ....3/10/1993....

DECISION SENT TO THE PARTIES ON
4/10/1993

AND ENTERED ON THE REGISTER
4/10/1993

T. Powell (Miss) ....

FOR SECRETARY OF THE TRIBUNALS

The tribunal will usually hold a further hearing to decide the amount of compensation payable, from which Huco Engineering Ltd. will be able to deduct any state benefits received by Mr. Fraser before they pay it to him. Huco Engineering Ltd. will then have to pay over to the Department of Social Security the amount of any such benefits.

Other tribunals

As we see from John Fraser's case, industrial tribunals operate like a court in first establishing the facts and then applying the law to those facts. Either party can appeal on a point of law to the Employment Appeals Tribunal, whose decisions are reported and become precedents for future cases. The role of the industrial tribunals is, therefore, basically judicial. Many kinds of tribunal operate in this way. Others have to exercise a discretion and the merits of their decisions are usually not open to question. Thus, government officials dispense a great range and variety of welfare benefits. Their decisions are invariably open to review by a tribunal which, if it does not uphold the official's decision, must substitute its own view of how the discretion should have been exercised. In this, they may be guided by reports of earlier appeal cases.

For the most part, tribunals are set up to see that the individual citizen receives justice at the hands of persons in authority, but this is not the whole picture. Others are designed to deal with rights as between one individual and another. Thus, there are several kinds of tribunal which fix rents and determine other matters as such between landlord and tenant.

Collectively, tribunals are sometimes referred to as "administrative tribunals," but this is somewhat misleading in view of their predominantly judicial nature. The phrase should, perhaps, be understood to refer to the administrative system of benefits, etc., to which a tribunal may be attached.

Administrative tribunals have been established because they provide a relatively cheap method of resolving disputes (where often the value of the claim is small) and because they provide a relatively fast system of dispensing justice. Further administrative tribunals relieve the ordinary courts of what would otherwise be an overwhelming volume of cases.

Another reason for establishing a tribunal rather than providing a remedy through the courts is that it makes it possible to constitute a body and its procedures to suit the particular subject matter. This applies particularly to the composition of the membership, which is invariably drawn from persons having relevant specialised knowledge and experience. Many tribunals deal with highly technical subjects, in which lawyers regularly appear as representatives. Only a short list can be given here of the tribunals before which a firm of solicitors which does not specialise might be called on to advise and appear.

	Subject Matter includes
Lands Tribunal	Appeals against local authorities on compulsory purchase compensation; appeals from Valuation Courts on rating assessments; applications for removal or variations of restrictive covenants.
Mental Health Review Tribunal	Review of compulsory detention of mentally disordered patients in hospital.
Commissioners for Income Tax	Appeals against assessments by Income Tax Inspectors.
Immigration Appeals Adjudicators and Tribunal	Appeals against decisions by Home Office to refuse entry or to deport aliens.
Social Security Appeal Tribunal	Appeals against refusal/curtailment of contributory benefits: unemployment benefit, sickness benefit, pensions and against decisions relating to non-contributory benefits

Tribunals and the courts

Tribunals have no enforcement machinery. Subject to any right of appeal, the order or decision of a tribunal for the payment of a sum of money is enforced by application to the County Court for an order. Application is made *ex parte* to the court for the district in which the person due to pay residues or carries on business, by filing an affidavit verifying the amount payable and at the same time producing the original award and filing a copy. The application is heard by the District Judge (C.C.R., Ord. 25, r. 12). Where a tribunal makes an order for costs, these can usually be taxed in the County Court.

Rights of appeal from the decisions of a tribunal are specified in the statute or regulation setting it up. Appeals on fact, if available, are invariably confined to review bodies within the tribunal system concerned. Provision is often made for appeal on a point of law to the High Court (usually to a single judge of the Queen's Bench Division) or the Court of Appeal (as in the case of the Employment Appeal Tribunal, with leave). In such cases a further appeal with leave lies to the House of Lords.

Where no express provision is made for appeal on a point of law, it is still possible for an aggrieved party to apply to the High Court for a Judicial Review (R.S.C., Ord. 53) provided the point at issue comes within the scope of one of the prerogative orders of *certiorari, mandamus* or prohibition. Certiorari and prohibition are available where there has been a want or excess of jurisdiction or a denial of natural justice. *Certiorari* can also be had to quash a decision the record of which shows an error of law. *Mandamus* is appropriate where a tribunal has wrongly declined to hear an application.

ADMINISTRATIVE PROCEEDINGS

Public powers and private rights

Central government, the local authorities and certain other public bodies have many statutory powers and responsibilities that can interfere with the lives of citizens, their property rights and the amenities of the area in which they live. Decisions made by such bodies are influenced by their political aims and their views on what is good for the community. Unlike tribunals, whose decisions are judicial in character, the decisions of such authorities are essentially administrative. However, when those decisions affect, for instance, the use and employment of a person's property, a balance has to be drawn between the public good on the one hand and the freedom of the individual from outside interference on the other. There must be some guarantee that statutory powers that affect individuals adversely are not exercised in a high handed and unconscionable way.

Invariably, when a statute confers a power to make lasting changes in private rights and amenities it imposes strict limits on the exercise of the power. In the first place, the circumstances justifying the exercise of the power are carefully defined. The authority which acts outside the prescribed limits is said to act *ultra vires*, that is, beyond its powers and its acts will be declared invalid by the courts. Then, the statute will lay down a procedure to be followed which, among other things, will ensure that all whose rights or interests may be affected receive proper notice of what is proposed. Failure to keep strictly to the procedure can also render the authority's acts void.

Thirdly, all interested persons must be able to object and to have their objections heard and fairly considered.

Lastly, and most importantly, the exercise of the power will be ineffective until it has been ratified by someone in authority whose function it is to make an objective judgment on the merits of the case presented by the authority and the grounds of opposition urged by the objectors.

To see how this works in practice, we will take one of the most commonly used statutory powers: compulsory purchase.

Compulsory purchase procedure

Land can be purchased compulsorily by the central government, local authorities and certain other public bodies for a great variety of purposes. The procedures vary, depending on the purpose for which the land is required. We will here briefly sketch the steps in the acquisition of land for redevelopment by a local authority. They are laid down partly in the relevant statutes, for example the Acquisition of Land Act 1981, partly in the Compulsory Purchase of Land Regulations 1990 and partly in Rules made by the Lord Chancellor.

First, a map is prepared of the area to be acquired. Next a resolution is drafted defining the area and setting out the statutory power for which the land is needed. When the resolution has been passed by the acquiring authority, it is usually referred to the authority's legal office to investigate the ownership and occupation of all the properties and sites in the area. This enables a schedule of owners and occupiers to be drawn up which is then incorporated, with the map, in an order. The order, which is in a form prescribed by the Regulations, is now sealed with the authority's seal.

The order is now ready to be submitted to the appropriate Minister for confirmation. Before doing this, however, notice must be given of the intention to do so. Formal notices are prepared which are published in local newspapers. Individual notices are also served on all the persons listed in the schedule to the order. Many authorities at this stage send out with the notices a statement of their reasons for making the order.

The notices invite persons who may be affected to submit to the Minister within the time allowed objections to the proposals.

Having published and served the notices, the authority submit the order to the Minister. if objections are received, copies are sent to the authority. Unless the objections received are withdrawn, a public local inquiry (or, occasionally, a private hearing) must be held. For this purpose, the Minister nominates an inspector, who is usually an official of his Department and notifies the date, time and place in the locality, where the inquiry will be held.

If the authority has not yet sent out a statement of its reasons for making the order it must now send it to all statutory objectors, that is to say, objectors who are listed in the schedule to the order as having an interest. The statement is accompanied by a list of the documents the authority will produce at the hearing. The statement may also be seen by other interested persons. All are given the opportunity to see any supporting maps, plans other documents and to take copies.

The inspector presiding over the inquiry has a discretion to decide how the hearing shall be conducted, but invariably the acquiring authority begins and has the right of making a final reply. The acquiring authority may appear by an officer or by counsel or a solicitor and any other person can appear in person or by counsel, a solicitor or any other person.

Evidence is presented and cross-examined as in court, but witnesses do not take the oath.

The inspector is free to visit and inspect the land before or during the hearing without announcing the fact. If he decides to make an inspection at the close of the inquiry, however, he must announce the date and time during the hearing and the authority's representatives and the objectors are entitled to accompany him. Such an inspection must be made if the authority or a statutory objector requests it.

Following the close of the inquiry the inspector makes a report to his Minister with his findings of fact and his recommendations on whether the order should be confirmed. The Minister then notifies his decision and the reasons for the conclusion reached. The decision is accompanied by a copy of the inspector's report or at least a summary of his conclusions and recommendations.

Notice of the confirmation is now given by the authority to all to whom notice of the order had been given and is published in the local newspaper. Thereafter, any person who is aggrieved by the order, *i.e.* thinks he has been injured or adversely affected thereby, may within six weeks of the notification appeal to the High Court. The right of appeal, however, is limited to two grounds:

(a) that the applicant has been seriously prejudiced by failure to observe correct procedures: or

(b) that the order is *ultra vires*.

Subject to any appeal, the authority has three years in which to serve a notice to treat on persons having a legal interest in any land within the area of the order. This invites the submission of claims for compensation for the purchase of the interest. This is the signal for negotiations to start up between the claimant and the authority, or their respective valuers. If agreement is reached, the ownership is transferred by the normal conveyancing procedures, although no contract is usually called for. If agreement is not reached, the claimant can apply to the Lands Tribunal to determine the compensation. The matter then again becomes contentious and the case has to be worked up on both sides for submission to the Tribunal. There solicitors and counsel regularly appear on behalf of the parties and expert evidence is given by valuers for each of them. When the Tribunal has determined the value, the land is transferred by the normal conveyancing procedures.

The parliamentary and local commissioners

We have taken over from the Scandinavian countries the concept of the Ombudsman ("Grievance Man"), as these Commissioners are popularly known. They deal with complaints by members of the public of maladministration on the part of public or local authorities. They are usually resorted to in circumstances where there is no definite breach of the law, but the conduct of the authority has been of a lower standard than the public are entitled to expect. It may be that delay by an authority in dealing with a matter has inconvenienced or prejudiced a person's position. Or, there may have been inconsistency of action between one citizen and another.

As the Commissioner has no executive powers, the result of an application is often more of a comfort to the disgruntled resident than a remedy. It is at the same time true that authorities have compensated applicants at the request of the Commissioner and invariably carry out any recommendations to avoid a repetition of the event.

There are two kinds of Commissioner, the Parliamentary Commissioner and the Local Commissioner.

The Parliamentary Commissioner can only investigate a complaint if it is referred to him via an M.P.—not necessarily the complainant's own M.P. He and his staff have powers which the M.P. lacks, namely to look at the Department's files of papers, to question the staff involved and to examine all the facts with great care. A complaint cannot be made about the merits of a decision, but only about bad administrative conduct of official duties. This covers such matters as delay, neglect, bias, rudeness, wrong advice and even corruption, although the latter is very rare.

The same Commissioner can also deal with complaints against the National Health Service. Here the intervention of an M.P. is not necessary but matters of medical treatment as such cannot be investigated. (Of course a claim for negligence could be brought in the courts).

The Local Government Commissioner will not normally take a case until the complainant has asked for the help of an elected member of the local authority concerned. In this way it is hoped that the authority will itself investigate the complaint. However if an approach to a local councillor is not successful, a reference may be made to the Commissioner's office.

As an alternative informal way of obtaining assistance it is often worthwhile to write to one's M.P.

An M.P. can often help a constituent by sending a letter for the aggrieved person to the relevant Minister. This will then receive high level attention within the Civil Service and a full explanation will be given to the M.P. Often, the constituent will receive more favourable treatment than previously.

ARBITRATION

Introduction

Arbitration is specified in some statutes as the method for settling disputes thereunder. More usually, it is the method chosen by agreement to exclude court action. An arbitration agreement may be a document drawn up in consequence of a dispute having arisen or it may be a clause in a contract to cover the contingency of a dispute arising. Documents which may be expected to contain arbitration clauses include leases, building agreements and commercial agreements. Arbitration is particularly favoured in contracts involving scientific or technical matters and in those where trade across national boundaries is involved. It can be a quicker process than court action and is much less formal. Being an entirely private process, it can be the means of avoiding unwelcome publicity. It is not necessarily cheaper in all cases, because the fees of the arbitrator can be heavy.

In its informality, arbitration is not unlike proceedings before a tribunal, but the similarities are superficial. The framework within which all arbitrations based on written agreements are conducted is provided by the Arbitration Acts 1950 and 1979. These Acts regulate the appointment of arbitrators and the procedure of arbitrations and confer powers on arbitrators comparable with those enjoyed by judges. They also lay down how awards are to be enforced. It should, at the same time, be borne in mind that many of the provisions of the Acts are prefaced by: "unless a contrary intention is expressed therein." The parties have therefore wide power to decide for themselves how the proceedings shall be conducted. References in this section to an arbitrator should be taken to include more than one where several are appointed. Agreements usually stipulate either a single arbitrator or three. In the latter case, two may be named assessors. Where more than one arbitrator is appointed the decision is by majority and this applies equally where two of the three are appointed as assessors.

Whether there is a valid arbitration agreement, the right of the parties to litigate in court is excluded and if a party attempts to bring court proceedings, they will be stayed on the application of the other party. But a party is not prevented from recovering, in court, a sum of money under the contract if liability is not disputed.

The steps in an arbitration may be:

(1) Selection of arbitrator
(2) Arbitrator accepts reference
(3) Preliminary meeting for directions
(4) Hearing
(5) Award

These steps are now commented upon.

Selection of arbitrator

The person called on to act may be named in the agreement or the means of appointment may be specified therein (*e.g.* "by the President of the RIBA" or "by the Court"). If the agreement is silent on selection or if the means laid down cannot be used (death of named arbitrator, etc.) the court has power to make the appointment on the application of one of the parties. It is often the ability to choose an arbitrator for his professional, technical or scientific knowledge or experience that makes arbitration the most advantageous way of dealing with disputes.

Acceptance of reference

The use of arbitration is referred to as a "reference" or "submission" to arbitration. The solicitor to the party initiating the process writes to the nominated arbitrator and asks him to confirm that he will accept the office. There is usually some discussion at this stage of the fees to be paid for his services. The prudent solicitor will get these agreed, if possible, with the solicitor for the other party.

The amount of information to be given to the prospective arbitrator will depend on how far he has been previously involved with the subject matter of the dispute and the contract between the parties. In the case of one newly nominated with no previous knowledge, he should have the original contract out of which the dispute arises, the arbitration agreement, if separate, a summary of the events leading to the dispute and the substance of the claim.

Once appointed, an arbitrator cannot be removed without an order of the court.

Preliminary meeting

The Arbitrator calls the parties together to settle questions of procedure to facilitate the hearing. This is equivalent to the pleadings stage in the court. The arbitrator is empowered to make orders like those a judge or master can make. They are referred to by the same terms: particulars of claim, defence, discovery and so on. As an alternative to applying to an arbitrator, a party can apply to the High Court where and Order for Directions will be issued by a master of the Queen's Bench Division.

Further preliminary meetings will be arranged as necessary.

The hearing

This follows the pattern of a civil court trial. Provided he observes the rules of natural justice and acts fairly between the parties, the arbitrator is not bound to follow strictly the practice of the court, but it is normal for him so to do. Witnesses do not have to be sworn but almost invariably are.

Representation can be in person, by solicitor or counsel. Before briefing counsel a solicitor normally informs the opponent's solicitor so that he may decide whether to have counsel.

The order of speeches and examination of witnesses are as in court. Strict rules of evidence apply and also the rules on privilege. The attendance of witnesses can be compelled by the issue of a subpoena in the High Court. The arbitrator must rely on his own careful notes if arrangements are not made between the parties for a shorthand writer or a tape-recorder to be provided.

A point which solicitors take into account when advising on an agreement to submit disputes to arbitration is that there is no general right of appeal from the award of the arbitrator. There is a limited right of appeal to the High Court on a question of law. The Court's decision on such an appeal may include a reference back to the arbitrator for a new award, based on the Court's finding on the law. It is even possible for a point of law to be referred to the High Court before the arbitrator gives his award, but only where the Court is satisfied that this will save substantial costs. Further appeal from the High Court to the Court of Appeal is only possible where there are special grounds and the Court grants leave. This is possible where the legal issue raised is one of general public importance (Arbitration Act 1979).

The award

The arbitrator usually closes the hearing with a statement that the award is reserved. This gives him the opportunity to study the papers and his notes and write up his considered conclusions and award. The party bringing the proceedings is usually the one notified that the award is to be published and his solicitor takes up the original signed document. The opponent's solicitor receives a copy. The arbitrator is entitled to withhold publication until his fees are paid. Thus, where the respondent is ordered to pay the costs, the claimant may have to pay the costs to recover them from the respondent.

The arbitrator has the same discretion to impose costs on a party as the court has. He may also be asked to tax the bill, but if not it can be taxed by the taxing master of the court.

Enforcement of award

An award may be for the payment of a sum of money or it may require some positive act of specific performance, such as the conveyance of land to the other party. If the terms of the award are not promptly and willingly carried out by the losing party, the successful party can apply to the High Court for leave to enter judgment in the terms of the award or he may apply directly for leave to enforce the award (R.S.C., Ord. 73).

CHAPTER 3

BUSINESSES

PARTNERSHIP AND LIMITED COMPANY

In the United Kingdom there are many ways of carrying on business: the most basic form of so doing is as a sole trader (also called a sole proprietor). A partnership is a more complex form of trading organisation and is subject to a greater number of restrictions and regulations than a sole trader. More complex still is the limited company. There are two principal types of limited company—the private and the public. The distinction between these will be discussed in greater detail in the third section of this chapter. It is sufficient to know that the private limited company is intended to enable small trading organisations to exist with the advantages that incorporation offers (see later) without having to satisfy great formalities. Often a private company will consist of the members of one family (frequently husband and wife), running a business—say a grocery store, sweet shop or tailoring factory. The public limited company is generally larger and raises the money which it needs to trade from the public.

In some cases a public limited company may be a nationalised industry. In these cases the Government has acquired at least 51 per cent. (a controlling proportion) of the voting share capital (see later). Not all nationalised industries, however, are public limited companies. Some are statutory corporations which are run and governed according to the Act which creates them. An example of this would be British Rail.

Accordingly, an individual who wishes to commence trading must decide which form his business is to take. The easiest course is to become a sole trader, but that does not mean that there are no requirements upon him. For example, the law imposes an obligation to keep proper books of account for income tax purposes; not all premises can be used as business premises—planning permission may be needed; if he trades under a name other than his own he must disclose on all stationery and premises details of his ownership of the business; there are many other legal rules which are intended to protect the consumer. Trading as a sole proprietor may, however, be more precarious than trading as part of a business enterprise. For example, he is exclusively liable for any debts which he incurs and if he fails to make payment he may be sued in a personal capacity. The effect of this is that everything that he may own is placed at risk. In addition a sole proprietor may have difficulty in raising finance to start his business; he is self-reliant and must have the security upon which to persuade others to lend.

Accordingly, many individuals do not operate alone but with others and organise their trading affairs as a company or partnership.

A partnership may arise whenever persons carry on a business in common with a view of a profit. It is defined in section 1 of the Partnership Act 1890. The essence of the organisation is the profit motive; and

97

"partnership" is the description of the relationship which exists between those who carry out the business. No formality is necessary for the creation of the relationship. The only requirement appears to be that there must be an agreement between the partners. Many partnerships encapsulate the terms of the agreement in a deed or articles signed by each partner. A partnership may be referred to as a firm. Frequently a limited company is colloquially referred to in the same way; it is not, however, legally correct and this usage should be avoided.

The members of a partnership are each personally liable to the full extent of any debts which have been incurred by it. The only circumstances in which a partner may place a limit on his liability is where he is a member of a publicly registered limited partnership under the Limited Partnerships Act 1907. Even then at least one partner must remain fully liable for the partnership and a limited partner may be so liable while he takes part in the management of the company. Unlike a limited company (see below) a partnership has no independent legal personality: each member (whether he is concerned in the management of the organisation or not) is deemed to act on behalf of his fellow partners so as to bind them for any act done in carrying on in the usual way business of the kind carried on by the firm.

A limited company is a wholly different concept. It is a notion which takes effect only if the relevant statutory provisions have been complied with. The provisions which set out its nature and procedure and which govern its formation and conduct are set out in the Companies Act 1985 (an Act consolidating previous legislation concerned with company law) and the Companies Act 1989 which introduced many important changes in the law.

It is important to recall that the word "company" alone does not necessarily mean a limited company. The word is also used to refer to a partnership, as in, for instance, "Dawkiss & Co."

The expression "limited" means that its members (shareholders or sometimes guarantors) have limited liability. Their liability is restricted to a certain sum agreed in advance; that is, at least before any member agrees to purchase a share or enter into a guarantee. It is this principle which is, in practical terms, the most significant distinguishing feature of a limited company. An individual may become a member without placing his home or possessions at risk in the event of the company's failure. This situation is possible because a company has a legal personality which is independent from that of its members. A person who contracts with a limited company does not enter into a contract with its members. Its members are liable to the company only for what they have contracted to pay for its shares or by way of guarantee: that sum can only be called up by the company acting through its agents (directors, secretary, managers, etc.) or by a liquidator who takes over the conduct of a limited company for the purposes of winding it up. A creditor may not, therefore, sue a member of a company directly for any part of the agreed sum which has not been paid. If a company is wound up, the intervention of a liquidator is essential to the enforcement of payment by a member. It may be wise to note here that there are a few situations where this may not apply. For these see "Lifting the Corporate Veil" below.

The legal theory which distinguishes the notions of partnership and limited company gives an indication of the choice which a prospective businessman may have to make. It is not, of course, only these distinctions which are relevant. The principal pertinent matters are set out below:

(1) He must decide whether he and his associate or associates are prepared to take the financial risks and responsibilities of partnership without the protection of limited liability and corporate personality. He must consider not only the protection of his individual property from the company's creditors, but also the risk that partnership property will be seized as charged by creditors of a partner who has contracted debts unconnected with the partnership. These risks, as have been explained, are lessened by the formation of a limited company.

(2) He must consider whether he wishes to found a business which may have a changing and fluctuating membership or which is to have a fixed membership. For example, a firm created to undertake a single enterprise may not need provision for new members; on the other hand a man seeking to establish a business which is to survive his death or which is intended to operate on a wide scale may need to provide for new members to control the business or to provide new capital. If he wishes the members of the organisation to be able to leave and joint then at first sight it may be more appropriate to choose a limited company. Because the limited company has an independent personality a change of membership does not affect its corporate status. As a partnership, on the other hand, is a relationship between persons, a change of membership will clearly change the relationship and the partnership will dissolve. It is possible for this effect to be avoided if the articles of partnership provide otherwise although it does not automatically follow that a person joining an existing partnership (an incoming partner) will be bound by the terms of the original partnership. He may not be bound by any terms, for instance, of which he had no knowledge.

The corollary of a change of membership is a change of management of the organisation. A partnership will almost invariably be run by the partners—it therefore attracts not only the strengths but the weaknesses of its individual members. For example, unless there is express provision to the contrary, a partnership will not be dissolved because a partner becomes an alcoholic, or a spendthrift, or goes insane. The existence of the relationship is not threatened by the personality of its members. On the other hand, if a director or senior manager of a limited company suffers a similar disability, he may (subject, of course, to the law of contract and unfair dismissal) be dismissed or retire without affecting the corporate structure of the company.

(3) A company can hold property (land and chattels) in its own name. This has three advantages. First, it may be beneficial in some cases for the purposes of taxation; secondly, demonstrable assets can make it easier for a company to borrow money. Any loan can then be secured by a charge on the company property rather than by looking to directors or members for a guarantee. Thirdly, ownership of property by a limited company rather than its members facilitates change of membership.

(4) A prospective businessman must consider whether he wishes the

members of the organisation to be its managers. If he wishes the membership of the organisation merely to provide financial backing, a limited company may be preferable. Members (who may have no knowledge of the business issues) may provide capital money, by purchasing shares for example. The company may then operate on the basis of this capital. Management of the company may be carried out by better experienced officers (directors and secretary). If a prospective businessman does not wish to be involved in the running of the business which he is to form he may delegate that responsibility even if he decides to form a partnership. He would then be a non-executive partner (called a "sleeping partner"). This would not have the effect of delegating his liabilities. He would continue to be liable personally for the partnership debts. The limited company, therefore, continues to offer an advantage.

(5) A further advantage which a limited company may offer is that there is no upper restriction upon the number of members which it may have. The minimum requirements for any limited company must have two directors and secretary. A private company must have at least one director and a secretary (who may not be the same person). A member may be a director and/or a secretary. The result is that in order to form a limited company, at least two people must be involved. The same is true of a partnership. The relationship cannot exist without at least two members. For a partnership, however, the usual rule is that there is an upper limit on the number of people who may be members. The upper limit on the number of partners is generally 20 (except for banking partnerships where the number may be 10). Certain types of partnerships may be exempted from this general rule, however. Notable examples are solicitors' partnerships, partnerships of patent agents, partnerships of surveyors, auctioneers, valuers and estate agents and partnerships of consulting engineers. In each case some or all of the partners are required to be members of a specified professional body in order to qualify for the exemption. For a business which is anticipated to grow quickly and to require a substantial amount of capital to start trading this restriction may be serious.

(6) A limited company may have greater ease in borrowing money than either a sole proprietor or partnership. There is at least one practical reason for this. A limited company's borrowing may be secured in favour of the creditor by a "floating charge." This is a charge over company property which is of particular use when the assets of the company are not fixed—the best example of a fixed asset is land. A company which does not hold any or much land may nevertheless have valuable non-fixed assets such as stock-in-trade, or debts due to it, or goodwill. Goodwill may be broadly described as an ability to earn money through trade without the need for substantial capital. The nature of a floating charge is that it is a charge on some or all of the non-fixed assets of a company present and future. The company can continue to deal with the assets because a floating charge does not prevent the sale and replacement of assets in the usual course of business. The most common form of floating charge is given to a bank often coupled with a personal guarantee by the directors. The charge may become fixed on a certain date or on the happening of an event such as a failure by the company to

meet the interest or capital repayment of the loan. The charge then becomes enforceable over all or some of the assets of the limited company on that date or event. Where a company creates a charge it must register particulars of it with the Registrar of Companies within 21 days. The "fixing" of a floating charge is known as crystallisation. Although there is no reason in principle why a floating charge should not be available to a sole proprietor or partnership, as a matter of law it is difficult to create a valid floating charge except on the assets of the company. The reason is this and it is a technical one:

A floating charge on chattels is an attempt to "mortgage" them—that is, to give another an interest in the chattels while keeping them in the possession of the organisation. The Bills of Sale Acts 1878 to 1882 provide that such an arrangement must be registered in the Bill of Sale Registry as a bill of sale. The bill would also need to be in a statutory form which requires the goods charged to be set out. As has been indicated the nature of the floating charge is such that the exact goods cannot be specified at the time that the charge is entered into. Charges entered into by companies, however, are expressly excluded from the provisions of the Bills of Sale Acts 1878 to 1882.

If an individual goes bankrupt while he has goods in his possession with the consent of the owner and which are reputed to be his, those goods pass to the trustee in bankruptcy and third-party rights are lost. This does not apply to limited companies so the floating charge is not, therefore, deprived of its efficacy.

The one great advantage to a borrower which a floating charge has over a fixed charge is that, until crystallisation, it can deal freely with the charged assets without the permission of the lender. However this very point is also a disadvantage to the lender because he cannot be sure of the value of his security until crystallisation.

Accordingly, the prospective business person must weigh up the relative borrowing capacities of the organisations that he wishes to establish. It must be noted, however, that in practice the small business, even if trading as a company, may be required to provide a guarantor for its debts. This will usually be by a director or shareholder. This requirement lessens the distinction between the relative borrowing powers of companies and partnerships.

(7) All the practical matters discussed so far which a prospective business person must consider have shown the limited company in a more favourable light than a partnership. However, a partnership has some advantages. One of these is the ease of its formation. It has previously been explained that all that is necessary for the creation of a partnership is an agreement between the partners. It can be a mere oral agreement. On the other hand, the creation of a company has some attendant formality and expense. This will be dealt with in greater detail later. The promoters of a limited company (principally those involved in or responsible for its creation) have to fill in certain forms and draw up a Memorandum and Articles of Association which must be filed with the Registrar of Companies with the relevant fee. These documents are available for inspection by the public. It follows that the formation of a limited company may attract greater publicity than the formation of a partnership.

(8) The running formalities of a limited company are also greater than those of a partnership. A number of registers must be maintained by the company; certain matters must consistently be registered at the Companies Registry, in particular details of the registered office, its officers, changes in its share capital, any charges taken out over company property and its annual returns. These documents are open to public inspection. A company must also set out full details of its name, place of registration, registered number and address of its registered office on its notepaper and other business documents. Failure to comply with these formalities can result in criminal sanctions being taken against company directors and even in the company being struck off the register of companies. In the latter event it would lose its corporate status Where a partnership has been created, these running formalities do not apply. In particular a partnership is entitled to keep its annual accounts confidential.

(9) A prospective business person should consider, too, the *ultra vires* rule. A company is entitled to do only that which is described in its Memorandum (see below) and may be prevented from exceeding those powers (that is, acting *ultra vires*) by the courts. A partnership may be free from this restriction, although if there is a partnership agreement a partner may be restrained by the other partners from breaking its provisions. However, the importance of this difference has been drastically lessened by changes introduced by the Companies Act 1989 which virtually abolish the *ultra vires* rule (see later).

(10) A partnership has no rules about the maintenance and raising of capital. A limited company has. A private limited company has no minimum share capital which must be raised. A public limited company (p.l.c.), however, must at present have an issued capital of £50,000 of which at least one-quarter must have been paid for by its members before the company may legitimately trade. However, both a private and public limited company are subject to rules concerning the maintenance, increase or reduction of capital. A partnership may vary its capital in accordance with the partnership agreement; its financial situation is, in that respect, more fluid. These advantages and disadvantages are summarised in the following table.

Partnership and limited company compared

Partnership	Limited Company
1. Advantages	
(a) Fewer formation formalities and expenses than limited company.	(a) Has registration expenses and considerable formality and capital duty to pay when shares are issued (see below).
(b) Fewer running formalities.	(b) Has very formal and complex rules about its day to day running, particularly regarding corporate finance.
(c) Has confidential accounts.	(c) Has to file accounts at the Companies Registry where they are available for public inspection.

(d) No ultra vires limitations.	(d) Activities not provided for in the Memorandum and Articles may be ultra vires.
	2. Advantages.
(a) No corporate personality.	(a) Corporate personality.
(b) Partners are personally liable.	(b) Limited liability.
(c) Unless specifically agree, partnership ends on the death of a partner and no provision for new members.	(c) Membership can change and therefore perpetual succession possible.
(d) Partners have to hold property in their names.	(d) Company can hold property in own name.
(e) Members who are not managers are still liable as though they were.	(e) Members and managers need not be the same.
(f) Share in business not transferable except by agreement.	(f) Shares are freely transferable (although private companies often restrict transfer in their Articles).
(g) Generally, not more than 20 partners may be in a firm.	(g) Minimum limitation on number of members only.
(h) Borrowing harder—no floating charges possible.	(h) Can find borrowing more easy.

There now follows a case-study which illustrates the setting-up of a new partnership.

PARTNERSHIP

Jack Abel, who is a senior legal executive dealing with much of the work of the company and partnership department of Messrs. Makepiece and Streiff, receives a telephone call from Mr. Drury asking for some preliminary advice about establishing a partnership. Jack's secretary, Julie, makes an appointment for Mr. Drury to come into the office for a general discussion and so that Jack could take some detailed instructions, if relevant.

Mr. Drury has for some years been trading as a sole proprietor. He buys wines from manufacturers and sometimes importers and sells them to the public. He has a small shop in the busy High Street of Barset. He wishes to join in partnership with Colonel Drinkwater who, after having left the army, has become a wine taster and importer of quality wines of some distinction. The Colonel has some valuable business contacts in the wine trade which he can use, but has to date developed no satisfactory means of selling the wines which he enjoys to the public at large. Another interested party is Mr. Brewer, who is a chartered accountant in a local firm and who is willing to lend to Mr. Drury and Colonel Drinkwater the sum of £15,000 to improve the shop currently owned by Mr. Drury. He has suggested that he should be repaid out of the profits of the partnership plus interest. He has suggested that the rate of interest should be 2 per cent. above the rate declared at any time as the Base Rate by the London Clearing Banks.

Jack's attendance note sets out the matters discussed.

MAKEPIECE & STREIFF

ATTENDANCE NOTE

NOTE OF: Interview/Tel.Con.   DATE: 5th February 1994

CLIENT: Alan Drury   ADDRESS: "The Flourishing Grape",
                                              11 High Street, Barset.

MATTER: Setting up business
              with Colonel Drinkwater
TAKEN BY: J.A.   TIME: 2.00 p.m.

Explaining that there are no legal requirements governing the formation of a partnership, but that it is wiser to avoid future squabbles by
drawing up a form of agreement. Explaining that it does not follow from
the fact that Mr. Brewer wishes to lend a sum of money in return for payments which are derived from the profits of the business that he must be a
partner. Advising that he can alternatively enter into a loan agreement
with the partnership between Mr. Drury and Colonel Drinkwater.

Explaining the need for trust and confidence between partners.

Advising that the property in the existing shop could be conveyed to the
partnership once it is formed or could be kept by Mr. Drury and held on
trust for the benefit of the partnership so long as it is in existence, or could
be let to the partnership for a nominal or market value rent. Being
instructed that the premises would be let to the partnership.

Being instructed that the intended distribution of profits is to be in
equal parts save that until the capital sum of £15,000 plus profits, interest
is paid to Mr. Brewer he should receive a third of the profits. Distribution
of capital on dissolution to be the value of the leasehold premises and the
rent paid plus any capital contributions by Mr. Drury during the partnership to be repaid to him and the goodwill value of Colonel Drinkwater's
business connections plus any contributions to capital made during the
partnership to be repaid to him. If capital value of partnership exceeds
these contributions, the excess to be apportioned rateably. Explaining the
effect of capital and income losses to the partnership and partners' liability.

Being instructed that the name of the partnership should be the name of
Mr. Drury's sole trading operation, i.e. "The Flourishing Grape". Advising as to the disclosure provisions under the Business Names Act 1985.

Explaining the advantages/disadvantages of partnership as against
Limited Company. Being instructed that the parties definitely wanted a
partnership but might form a limited company later. Main reason being
confidentiality of accounts and lack of "formality". Anticipate no cash
flow problems so no real need for limited liability.

2.45 p.m.   Jack Abel

Notes

Jack has noted the advice that he has given and some of the important
matters which will be needed to draw up a draft deed of partnership.

It has already been seen that a partnership is the relation that subsists
between persons carrying on a business with a view to a profit and that
no particular formalities are required by the law in order that this rela-

tionship may come into existence. The relationship can in some cases be deemed to subsist by virtue of the behaviour of the alleged parties. The existence of the relationship is then dependent upon evidence. It is, however, desirable that partners who wish to create a longstanding and stable firm should draw up a partnership agreement so that the rights and liabilities of the partners can be determined. In particular, certain partners may wish to preserve rights and privileges which are distinct from those of other partners; for instance, it is presumed by the Partnership Act 1890 that, subject to any special agreement, expressed or implied, all partners are entitled to share equally in the capital and profits of the business and most contribute equally to the losses whether of capital or otherwise sustained by the firm. It may be agreed at the time of the entry into the agreement for partnership that one partner should receive, say, three-quarters of the profits: the advantages of a document which records this are obvious.

Furthermore it is usual for many partnerships to include provisions which deal with the death or bankruptcy of a partner. The death of one partner will, for example, bring the partnership to an end. Where the partnership is a large one it may be desirable for the partnership to survive the death of one partner. Although the courts may deem that a new partnership arises in the same terms as the old one, the advantages of recording what is to happen on the death of a partner are self-evident.

In this instance it is particularly important that a partnership agreement deals with what is to happen to the business premises already owned by Mr. Drury. He has told Jack that he wishes to keep the premises in his own name but that they should be used for the benefit of the partnership. Jack has explained that this can either be done by holding the freehold of the premises on trust for the use of the partnership or by granting a lease of the premises to the partnership. In the former case the trust would have to be declared or evidenced in writing to satisfy section 53 of the Law of Property Act 1925. On the other hand, Mr. Drury may retain greater control over the use of the premises and protect himself better against a failure of the partnership if he is a creditor of the partnership rather than a trustee. Accordingly he decided, on Jack's advice, to let the premises to the partnership.

The intentions of Colonel Drinkwater and Mr. Drury do not appear to be the same as those of Mr. Brewer. That is why Jack questioned the necessity of joining him in partnership. His role is principally that of a money-lender seeking to recover the £15,000 that he has offered to lend, plus interest. The disadvantage of his being a partner rather than an outsider is, however, that should the business fail he may not be able to seek redress against the other partners for recovery of the loan. If he is not a partner he can take proceedings for recovery of the loan against each of the partners personally in the same way as any other creditor (although he may rank as a deferred creditor; that is, one whose right to recover the debt takes effect only after other creditors of the partnership have been paid). A further disadvantage of taking Mr. Brewer into partnership is that event after the £15,000 plus interest has been paid out of the profits of the firm he would still be a partner and in a position to bind the firm in contracts with third parties provided always that he appeared to be carrying on a business of the kind carrying on by the firm in the normal way.

It is largely for the above reason that Jack stressed the need for confidence between partners. Every partner is an agent of the firm for the purpose of the business of the partnership. So, if a partner enters a contrast of a kind which the partnership would normally enter into the other partners will be bound by that contract even if it is in fact contracted for the benefit of the partner personally, and even though the partner had no actual authority to enter into the agreement. The only exception to that rule may arise where the third party with whom the unauthorised contract was created knew at the time of entering the contract that the person had no authority or did not know or did not believe that the person was a partner. Furthermore, if one partner causes a third party loss or injury or misapplies money or property belonging to a third party but which is in the custody of the firm, the firm may be liable to the full extent. The firm will also be liable where a partner receives and misapplies money or property even though he may have had no authority to receive it provided that he appeared to have been acting within his authority. In a nutshell, it is the partners who bear the risk of each other's carelessness and fraud, not innocent third parties.

A partner is, however, only liable for events which occur during his partnership. He is not liable for matters which arise before he becomes a partner or after he leaves the partnership, although he may be liable for matters which arose during the time that he was a partner even after he has left the firm unless he is specifically released by agreement with the other partners and creditors of the firm.

It is important that the partnership deed deals with the distribution of profits and capital upon the dissolution of the firm. Jack has taken instructions as to the parties' intentions, as, indeed he has as to the distribution of profits and contribution of capital during the life of the business. If no other agreement is made, the contributions and distributions will be governed by the Partnership Act 1890. These are that:

(a) Losses (including capital losses and deficiencies) are met first out of profits, then capital, then by the partners personally in the proportion to which they were entitled to share the profits of the firm before and on distribution;

(b) The assets of the firm (including capital contributions by the partners) are applied in the following order of priority;

(1) To meet debts and liabilities to third parties.

(2) Paying advances to the partners which are due. Advances due to partners are usually where a partner has lent money to the firm which has not been repaid and which was not intended by him to be risked in business. The distinction between dealings with contributions of capital and advanced is frequently dealt with in the partnership agreement.

(3) Paying to each partner rateably what is due to him by way of capital.

(4) Paying to each partner the residue in the proportion in which profits are payable.

The determination of the name of the firm is very important. Although it is no longer necessary for Jack to register the firm name (the

Business Names Registry was abolished in 1982), there are certain obligations under the Business Names Act 1985 upon businesses which do not trade under the names of the owners to give disclosure of the name or names of the owners of the business and, for each owner, a business or other address within Great Britain. The address must be one at which documents can be served if necessary. Disclosure is given by showing the relevant information legibly on all:
—business letters,
—written orders for the supply of goods or services,
—invoices and receipts issued in the course of the business,
—written demands for payment of debts arising in the course of business.

This information must also be displayed at any premises where the business is carried on and to which customers or suppliers have access.

In addition, it is important to remember that in selecting a firm name it must not, by itself, or together with its manner of carrying on business, or the goods to which the name is to apply, mislead the public to the detriment of a rival business. The use of any such misleading name may, in the above circumstances, be restrained by a passing-off action. This is an action in tort and the person or business whose rights have been infringed may be able to prevent the organisation from using that name by injunction. As Mr. Drury has been using the name for some time Jack does not forsee that there is likely to be a problem in this respect.

Jack did not, in the circumstances of the partnership proposed by Mr. Drury, need to explain to him that he would not be permitted to enter into a partnership of more than 20 people. For greater details of this restriction see the section of this chapter entitled "Partnership and Limited Company" above.

Jack then drew up a draft deed of partnership and submitted it to Mr. Amity, a partner in Messrs. Makepiece and Streiff, for his approval.

In drawing up the draft Jack has been able to refer to precedents drawn up previously by the firm for other partnerships as well as to other standard precedent books. He also keeps a checklist of principal matters with which he may be concerned. This list contains the following matters:

(1) The name of the firm;
(2) Commencement date and duration of the partnership;
(3) Place of partnership business;
(4) Holding of partnership land or land used or occupied by the business;
(5) Payment of any premium by an incoming partner. (A premium is a sum payable by a person joining a partnership to the existing partners. If there is no deed of partnership but only a written agreement, the premium can constitute clear evidence that consideration has been provided in respect of the new partner's receipt of benefits in accordance with the agreement).
(6) Capital contributions and ownership. Whether any interest will be paid on any capital contributed.
(7) The proportions in which profits and losses will be shared. Will

there be a future variation of these proportions? Will any partner receive a "salary" before the profits are distributed?

(8) To what date will the accounts be drawn in each year? (This is frequently left to be decided by the firm's accountant, who is often also closely concerned with the formation of the firm).

(9) Name of firm's bankers. Who is to be an authorised signatory of the firm's cheques? Are the signatures of all partners needed for all cheques drawn on the account or only cheques over a certain value?

(10) The insurance that the firm will need.

(11) Must a partner devote his entire time and attention to the business or may be concerned or interested in another business run concurrently? What annual holiday is a partner entitled to take?

(12) Will there be a prohibition on the partners charging their interests in the firm?

(13) Will the partnership dissolve on the death, retirement or expulsion of a partner or will his share of the partnership vest in other partners? Would other partners be entitled to purchase his share in the partnership? If the share vests in the other partners or can, under the agreement, be bought by them, what payment is he, his estate or his widow to receive?

(14) Will an outgoing partner be restricted from competing with the firm, and if so, to what extent?

Not all of these matters have been reflected in Jack's draft, either because they are dealt with under the Partnership Act 1890 or because they are not relevant and in view of the size of the firm can appropriately be left out.

DEED OF PARTNERSHIP

THIS DEED OF PARTNERSHIP is made the 10th day of March 1994 between Alan Siegfried Drury of 41 Acacia Gardens, Barset in the County of Barsetshire (hereinafter called Mr. Drury) of the one part and Edward George Drinkwater of "The Mousehole", Iconfield, Near Barset in the County of Barsetshire (hereinafter called Colonel Drinkwater) of the other part.

WHEREAS Mr. Drury has agreed to carry on partnership with Colonel Drinkwater upon the terms of this Deed the business of wine trading importing and vending which has been carried on by Mr. Drury as a sole trader since 1981 under the name of "The Flourishing Grape" at 11 High Street, Barset in the County of Barsetshire.

NOW THIS DEED WITNESSETH AS FOLLOWS: *[defined terms]*

(1) Colonel Drinkwater and Mr. Drury (hereinafter called the partners) shall carry on business as a partnership from the 1st day of April 1994 under the name of "The Flourishing Grape" in continuation of the business of the same name (hereinafter called the "existing business").

(2) Subject to the provisions for dissolution hereinafter contained the partnership shall continue for the joint lives of the partners.

(3) The partnership business shall be carried on in the premises known as 11 High Street, Barset in the County of Barset where the existing business has been carried on by Mr. Drury and will be so carried on until the 31st day of

defined terms —use Initial Capitals.

March 1994 inclusive of that date and to which Mr. Drury is entitled in fee simple absolute.

(4) Mr. Drury agrees to grant a monthly tenancy of the said premises to the partnership commencing on 1st April 1994 on the following terms:

(a) The partnership shall pay to Mr. Drury a monthly rent of £500 payable in arrears on the last day of the month in which such rent fell due;

(b) The partnership will keep the interior of the said premises including the fixtures, fittings, sanitary apparatus, plumbing, lighting, heating and gas appliances in good repair and condition and will keep the same, including, without prejudice to the foregoing, any plate glass insured to the full value thereof against all usual risks;

(c) Mr. Drury will not give notice terminating the tenancy during the continuance of the partnership PROVIDED that if any part of the said rent (whether formally demanded or not) shall at any time be in arrear for more than 21 days or if the partnership shall be in breach of any of its obligations hereunder Mr. Drury shall be entitled at any time to enter on the said premises and determine the tenancy thereof.

(5) Mr. Drury shall carry on the existing business in its usual and proper course until the 31st day of March 1994 whereafter the profits and losses of the existing business shall belong to and be assumed by the partnership.

(6) The initial capital of the partnership shall consist of the sum of £75,000 being the agreed value of the assets of the business listed in the inventory named Schedule I and attached hereto and the goodwill of the existing business of which the total sum will be credited to the capital account of Mr. Drury and the sum of £2,500 being the agreed value of the goodwill of the wine trade business currently run by Colonel Drinkwater of which the total sum will be credited to the capital account of Colonel Drinkwater.

(7) The capital of the partnership shall belong to the partners in the proportions in which the amounts for the time being standing to the credit of their respective capital accounts bear to the total of such amounts.

(8) The profits of the partnership (including profits of a capital nature) remaining after the payment of the losses of the partnership shall be divided as to one third to James John Brewer of 41 Cattle Street, Barset, as to one third to Mr. Drury and as to the remaining third to Colonel Drinkwater until such time as the said James John Brewer shall have been paid the sum of £15,000 plus simple interest calculated on such part thereof as has not been paid to James John Brewer annually on 1st April at 2 per cent. above the Base Rate decided by the London Clearing Banks and any variations thereof. After £15,000 and such interest as aforesaid has been repaid the profits of the partnership calculated in the manner hereinbefore mentioned shall be divided between Mr. Drury and Colonel Drinkwater in equal parts.

(9) Mr. Drury and Colonel Drinkwater shall contribute equally towards partnership losses whether of capital or otherwise.

(10) Mr. Drury and Colonel Drinkwater shall be entitled to draw out of the partnership bank account sums not exceeding £200 each in any one month on account of his share of the profits. If the profit and loss account of the partnership shall show that in the period covered by the account any partner drew pursuant to the foregoing sentence in excess of the profits for that period, such partner shall repay the excess forthwith. Each partner shall be entitled to draw out of the partnership bank account the undrawn balance (if any) of his share of any profits shown in any such profit and loss account at any time after the account in question has been signed by the partners.

(11) Proper books of account shall be kept promptly posted and such books shall be available at all times for inspection by each of the partners and by the partnership accountants. A profit and loss account and balance sheet shall be prepared on the 19th day of March in every year by Messrs. Small Backward and Adder or whoever the partners shall from time to time agree shall be appointed as the partnership accountants. Every such account and balance sheet shall be signed by the partners.

(12) The bankers of the partnership shall be the Trusty Bank p.l.c. and all partnership monies not required for current expenses shall immediately upon receipt be paid into the said banking account and all cheques on such account shall be signed by both partners.

(13) Neither partners shall without the consent of the other:
    (a) engage directly or indirectly or be concerned or interested in any business other than that of the partnership;
    (b) enter into any bond or become bail or surety for any person or knowingly cause or suffer to be done anything whereby the partnership property may be taken in execution or otherwise endangered;
    (c) assign, mortgage or charge his share in the assets or profits of the partnership;
    (d) compromise or compound or (except upon payment in full) release or discharge any debt due to the partnership;
    (e) contract any partnership debt exceeding the sum of £4,000 in respect of any one transaction without the consent of the other.

(14) If either partner shall commit a breach of the terms of this agreement the other partner shall be at liberty within 3 calender months of becoming aware of such breach by notice in writing to the offending partner forthwith determine the partnership.

(15) In the determination of the partnership howsoever occasioned the assets and liabilities of the partnership shall be dealt with as follows:
    (a) Partnership losses (whether of capital or otherwise) shall be paid first out of profits, next out of capital and lastly by the partners in equal proportions;
    (b) Partnership capital shall be divided proportionally to the relative sums shown in the capital account of each partner.
    (c) Partnership profit shall be divided equally.
IN WITNESS etc.

To this deed will be appended an inventory of the assets of the existing business entitled "Schedule I." See clause (6) of the deed.

Once Jack has shown this to Mr. Amity for his approval he sends the draft to Mr. Drury. Mr. Drury comes to see Mr. Amity this time bringing Colonel Drinkwater with him and the document is "signed and delivered as his deed" by each intending partner and their respective signatures are then witnessed. The agreement is then binding upon both of them irrespective of whether either has provided consideration.

While they are there, Mr. Amity says a few words about dissolution of the partnership. As this is a partnership for the duration of their joint lives, it must be determined on the death of one of them. The partnership would also be brought to an end automatically be the termination of the enterprise, either as a result of the Partnership Act 1890 or on the time construction of the deed. By virtue of the Partnership Act 1890 the partnership would also be dissolved by the bankruptcy of a partner subject to any agreement between the partners. If one partner were to allow his share of the partnership property to be charged for his separate debt, the other partner would have the option by virtue of the Partnership Act 1890 to decide whether to treat the partnership as dissolved. Additionally this deed provides that partners are not to charge their property for their separate debts. For either to do so would constitute a breach of the agreement. By clause (14) the "innocent" partner would be entitled to give notice to determine the agreement. The partnership would also be dissolved if wine trading became illegal. In addition to these circumstances where dissolution (or the option to determine) arise automatically on the happening of an event, an "innocent" partner has the right to apply to the court for an order that the partnership be dissolved. The circumstances in which a dissolution may occur are set out in the following table.

Events giving rise to a dissolution

Events.	Conditions whereby dissolution becomes available on each event.
1. An event specified in the partnership agreement.	According to the terms of the agreement
2. Expiry of a fixed term.	ONLY where the agreement is for a fixed term e.g. 5 years, 20 years, AND subject to any agreement between the partners
3. Termination of a single adventure or undertaking.	ONLY where the agreement is entered into for a single adventure or undertaking i.e. a "one-off" transaction, AND subject to any agreement between the partners.
4. By a partner giving notice of his intention to dissolve.	ONLY where the agreement is entered into for an undefined time, AND subject to any agreement between the partners
5. Death or bankruptcy of any partner.	Subject to any agreement between the partners.
6. A partner allows his share of partnership property to be charged for his separate debt.	Dissolution is available at the option of the other partners.
7. An event makes it unlawful for the partnership to be carried on.	Dissolution is available in every case.
8. By the court on an application by a partner.	(a) Another partner is permanently incapable of performing his part of the partnership contract. (b) Another partner has been guilty of conduct that the court thinks is calculated prejudicially to affect the carrying on of the business.

Events.	Conditions whereby dissolution becomes available on each event.
	(c) Another partner wilfully or persistently commits a breach of the partnership agreement or otherwise conducts himself so that it is not reasonably practicable for the other partner or partners to carry on the business in partnership with him.
	(d) The partnership business can only be carried on at a loss.
	(e) The court considers that it would be just and equitable that the partnership be dissolved.
9. By the court under the Mental Health Act 1983.	The court may dissolve or give directions for the dissolution of a partnership of which "a patient" is a member. "A patient" is a person who the judge is satisfied is incapable of managing or administering his property and affairs by reason of mental disorder.

A final point should be borne in mind. There is one situation where a person who is not a partner of a firm may become liable to third parties as though he were a partner. Liability arises if a person conducts himself, or allows himself to be represented as a partner in a particular firm, on the basis of that representation. The most common example of the application of this principle is where a person allows his name to be used by the partnership, perhaps on a letter heading, after he has ceased to be a partner. The attachment of this liability is called "the doctrine of holding out."

LIMITED COMPANIES

General

It has already been observed that the limited company is more complex form of association than a partnership. It is entirely a creature of statute, and its nature, procedure, the rules governing its formation, conduct and winding-up are to be found principally in the Companies Act 1985 and 1989.

It has already been explained, too, that the outstanding feature of the limited company is the limited liability of its members. This is possible because the limited company has an independent legal personality—that is, one which is separate from that of its members (shareholders or guarantors). This independent legal personality (referred to also as its "corporate identity") can only be obtained if the company is formed in a manner authorised by the Companies Acts 1985 and 1989. This formation is called incorporation. The essence of incorporation is registration with the Companies Registry by the preparation and lodgment of certain specified documents. Provided that the documents are correct in form and detail the Registrar will register the company and grant a certificate of incorporation. It is not only companies with limited liability that may be incorporated. Companies which do not have limited liability may also be incorporated in accordance with the Companies Acts 1985 and 1989. All these companies are registered and can be identified by the registration number allocated to them by the Registrar.

The fact that a company is registered with limited liability does not mean that its members are free from all liability. The nature of membership of a company is such that money is to be paid to it by the member. Where membership takes the form of shareholding (which is the more common form of membership) a member purchases his interest in the company by receiving a share in exchange for a sum of money. Sometimes the sum of money is equal to the value of the share which is declared in the Memorandum of Association. For example, a company may have a share capital which is declared to be £100 which is divided into 100 shares with a value of £1. A member may buy, 25 shares for £25. Sometimes he may pay more or less than that price. In any event, his liability is to pay the price that he has agreed to pay for that share. If he pays the full price when he buys the share his liability to the company will be over. If he pays only part of the agreed price he will be liable to pay the balance if he is "called" upon to do so by the directors, or by the liquidator on a winding-up. "Calls" on shares may only be made by directors in accordance with the Memorandum and Articles of Association. He is not in general liable to the creditors of the company.

Where a company is limited by guarantee a member does not pay a price for a share but undertakes to pay a sum to the company in the event of its being wound up. For example, a member may be a guarantor of a company limited by guarantee in the sum of £5. Membership of a company of this type is common only where the company does not need capital in order to operate. This usually means that it is a non-profit-making enterprise such as "Friends" of a museum or art gallery, or a charity. In this instance, the liability of members is limited to the extent of the guarantee that has been given.

The practical application of the concept of limited liability can lead to some surprising results. Perhaps the most outstanding example of this occurs in the leading authority: *Salomon* v. *Salomon & Co. Ltd.* [1897] A.C. 22, H.L.:

Mr. Salomon with his wife and five children became directors of a company called Salomon & Co. Ltd. Mr. Salomon was the Managing Director and in complete control. The company bought Mr. Saloman's leather business from him for £30,000. This was an honest overestimation by him of the business's value. The company paid for the leather business by issuing shares to Mr. Salomon of a nominal value of £20,000 and by issuing "debentures" of £10,000. (A debenture is a form of secured loan to a company. In the event of non-payment the lender can enforce repayment by demanding the sale or transfer to him of any assets of the company which have been the subject of security). The debenture was secured over all the assets of the company. The business became insolvent. The company was wound up. The assets were sufficient to pay the sum secured by the debentures but not enough to pay the unsecured creditors of the company who collectively were owed £7,000. It was held that even though Mr. Salomon was a shareholder and director he was not liable to the creditors and was entitled to be paid out first and that unsecured creditors could therefore not recover their loss. Mr. Salomon and the company were of a different legal personality.

In addition to the liability which members have to make agreed payment to the company, they may in certain circumstances, which usually result from their own misconduct, lose their immunity and become subject to an increased liability. This is called "lifting the corporate veil" because it entails looking beyond the independent legal personality of the company into the reality of a transaction. The main occasions when the corporate veil may be lifted are:

(i) Where there are less than two members for more than six months. The statutory minimum number of members of a company is now two. Every member who knows that the company has been trading for more than six months with less than two members can be made liable for debts contracted after the end of the six-month period.

(ii) Where there has been fraudulent or wrongful trading. If it is discovered that business has been carried on with fraudulent intent, or the directors should have known that there was no prospect of avoiding an insolvent liquidation, the court may declare that any person who was knowingly responsible may be personally liable for all or any of the debts incurred, or indeed, for any other liabilities.

(iii) Where directors have failed to disclose their agency. Directors may be personally liable where they have not indicated that they were acting as agents of the company. They may also be personally liable where they have signed or authorised the signature of a bill of exchange, promissory note or order for goods or money and the name of the company does not appear in legible letters on the document.

(iv) Where the company is a mere sham or is being used as an instrument of fraud. The court will not allow a limited company to be used to perpetrate a fraud. For example, the court would prevent an individual member from using the independent legal personality of a company to evade an obligation which he has incurred personally. If, say, an individual undertakes not to solicit the customer of his former employer, the courts will not permit him to evade this by forming a company to solicit those customers. In the *Salomon* case (above), Mr. Salomon could not have been permitted by the court to benefit from its corporate personality if he had fraudulently, rather than honestly, overvalued his leather business.

(v) Where the Inland Revenue requires it. These examples are legion but outside the scope of this section.

The foundation documents

As we know Jack is a legal executive with Messrs. Makepiece and Streiff working in the companies department of the firm. He is assisted by George, a student of the Institute of Legal Executives. In November 1993 Jack was visited by Mr. Joseph Sharp. Mr. Sharp was a sole trader in the Barset market where he ran a vegetable stall. He did not have a vegetable shop in the town, but he wished to open one because his business had been so prosperous in recent years. He had heard other market traders talk about forming a private limited company and he wanted to know if it would be advantageous for him to do so. He was particularly motivated to take this step because his wife (who, together with their 17-year-old son, also helped on the market stall) was very worried about the expense of obtaining and opening shop premises. She thought that substantial debts might be incurred and she was freightened that the family might lose its home if the business could not pay its way.

Jack's attendance note appears below:

MAKEPIECE & STREIFF
ATTENDANCE NOTE

NOTE OF: Interview/~~Tel.Con.~~　　　　　DATE: 6/11/93

CLIENT: Joseph Sharp　　　　　ADDRESS: 51, Paradise Row, Barset

MATTER: Private Company formation

TAKEN BY: JA.　　　　　TIME: 10.00 p.m.

Being instructed that Mr. Sharp was a sole proprietor with a vegetable stall on Barset market assisted by wife and 17 year old son, Albert. Being instructed that Mr. Sharp wanted to expand the business but was worried about financial consequences of taking on shop premises, particularly concerning the matrimonial home which could be lost if the business failed.

Advising that the formation of a private limited company would protect the matrimonial home; explaining briefly the nature of independent legal personality. Explaining that there are, however, very strict rules governing U.K. companies which must be complied with strictly and which may provide for punishment of non-compliance by prosecution of the directors. Explaining that a director of an insolvent company may be prohibited from acting as a director of another company for up to 15 years. Explaining how fraudulent or wrongful trading would remove immunity from debts.

Advising that the company would need at least two members, a director and a secretary. Explaining that it is usual for the directors to be the members of the company. Being instructed that Mr. and Mrs. Sharp would both be directors and that Mrs. Sharp would be secretary. Both would be members. Albert not be a director until he becomes 18.

Being instructed that the company was to be limited by shares—share capital £100 to be divided into 100 £1 shares with equal rights.

Explaining that the goodwill of the market stall could be purchased in exchange for shares, and/or in another way, say by the issue of debentures.

Being instructed, that the shares were to be allocated initially as to 99 to Mr. Sharp and as to 1 to Mrs. Sharp in consideration or the goodwill of the business valued at £2,000.

> Advising as to the name of the company and the names which are not likely to be accepted by the Registrar of Companies. Being instructed that the proposed name of the company is Joseph Sharp (Vegetables) Limited.
> Advising that a Memorandum and Articles of Association are necessary. Being instructed to make such variations to Table A as are necessary.

Notes

Jack has been told by Mr. Sharp that the name of the company is to be "Joseph Sharp (Vegetables) Limited." It is always the job of the promoters of a company to choose its name, although free choice is fettered. The Secretary of State for Trade and Industry (acting through his Department) has power to refuse to register some names.

In choosing the name there are two factors which need to be considered. The first is whether the name is one which the Registrar *must* refuse to register as a matter of law. These names are prohibited by the Companies Act 1985 and are as follows:

(1) a name in which "limited," "public limited company" or "unlimited" or their Welsh equivalents or their abbreviations (*e.g.* Ltd., p.l.c.) appear other than at the end;

(2) a name which is the same as a name already appearing in the index kept by the Registrar;

(3) a name which the Secretary of State considers would constitute an offence if used. Examples of this would arise if the name were obscence or criminally libellous or if it were in some way an incitement to racial hatred;

(4) a name which the Secretary of State considers to be offensive.

The second factor to be considered is whether the name is one which, as a matter of law, needs the approval of the Secretary of State before it can be registered. Such a name is:

(1) one which gives the impression that it is connected in any way with Her Majesty's Government or with a local authority;

(2) one which includes any word or expression which is specified in regulations made by the Secretary of State. For example, a name that is misleading because it includes the word "worldwide" for a very small company is liable to be refused.

In addition to these matters, the Secretary of State has certain powers which may be exercised even after the company's name has been registered. The 1985 Act allows the Secretary of State within 12 months of registration to insist that a new company change its name if the name which it has registered is too similar to that of a company which is already registered. If this is not done by the Secretary of State, a company may change its own name by special resolution of the members. Additionally, any existing company can seek an injunction to prevent a new company from trading under the same or a similar name if there is likely to be any confusion which might adversely affect the existing company. Even if the first enterprise was not a company but a partnership or private trader, it may be able to prevent the new company from operating under the name. An injunction will not generally be available, however, if the two organisations are not competing in the same area. This cause of action is known as "passing-off" and constitutes a tort.

The Companies Act 1985 also provides for the Department of Trade and Industry to order a change of name if the registered name is so misleading as to the nature of the company's activities that it might cause harm to the public. There is a right of appeal to the courts against this order.

The documents of the company

Jack now has to draw up the Memorandum and Articles for Joseph Sharp (Vegetables) Limited. These are the foundation documents of a company and together they bind the company and its members contractually to all the provisions contained in them. The contract exists between the company and its members as well as between the individual members. It is, of course, subject to the provisions of the Companies Acts. A majority of members may sometimes vary the contract at a General Meeting of its members. The effect of this is to vary a contract between two or more individuals in circumstances where the consent of one or more may not have been given.

Jack draws up the Memorandum and Articles of the company first. As Joseph Sharp (Vegetables) Limited is to be a private company limited by shares, George knows that the form of the Memorandum must comply as nearly as possible with the form set out in Table B of the Companies (Tablex A-F) Regulations 1985.

There are six obligatory clauses in the Memorandum:

(1) The Name Clause
(2) The Registered Office Clause
(3) The Objects Clause
(4) The Limited Liability Clause
(5) The Capital Clause
(6) The Association Clause

The first five of these are number in the document which forms the Memorandum and the last is not.

(1) *The Name Clause*

It has already been made clear that choosing the name of a company may not always be an easy task. However, when the name has been chosen it will be recited in the Memorandum.

A company can trade under another name provided it makes this clear to its customers at its place of business and on its correspondence. These provisions are now contained in the Business Names Act 1985.

(2) *The Registered Office Clause*

Every company must have a registered office. Its location must be notified to the Registrar of Companies in a prescribed form. The Registrar will not register the company unless he has received a statement of its location in a prescribed form. The Memorandum of Association must state whether the registered office is to be in England, Wales or Scotland, although the actual address need not be specified.

The purpose of the Registered Office to enable a person to know where he can communicate with the company. For example, a writ may be served on a company by delivery or post to its registered office. The company need not have carried on business there, nor does there have to be any intention to do so. Sometimes the registered office of a company may be a place where another organisation carries on business, for example, the company's accountants or solicitors.

There are certain documents which are usually kept at the registered office unless otherwise stated. These are called the Statutory Documents or Statutory Books and their nature is set out in the section entitled "Company Management" below.

(3) *The Objects Clause*

Because a company is an artificial creation its powers to act in any way can only be those which are specifically allotted to it. The objects clause states what the powers of the company are to be. The company may not act outside or in excess of those powers. This restriction is called the *ultra vires* rule.

It is common practice nowadays to draft an objects clause in very wide terms so enabling a company to do anything that an individual could do. Furthermore, the objects clause in the Memorandum of Association may be altered by special resolution. However, the Companies Act 1989 effectively abolishes the *ultra vires* rule as far as a person dealing with a company is concerned and also further provides that where a company's memorandum states that the object of the company is to "carry on business as a general commercial company" the powers of the company will include power to carry on *any* trade or business whatsoever.

(4) *The Limited Liability Clause*

This states that the liability of the members is limited.

(5) *The Capital Clause*

This states the amount of the nominal capital, the number of shares into which it is divided and the amount of each share. It need not say anything else, unless there is more than one type of share (see below).

(6) *The Association Clause*

This is a clause whereby the subscribers declare that they desire to be formed into a company and that they agree to take at least one share each. This is followed by a tabular form in which the names and addresses and descriptions of the subscribers and the number of shares taken by each appear. The Memorandum should be signed by each subscriber in the presence of at least one witness opposite the number of shares which he agrees to take. In practice subscribers agree to take one share each although a larger number is to be allotted to them. The witness will attest the signature by signing the document also.

Accordingly, George draws up the Memorandum and submits it to Mr. Amity, the partner dealing with this department of work, for his approval. After approval has been given Mr. and Mrs. Sharp will be asked to come into the office again and sign the document in the presence of Mr. Amity. The way the Memorandum for Joseph Sharp (Vegetables) Limited is to look is shown below.

THE COMPANIES ACTS 1985 to 1989
COMPANY LIMITED BY SHARES
MEMORANDUM OF ASSOCIATION
of
JOSEPH SHARP (VEGETABLES) LIMITED

1st. The name of the company is "Joseph Sharp (Vegetables) Limited."
2nd. The Registered Office will be situate in England.
3rd. The objects for which the company is established are:
(i) To carry on business as wholesalers, retailers, importers, exporters, buyers and sellers of vegetables, fruit, canned food, packed food and articles and goods of any kind whether manufactured or not and whether perishable or intended for consumption or not.
(ii) To carry on any business which in the opinion of the directors of the company may seem capable of being conveniently carried on in connection with or as ancillary to the above business or businesses or which may be deemed by them to be capable directly or indirectly of enhancing the value of or rendering profitable any of the property of the company or of furthering any of its objects.
(iii) To purchase, take on, lease, exchange, hire or otherwise acquire any real or personal property or any interest in such property and to sell, lease, let on hire, develop such property, or otherwise turn the same to the advantage of the company.
(iv) To build, construct, maintain, alter, enlarge, pull down, remove or replace any buildings, works, plant and machinery necessary or convenient for the business of the company or to join with any person, firm or company for the doing of the things aforesaid.
(v) To borrow or raise money upon such terms and on such security as may be considered expedient and in particular by the issue or deposit of debentures or debenture stock and to secure the repayment of any money borrowed or raised or owing by mortgage, charge or lien upon the whole or any part of the undertaking, property and assets of the company whether present or future and including its uncalled capital.
(vi) To remunerate any person, firm or company in any manner and to pay all or any of the preliminary expenses of the company and of any company formed or promoted by the company.
(vii) To do all such things as in the discretion of the directors may be incidental or conducive to the attainment of the above objects or any of them.
4th. The liability of the members is limited.
5th. The share capital of the company is £100 divided into one hundred shares of £1 each.
We, the several persons whose names and addresses are subscribed are desirous of being formed into a company in pursuance of this Memorandum of Association and we respectively agree to take the number of shares set opposite our respective names.

Names, addresses and descriptions of Subscribers	Number of shares taken by each Subscriber
Joseph Sharp of 51 Paradise Row, Barset, in the county of Barsetshire. Greengrocer	ONE
Doreen May Sharp of 51 Paradise Row, Barset, in the county of Barsetshire. Greengrocer	ONE
Dated the day of	
Witness to the above signatures:–	

Jack has also been instructed to draft the Articles of Association. This is the more detailed of the two foundation documents and sets out more specifically the rights and liabilities of the members and the powers and duties of directors. A director may be made liable to the members of a company if he exceeds his powers.

A standard form of Articles of Association is set out in Table A of the Companies (Tables A-F) Regulations 1985. By statute, these are adopted if no other Articles apply. Accordingly, Charles could do one of four things:

(1) He could do nothing. Table A would then apply in full.

(2) He could draw up Articles of Association which adopt Table A in full.

(3) He could exclude Table A and set out the company's own Articles in full.

(4) He could set out the company's own Articles in part and include Table A in part. This is the most common course—but it is also the path to the greatest proportion of litigation. The advantage of this is that it enables a company to follow a standard pattern of internal regulation save for any desirable variations that are easy to spot in a simple form of Articles.

The matters with which the Articles usually deal are as follows:

(1) the exclusion, wholly or in part, of Table A (see above).

(2) the execution or adoption of a preliminary agreement, if any; agreements, if any; agreements made before the company is formed are not binding upon the company until the certificate of incorporation and a trading certificate have been granted, because the company has no legal personality. Accordingly the promoter or the other party acting as agent for the company will be personally liable on the contract until such time as it may be executed and adopted by the company after its incorporation.

(3) The allotment of shares by the directors; as a rule, application for shares is an offer to purchase those shares. The acceptance of the application is by allotment of those shares which must be notified to the applicant in accordance with special provisions. For there to be a valid

allotment there should usually be a validly constituted Board of Directors. A director's duty with regard to the allotment of shares is, as ever, to act in good faith for the best interest of the company. In the case of a public company, shares may not be allotted unless they are paid up at least to one-quarter of the nominal value plus the whole of any premium under the provisions of the Companies Act 1985.

(4) Calls and forfeiture for non-payment of calls. A shareholder is bound to pay the full amount unpaid on the value of his shares, unless the terms of the issue provide he does not have to pay the full amount immediately. The Articles will provide for the way in which payment is to be made, for instance, by fixed instalments or in response to calls. A call is a request by the directors of a company for payment of all or some of the unpaid balance of the nominal value of the shares. If the call is not answered by payment, the directors will not have a general power to require the shareholder to forfeit the shares unless this is specifically provided for in the Articles. If the shares are forfeited the shareholder will cease to be a member of the company.

(5) Transfer and transmission of shares. The Articles may impose restrictions on the transfer and transmission of shares. If they do not impose restrictions the shares will be freely transferable. In many cases the directors are given the power to refuse to register unacceptable transfers although exceptions are usually made for transfers to existing members/family. The difference between transfer and transmission is that a transfer denotes a voluntary passing of the rights and duties of a shareholder represented in a share whereas a transmission is concerned with the passing of a share by operating of law, *e.g.* on the death or bankruptcy of a shareholder.

(6) Increase of capital. Where a company limited by shares is concerned, the term "capital" refers to the share capital registered in the Memorandum. It is a nominal value only. The nominal share capital can be increased by approval of the shareholders followed by the issue of further shares. Under the 1985 Act directors are precluded from issuing shares unless authorised to do so either by the General Meeting or by the Articles. (Note that increasing the capital is distinct from raising money by selling shares at a higher price than their value. This is known as selling shares at a premium and it does not increase the nominal capital).

(7) Reduction of capital; a limited company registered under the Companies Acts and having a share capital may reduce its authorised capital in any way by passing a special resolution at a General Meeting of its members and subsequently obtaining the consent of the court. Since 1981 it has also been possible for a company to reduce its own issued share capital out of its distributable profits by purchasing its own shares. It must be permitted by the Articles of Association, and there are special provisions now contained in the 1985 Act designed to prevent the company from perpetrating a fraud on its members by the exercise of such a power. Private companies only may use capital for this purpose subject to very strict procedures.

(8) Borrowing powers; to enable a limited company to borrow money, power must be granted in its Articles of Association. It is also desirable for the Memorandum of Association to include such a power

in the objects clause, although the omission of this will not be fatal where the company is a trading company. A director must be given express authority in the Articles of Association in order to enable him to exercise the borrowing powers of a company on its behalf. This can be done in two ways. The Articles may contain a general clause empowering the directors to exercise all the powers which are exercisable by the company to borrow, or to exercise particular powers.

(9) General Meetings; the Articles will normally include a clause or clauses dealing with the Annual General Meeting and the procedure to be adopted before an Extraordinary General Meeting is held. A company must hold an Annual General Meeting to which its members must be invited within 15 months of the date of the last Annual General Meeting. (However, a private company can elect not to hold Annual General Meetings.) The Articles may deal, too, with the business to be conducted at the meeting. The business would usually be:

the declaration of a dividend to its members
discussion of the accounts
directors' reports
the appointment and remuneration of the company's auditors.

This is referred to as ordinary business. All other business is special business. The Articles will normally provide for an Extraordinary General Meeting to be called at any time when the directors may think fit. The Act also provides that the directors must call an Extraordinary General Meeting when called upon to do so by a specified proportion of its membership.

(10) Directors; the directors of a company are responsible for its management and they should, as a rule, make their decisions collectively at meetings known as Board meetings. In reality, this may be impractical, and the Articles may include provision for the implementation of the decisions that are contained in a resolution signed by those entitled to receive notice of a Board meeting, so that the requirement to meet is dispensed with. Where a Board meeting is held, the directors exercise their authority by way of resolution which is passed in a manner pre-' scribed in the Articles, *e.g.* by majority on a show of hands. The Articles may also provide for the appointment and remuneration of directors and their powers and duties.

(11) Declaration of a dividend; a company may pay a dividend subject to the provisions of the Companies Act 1985, and the Articles will usually specify in what proportion the dividend is payable to its members. If no reference is made to this in the Articles the dividend will normally be payable in proportion to the interests of the members. The dividend may only be paid out of profits available for distribution—it may not be paid out of the capital of the company. This applies even though the company may be a private company limited by shares. If the company is public, and is quoted on the Stock Exchange, the Stock Exchange should be notified.

(12) Accounts and auditing; these clauses will specify the way in which the accounts are to be kept and provide for the appointment of an auditor. The accounts must include a balance sheet showing the state of the company's affairs at the end of the accounting period, and a profit

and loss account. Both of these must give a true and fair view of the matters with which they purport to deal.

(13) Notices; it is incumbent upon the Board of Directors of a company to give notice of the Annual General Meeting and any Extraordinary General Meeting to all those members who are entitled to receive notices and to attend. The Articles may contain some details as to how this should be done and to whom the notice should be sent.

(14) Special provision for winding-up. Although there are statutory provisions for the voluntary and compulsory winding-up of companies, special provisions may also be included in the Articles.

Jack has drawn up a form of Articles which adopts Table A in part but with variations to cater for the small size of the company. This also is submitted to Mr. Amity for his approval.

THE COMPANIES ACTS 1985 to 1989
COMPANY LIMITED BY SHARES
ARTICLES OF ASSOCIATION
of
JOSEPH SHARP (VEGETABLES) LIMITED

Preliminary

(1)(a) Save as hereinafter provided the Regulations contained in Table A in the Companies (Tables A to F) Regulations 1985 (hereinafter referred to as Table A) shall apply to the Company.

(b) In these Articles the expression "the Act" means the Companies Act 1985.

(2) The Company is a private Company.

(3) The Directors shall pay all expenses incident to the formation and promotion of the Company and any agreement properly entered into in connection therewith by the promoters hereof is hereby adopted or executed.

Shares

(4) The capital of the Company is £100 divided into 100 shares of £1 each such shares being numbered 1 to 100 inclusive.

(5) The shares shall be at the disposal of the Directors who (for the purposes of s.80 of the Act) may allot, grant options over, or otherwise dispose of them to such persons at such times and on such terms and in such manner as they think fit, save that the Directors may not allot or agree to allot or grant options over or otherwise dispose of any share with a view to its being put on sale to the public, nor shall any such shares be allotted to a value of more than one third of the share capital of the Company. This authority shall expire five years from the date of incorporation.

Calls and forfeiture of shares

(6) The Directors may from time to time make calls upon the members in respect of any moneys unpaid on their shares (whether on account of their nominal value or by way of premium and not by the conditions of allotment thereof made payable at fixed times, provided that no call shall exceed one quarter of the nominal value of the share or be payable at less than one month from the date fixed for the payment of the last preceding call, and each member shall (subject to receiving at least 14 days' notice specifying the time or times and place) pay the amount called on his shares.

(7) If a member fails to pay any call or instalment of a call on the day appointed for payment thereof, the Directors may, at any time thereafter during such time as any part of the call remains unpaid serve a notice on him

requiring payment of so much of the call as may be specified or so much of any instalment thereof as is unpaid on or before a date not being less than 14 days from the date of service thereof and stating that failure to make such payment may enable the Directors by resolution to forfeit any share in respect of which a notice has been served.

Transfer and transmission of shares

(8) The instrument of transfer of any share shall be executed by or on behalf of the transferor and the transferor shall be deemed to remain a holder of the share until the name of the transferee is entered in the register of members in respect thereof.

(9) The Directors may decline to register the transfer of a share to a person of whom they shall not approve.

(10) In the case of the death of a member the survivor, or survivors, where the deceased was a joint holder, and the legal personal representatives of the deceased where he was a sole holder, shall be the only persons recognised by the company as having any title to his interest in the shares, but nothing herein contained shall release the estate of a deceased joint holder from any liability in respect of any share which has been jointly held by him with other persons.

(12) In the case of the death of a member the Directors shall have the same right to decline or suspend registration as they would have had in the case of a transfer of the share by that member before his death. Such right shall also exist where a person has become entitled to a share in consequence of the bankruptcy of a member.

Purchase of issued share capital

(13) The company shall have the right at any time when the Directors thereof think fit to repurchase any issued shares, whether those shares were issued as redeemable shares or not, and the purchase of such shares may be out of the capital hereof as well as out of any profits available for distribution. This power shall be exercised in accordance with the provisions of Part V of the Companies Act 1985.

General Meeting

(14) Every notice convening a general meeting shall comply with the provisions of section 372 of the Companies Act 1985, as to the giving of information to Members in regard to their right to appoint proxies; and notices of and other communications relating to any general meeting which any member is entitled to receive shall be sent to the Auditor for the time being of the Company.

(15) Clause 41 of Table A shall be read and constructed as if the words "Meeting shall be dissolved" were substituted for the words "meeting shall stand adjourned to the same day in the next week . . . may determine."

Borrowing powers

(16) The Directors may exercise all the powers of the company to borrow money and to mortgage or charge its undertaking, property or uncalled capital or any part thereof, and may issue debentures, debenture stock and other stock or securities whether outright or as security for any debt, liability or obligation of the company or of any third party.

Directors

(17) Unless or until the company in General Meeting shall otherwise determine, the number of Directors shall not be less than one nor more than seven. If and so long as there is a sole Director such Director may act alone in

exercising all the powers and authorities vested in the Directors and which are not required to be exercised by the company in general meeting.

(18) Any Director may appoint any person approved by the Board to be an alternate Director and such appointment shall effect and such appointee shall whilst he holds office as an alternate Director be entitled to receive notice of meetings of Directors and to attend and vote thereat, but he shall not be entitled to receive any remuneration from the company otherwise than out of the remuneration of the director appointing him and agreed between the said Director and the appointee. Such appointment may be revoked at any time by the appointor or by a resolution of the Directors or by an ordinary resolution of the company in general meeting. Any appointment or revocation made under this clause shall be in writing under the hand of the Director making the same.

Dividends

(19) The company may in general meeting declare dividends but no dividend shall exceed the amount recommended by the Directors, which amount shall not in any case be greater than six tenths of the profits of the company.

(20) The Directors shall, before recommending any dividend, set aside out of the profits of the company such sums as they think proper as a reserve or reserves being equal to or more than four tenths of such profits and these sums shall be available for any purpose for which the profits of a company may be properly applied, including long or short term investment in any lawful enterprise which may, in the view of the Directors, yield a profitable return.

Accounts and audit

(21) The Directors shall cause accounting records to be kept in accordance with section 221 of the Companies Act 1985 and auditors shall be appointed and their duties regulated in accordance therewith and with Part XI of the Companies Act 1985 and Part II of the Companies Act 1989.

Notices

(22) A notice may be given by the company to any member personally or by sending it to him or to his registered address, or (if he has no registered address within the U.K.) to the address, if any, within the United Kingdom supplied by him to the company for the giving of notice to him. Where a notice is sent by post, service of the notice shall be deemed to be effected by properly addressing, prepaying and posting a letter containing the notice, and to have been effected in the case of a notice of a meeting at the expiration of 24 hours after the letter containing the same is posted, and, in any other case, at the time when the letter would be delivered in the ordinary course of posting.

(23) If the company shall be wound up the liquidator may with sanction of an extraordinary resolution of the company any other sanction required by the Act, divide amongst the members in specie or kind the whole or any part of the assets of the company (whether they be property of a like kind or not) and may, for such purpose set such value as he may deem fair upon any property to be divided as aforesaid and may determine how such division shall be carried out as between the members or different classes of members.

Formation of a company

Once Mr. Sharp has approved the Memorandum and Articles, and when they have been signed by Mr. and Mrs. Sharp and their signatures witnessed, these documents are ready for presentation to the Registrar of Companies.

The Memorandum and Articles are not the only documents which Jack must lodge, however. He must also complete the lodge the following documents:

(1) The Declaration of Compliance (the Statutory Declaration) (G12). This declaration is made on a standard form and is made either by a solicitor engaged in the formation of the company or by a person named in the Articles as a director or secretary of the company. It declares that all the provisions in the Acts have been complied with, and its purpose is, presumably, to ensure that those involve in registering and forming the company take reasonable care. However, as the Registrar's staff check all the documents carefully, its actual value may be limited.

George completes this form in so far as he can but it is for Mr. Amity, under whose supervision he has undertaken this work, to make the declaration. It must be witnessed by someone who has the power to witness oaths.

(2) The statement of first directors and secretary and intended situation of registered office. (Form G10). This must be signed by all those who subscribed to the Memorandum (or their agents) and the consent of all those named as the directors and secretary must be obtained. In this case the directors and secretary are also the subscribers to the Memorandum. The address of the Registered Office must correspond with the detail given in the Registered Office clause of the Memorandum. The address of the Registered Office must correspond with the detail given in the Registered Office clause of the Memorandum.

These are the only forms which are inittially required to be lodged if the company is a private company. The registration fee, currently £50, must also be sent.

The documents completed by Jack appear at pp. 128–132.

Once the documents sent by George are received at the Companies Registry in Cardiff they will be examined by the Registrar's staff to see if they in fact comply with the requirements of the Companies Acts. There may be a preliminary examination of the documents prior to the payment of the registration fee, but this is likely to happen only if the documents are delivered by hand. If the documents are all in good order, then the Registrar must sign and issue the Certificate of Incorporation. The Certificate of Incorporation is thought to be conclusive evidence that all the requirements of the Acts have been complied with.

If the documents are not in accordance with the requirements of the Acts the Registrar may not register the company.

In this case Jack receives the Certificate of Incorporation from the Registrar. The company now has an independent personality and can trade in its own name. The Certificate appears below.

[ROYAL CREST OMITTED]

CERTIFICATE OF INCORPORATION

No. 1487304

I hereby certify that

JOSEPH SHARP (VEGETABLES) LIMITED

is this day incorporated under the Companies Acts 1985 to 1989 as a private company and that the Company is Limited.

Given under my hand at Cardiff the 29th JANUARY 1994

JOHN BLOGGS
Assistant Registrar of Companies

G

COMPANIES FORM No. 12

Statutory Declaration of compliance with requirements on application for registration of a company

12

Pursuant to section 12(3) of the Companies Act 1985

To the Registrar of Companies

For official use   For official use

Name of company

*   JOSEPH SHARP (VEGETABLES) LIMITED

I,   CLEMENT AMITY

of   Messrs. Makepiece and Streiff, Bank Chambers

Barset, in the County of Barsetshire.

do solemnly and sincerely declare that I am a [Solicitor engaged in the formation of the company]†
[person named as director or secretary of the company in the statement delivered to the registrar
under section 10(2)]† and that all the requirements of the above Act in respect of the registration of the
above company and of matters precedent and incidental to it have been complied with,

And I make this solemn declaration conscientiously believing the same to be true and by virtue of the
provisions of the Statutory Declarations Act 1835

Declared at   Messrs Popple, Copplewhite and

Brown, 14a Bank Chambers, Barset,

Barsetshire

the   Fourteenth   day of   December

One thousand nine hundred and   Ninety Three

before me   *Findar Horton*

A Commissioner for Oaths or Notary Public or Justice of
the Peace or Solicitor having the powers conferred on a
Commissioner for Oaths.

Declarant to sign below

Clement Amity

Presentor's name address and
reference (if any):

Makepiece & Streiff
Bank Chambers
Barset
Barsetshire

Ref: CA/JA/Sharp

For official Use

New Companies Section	Post room

Companies G12

5017173
* * *

OYEZ

CHA1

This form should be completed in black.

10

Statement of first directors and secretary and intended situation of registered office

Company name *(in full)*

CN		For official use

JOSEPH SHARP (VEGETABLES) LIMITED

Registered office of the company on incorporation.

RO   31 BARKING ROAD

Post town   BARSET

County/Region   BARSETSHIRE

Postcode   BA16 1AL

If the memorandum is delivered by an agent for the subscribers of the memorandum mark 'X' in the box opposite and give the agent's name and address.

X

Name   MESSRS MAKEPIECE AND STREIFF

RA   BANK CHAMBERS

Post town   BARSET

County/Region   BARSETSHIRE

Postcode   BA16 3AL

Number of continuation sheets attached

To whom should Companies House direct any enquiries about the information shown in this form?

MAKEPIECE AND STREIFF   Ref: CA/JA/Sharp

BANK CHAMBERS

BARSET   Postcode   BA16 3AL

Telephone   Barchester 4321   Extension

Page 1

Company Secretary *(See notes 1 - 5)*

Name

*Style/Title | **CS** | MRS

Forenames | DOREEN MAY

Surname | SHARP

*Honours etc

Previous forenames

Previous surname

Address | **AD** | 51 Paradise Row

Usual residential address must be given.
In the case of a corporation, give the
registered or principal office address.

Post town | Barset

County/Region | Barsetshire

Postcode | BA16 2AL | Country | Great Britain

I consent to act as secretary of the company named on page 1

Consent signature | Signed | *D M Sharp* | Date 14th December 1993

Directors *(See notes 1 - 5)*

Please list directors in alphabetical order.

Name

*Style/Title | **CD** | MR

Forenames | JOSEPH

Surname | SHARP

*Honours etc

Previous forenames

Previous surname

Address | **AD** | 51 Paradise Road

Usual residential address must be given.
In the case of a corporation, give the
registered or principal office address.

Post town | Barset

County/Region | Barsetshire

Postcode | BA16 2AL | Country | Great Britain

Date of birth | **DO**

Nationality | **NA** | British

Business occupation | **OC** | Director

Other directorships | **OD**

* Voluntary details

I consent to act as director of the company named on page 1

Page 2 | **Consent signature** | Signed | *Joseph Sharp* | Date 14th December 1993

Directors (continued)

(See notes 1 - 5)

Name	*Style/Title	**CD** MRS
	Forenames	DOREEN MAY
	Surname	SHARP
	*Honours etc	
	Previous forenames	
	Previous surname	

Address

Usual residential address must be given. In the case of a corporation, give the registered or principal office address.

AD 51 Paradise Row

Post town   Barset

County/Region   Barsetshire

Postcode BA16 2AL   Country Great Britain

Date of birth   **DO**

Nationality **NA** British

Business occupation   **OC**   Director

Other directorships   **OD**

* Voluntary details

I consent to act as director of the company named on page 1

Consent signature   Signed *Ø M Sharp*   Date *14th December 1993*

Delete if the form is signed by the subscribers.

Makepiece & Streiff

Signature of agent on behalf of all subscribers   Date *14 th December 1993*

Delete if the form is signed by an agent on behalf of all the subscribers.

All the subscribers must sign either personally or by a person or persons authorised to sign for them.

Signed	Date
Signed	Date
Signed	Date
Signed	Date
Signed	Date
Signed	Date

Page 3

Notes

1 Show for an individual the full forenames NOT INITIALS and surname together with any previous forenames or surname(s).

If the director or secretary is a corporation or Scottish firm - show the corporate or firm name on the surname line.

Give previous forenames or surname except that:

· for a married woman, the name by which she was known before marriage need not be given,

· names not used since the age of 18 or for at least 20 years need not be given.

In the case of a peer, or an individual usually known by a British title, you may state the title instead of or in addition to the forenames and surname and you need not give the name by which that person was known before he or she adopted the title or succeeded to it.

Address:

Give the usual residential address.

In the case of a corporation or Scottish firm give the registered or principal office.

2 Directors known by another description:

A director includes any person who occupies that position even if called by a different name, for example, governor, member of council. It also includes a shadow director.

3 Directors details:

Show for each individual director their date of birth, business occupation and nationality.
The date of birth must be given for every individual director.

4 Other directorships:

Give the name of every company of which the individual concerned is a director or has been a director at any time in the past 5 years. You may exclude a company which either **is** or at **all times during the past 5 years** when the person was a director **was**:

· dormant,

· a parent company which wholly owned the company making the return,

· a wholly owned subsidiary of the company making the return,

· another wholly owned subsidiary of the same parent company.

If there is insufficient space on the form for other directorships you may use a separate sheet of paper.

5 Use photocopies of page 2 to provide details of joint secretaries or additional directors and include the company's name and number.

6 The address for companies registered in England and Wales is:-

The Registrar of Companies
Companies House
Crown Way
Cardiff
CF4 3UZ

or, for companies registered in Scotland:-

The Registrar of Companies
Companies House
100-102 George Street
Edinburgh
EH2 3DJ

OYEZ The Solicitor's Law Stationery Society Ltd., Oyez House, 27 Crimscott Street, London SE1 5TS

1990 Edition
9.90 F17984
5017288
★ ★ ★

Companies 10

The company which has been formed is a private limited company. The procedure for forming a public limited company may be different in part. There is an additional document to those set out above which must be lodged. That is, a form of application to commence business and of declaration of particulars must be sent to the Registrar. This form asks for a certificate to start trading and for that purpose a director or secretary of the company declares:

(a) that the nominal value of the company's allotted share capital is at least £50,000;

(b) the amount already paid up on the allotted share capital;

(c) the amount of any preliminary expenses of the company and by whom they are payable or paid; and

(d) any remuneration given to a promoter.

Jack has previously acted for a public limited company: Euroxplore Minerals and Mines p.l.c. The relevant form appears below.

Once this has been submitted, the Registrar will review all the documents. As with the private limited company he may grant a Certificate of Incorporation. That has the effect of vesting corporate status in a public limited company, but does not entitle it to trade. A Certificate of Compliance is needed before the company can trade. It will not be granted unless the Registrar is satisfied that the company has complied with the requirements as to the authorised minimum allotted and paid-up share capital. If a public company does business or borrows without that certificate the directors commit a criminal offence. They are, in addition, personally responsible for seeing that any contract is performed or liability discharged.

A public company which does not receive a Certificate of Compliance within a year of its initial registration may be wound up.

SECURITIES

There are two primary ways in which a company can raise money; by issuing and allotting shares and by issuing debentures. There is a distinction between these. A person who is a shareholder may be a member of the company (although not every shareholder need be. It depends on the rights and liabilities attached to the class of share which is held). A person who is a debenture holder is not a member of the company but is a creditor. Most debentures have the effect of securing a loan which is made to the company against the assets of the company. Accordingly, the power of a company to issue debentures is not restricted by the nominal share capital of the company.

Shares

The exact nature of a share has always been rather perplexing. A shareholder does not have any right to any of the company's property while the company is in existence, although on a winding-up of the company he may be entitled to the return of the capital. A shareholder may have certain rights regarding the payment of a dividend to him but these rights are limited. A dividend is a periodical payment by the company to those of its members who are entitled to receive such payments by virtue of their shareholding. The payment is made out of the profits of the company which are available for distribution. The method of declaring a dividend is at the directors' discretion subject to the wording of the Articles. It is possible for the members of the company to vote to reduce the dividend in a General Meeting, but they have no power to raise it. A dividend only becomes a debt due to a member when declared in a General Meeting.

COMPANIES FORM No. 117

Application by a public company for certificate to commence business and statutory declaration in support

117

Please do not write in this margin

Pursuant to section 117 of the Companies Act 1985

Please complete legibly, preferably in black type, or bold block lettering

To the Registrar of Companies

For official use   Company number

Name of company

*Insert full name of company

• EUROXPLORE MINERALS & MINES p.l.c.

applies for a certificate that it is entitled to do business and exercise borrowing powers.

For that purpose I,   CONRAD ASPINALL

of   EUROXPLORE MINERALS & MINES p.l.c.

†Delete as appropriate

[The Secretary][A Director]† of the above company,

do solemnly and sincerely declare that;

1   the nominal value of the company's allotted share capital is not less than the authorised minimum

2   the amount paid up on the allotted share capital of the company at the time of this application is   £ 24,000

3   the [estimated]† amount of the preliminary expenses of the company is

and [has been paid][is payable]† by   £ 5,000

§ Insert name of person(s) by whom expenses paid or payable

§   CONRAD ASPINALL

FOREIGN FIELD EXPLORATION p.l.c.

Presentor's name address and reference (if any):

Makepiece and Streiff
Bank Chambers
Barset
Barsetshire
Ref: CA/JA/Sharp

For official use
General Section

Post room

Page 1

[4a.   no amount or benefit has been paid or given or is intended to be paid or given to any of the promoters of the company]*

[4b.   the amount or benefit paid or given or intended to be paid or given to any promoter of the company is:]*

Promoter No. 1;
The amount paid or intended to be paid to him £ 500
Any benefit given or intended to be given to him   None
The consideration for such payment or benefit   None

Promoter No. 2;
The amount paid or intended to be paid to him £
Any benefit given or intended to be given to him
The consideration for such payment or benefit

Promoter No. 3;
The amount paid or intended to be paid to him £
Any benefit given or intended to be given to him
The consideration for such payment or benefit

Promoter No. 4;
The amount paid or intended to be paid to him £
Any benefit given or intended to be given to him
The consideration for such payment or benefit

And I make this solemn declaration conscientiously believing the same to be true and by virtue of the provisions of the Statutory Declarations Act 1835.

Declared at St Augustines House

Rodring

Barsetshire

the 19th day of February

one thousand nine hundred and Ninety four

before me Findar Horton

A Commissioner for Oaths or Notary Public or Justice of the Peace or Solicitor having the powers conferred on a Commissioner for Oaths.

Declarant to sign below

C Aspinall

Companies G117

In addition to the legal relationship described above between the shareholder and the company a legal relationship is also created between the shareholders themselves. This relationship is a series of mutual covenants entered into by all the shareholders and is in terms of the regulations laid down in the constitutional documents; the Memorandum and Articles.

Becoming a shareholder

When a company is formed it must specify in the capital clause of its Memorandum of Association what its authorised capital is to be. The orthodox way of calculating this is to assess the financial requirements of the company at its inception until such time as it will generate profits sufficient to be self-financing. Usually, a safety margin will be added, and the total will be authorised share capital specified in the Memorandum. it is then divided up into a number of shares. Each share will have a nominal value. So, for example, if the estimated requirements are £1,000 that may become the authority share capital. This might then be divided into 1,000 shares with a nominal value of £1. The nominal value is also called the par value.

The company then issues shares to people who pay consideration to the company. The consideration is the promise to pay at least the nominal value of the share if called upon to do so. This may be more or less than the nominal value of the share. The price at which they are issued (or transferred) does not depend upon their nominal value but upon their commercial value, which may fluctuate. Where the company is a public company quoted on the Stock Exchange the commercial value of the share will normally be that which is quoted on the Exchange at any given time. If the company is a private company the commercial value of the share will, of course, be a matter of private bargain.

If a shareholder has been paid less than the agreed value of the share, it is said to be a partly-paid share. The company may, as has been seen in this chapter, make calls on these shares. This requires the shareholder to pay all or some of the unpaid value of the share. Once a shareholder has paid the value of the share he is not liable to any further extent for the liabilities of the company. Compare the liability of a guarantor, or a shareholder of a company in which liability is not limited.

The sum total of the nominal value of all the shares that have been issued by the company to all the shareholders is known as the issued capital. The issued capital may therefore be less than or equal to the authorised share capital, but it can never be greater.

Where the company is a public limited company, its shares may be bought and sold like any other item of personal property, subject to the restrictions contained in the Articles. It is, however, necessary that a shareholder shall have agreed to take the shares and that his name shall have been entered on the Register of Members. It is usual for a company to issue a document under seal indicating that the holder has a title to the shares. This is called a share certificate.

Classes of shareholding

Usually, each share in a company is exactly the same as any other share in that company and all are said to rank *"pari passu,"* that is, equally. Each shareholder will expect a right to vote, a right to share in the profits of the company and a right to share in any return of capital in a winding-up of the company or otherwise. It is possible, however, to create shares where the rights which shareholders have differ dependent upon the type, or class, of share held.

Where shares exist with different rights each group of shares that are identical is known as a class of shares. There is no limit to the number of classes which can exist. Also, there is no established distinction between the way in which the rights attached to each class of share may differ. For instance, one class of share may give shareholders the right to vote at a General Meeting whereas another may not. One class may entitle a holder to receive a dividend, another may not.

Preference shares

There is no legal definition of a preference share and there are many different ways in which preference shares are issued. Their distinguishing feature is that they can in some way outrank other shares. Usually, this ranking will relate to the distribution of profits. For instance, a "10 per cent. preference share" is one where its holder is entitled to a 10 per cent. return on a nominal value of his shares from the company's profits which are available for distribution before any other class of shareholding receives a return. So it is said that the class the class is a preferred class.

Deferred shares

These shares are rare. They are also called Founders shares and would be mentioned in the capital clauses of the Memorandum of Association. If they are truly Founders shares they will be subscribed for by the promoters of the company. Deferred shares are the reverse of preferred shares. Whereas preferred shares are to be dealt with in priority to other shares, ordinary shares may take priority over deferred shares. Frequently founders accept deferred shares in order to give other shareholders confidence in the good faith of the proposed company.

Ordinary shares

Shareholders who hold ordinary shares generally carry the bulk of the risk of the business and stand to receive the bulk of the profits. They are frequently referred to as equity shareholders for that reason. When the company declares a dividend and any distribution provided for in the Articles to preferred creditors has occurred, the whole of the dividend is available for the ordinary shareholders.

If the company is wound up the ordinary shareholders are entitled to a division of all the assets which remain after the debts and other liabilities of the company have been met and after the capital of the shares has been repaid.

It is not necessary for all ordinary shares to be of the same class. For example, companies may issue ordinary shares which do not carry voting rights. This enables a company to increase its financial input without losing any proportion of the control which is exercised by its membership. It is a practice which is not encouraged by the Stock Exchange because it permits the rights of other shareholders to be abused.

Debentures

It has been stated above that the major distinction between shareholding and debenture holding is that the former gives a beneficial interest in the company whereas the latter is usually a form of secured lending by the debenture holder (the creditor) to the company (the debtor).

Just as the terms of a particular class of share are a matter of contract, it is possible to contract for particular types of debenture. Sometimes debenture holding can be similar to shareholding. For instance, some preferred shares may appear to be almost identical to some debentures. There is, however, one overriding distinction. If interest is to be paid on a loan then it has to be paid whether or not the company makes a profit. On the other hand, dividends are only payable on shares if the company has made a profit which is available for distribution, and the directors believe that part of the profit should be paid out as a dividend.

A debenture can include any form of long-term borrowing. It is normally secured by way of a charge on the property of the company. So, for instance, a mortgage, such as a bank, building society, insurance company, etc., may be a debenture holder, even though the mortgagee may have other remedies in the case of non-payment, such as the right to require the company to forfeit the mortgaged land.

COMPANY MANAGEMENT

The last four sections have shown the principles behind, and formation of, a company as a distinct legal personality. It is, however, an artificial personality and its actions must be controlled by human personalities who are its officers or employees.

Directors

Appointment. The Memorandum and Articles will provide for the appointment of a company's principal agents or officers, called directors, who are empowered to appoint a Managing Director. He will be in actual control of the day-to-day running of the company. Each director appointed acts as an agent of the company but none is agent of another director. So, in the case study shown above, Mr. & Mrs. Sharp are both directors and agents of Joseph Sharp (Vegetables) Limited but not of each other.

It is usual for the subcribers to the Memorandum to appoint the first directors and thereafter for the directors to retire in rotation. These vacancies are then filled at the Annual General Meeting of the members (see below). However in the case of private companies, provisions for retirement by rotation are often removed so that directors hold office permanently until death, voluntary retirement or removal from office. Vacancies other than rotational vacancies may be filled by an appointee of the other directors. It follows that any member who holds 51 per cent. of the voting shares (for example, the Government as a member of some nationalised industries) is very likely to be able to control the holding of directorships in a company.

Powers and duties

The powers which are exercised by directors (known collectively as the Board of Directors) will depend upon the Articles of Association. If Table A has been adopted the directors "and no one else" are responsible for the management of the company save where matters have been delegated by statute or by words elsewhere in the Articles or by way of lawful delegation from the directors to a General Meeting. If the directors fail to exercise their powers the General Meeting of members may exercise the powers for them. So if there were to be a deadlock on the Board or if there were to be no directors, for instance, the General Meeting may act. Notably these provisions may help Joseph Sharp (Vegetables) Limited even though the directors and the shareholders are the same because Mr. Sharp holds the controlling interest. He holds 99 per cent. of the shares. All the shares carry voting rights. It follows that he has 99 per cent. of the voting rights.

Directors have a "fiduciary duty" to their principal, the company. They must not make "secret profits" out of their position. They must act in good faith in the best interests of the company and must act with care and skill. A director is not, however, required to act with greater care and skill than may reasonably be expected of a person with his knowledge and experience; he is not bound to give continuous attention to the affairs of the company and he may entrust other officials of the company to carry out tasks for him.

A director has a duty towards the employees of a company too. He must have regard to their interests in general as well as to the interests of the members.

Removal

Members of the company have the power to remove directors by ordinary resolution at a General Meeting. This is expressed in the 1985 Act to be so despite anything in the Articles to the contrary, although 28 days' notice has to be given to the company which in turn must give notice to the director whose removal is proposed. He is entitled to be heard at the Meeting and he may require the company to circulate his representations.

The Managing Director

Under Table A the directors are entitled to appoint one or more of their number to be Managing Director(s). They may appoint him for as long, and upon such terms, as they think fit. He is salaried and may frequently receive a salary which is determined by the Board of Directors. His function is to exercise those powers which are delegated to him by the Board of Directors. He does not retire by rotation.

The Secretary

Technically, the company secretary is not concerned with the management of the company. However, the Articles may impose managerial functions upon him. The secretary's pure function is to take a charge of the documentation required by the Companies Acts and to ensure that all returns to the Companies Registry are made in good order and on time. All companies must have a secretary. If the company is a public company the directors must take all reasonable steps to secure that the secretary is a person who has the necessary knowledge and experience and who has been:

(a) the secretary or an assistant or deputy secretary of that company; or

(b) the secretary of another public company; or

(c) has a specified professional qualification such as barrister, solicitor, accountant or member of the Institute of Chartered Secretaries and Administrators.

Auditors

A company must appoint auditors to report to the members on the accounts of the company as well as on the balance sheet and profit and loss account. The first auditors may be appointed by the directors of the company although the General Meeting of members must appoint auditors to hold office for the following year. A private company may elect to dispense with the annual appointment of auditors. There are special rules about changing a company's auditors.

First meeting of directors

The first meeting of directors is an important event. The solicitor responsible for forming the company will attend and report the incorporation of the company to the directors.

Jack has drawn up the agenda for the first meeting of directors to be held in Mr. Amity's office on February 1, 1994. Mr. and Mrs. Sharp will attend.

JOSEPH SHARP (VEGETABLES) LIMITED

Agenda for First Meeting of Directors

1. Mr. Amity to report that Joseph Sharp (Vegetables) Limited has been incorporated.

2. Mr. Amity to report as to the directors, secretary and registered office.

3. Chairman of the Board of Directors to be appointed.

4. The common seal of the company to be adopted.

5. Auditors to be appointed.

6. The accounting reference date to be fixed.

7. Bankers to be appointed and signatories to the account to be authorised.

8. Shares to be allotted and FORM 88(2) completed (see p. 135).

9. Share certificates to be sealed.

10. To register for the purposes of V.A.T.

11. Notification of share interests by directors if any.

12. General notice as to interests in contracts.

13. Costs of formation to be approved for payment to Messrs. Makepiece and Streiff.

These are the matters which are to be discussed. They are principally of an administrative nature which enable the effective management of the company. Following this meeting notice of the accounting reference date will be sent to the Registrar of Companies in form G224. It is the date to which the company's accounts will be made up. It appears below.

Meetings

There are now only two types of meeting of the members of a company: the Annual General Meeting, and an Extraordinary General Meeting. Each of these is governed largely by the constitution of the company but it is also governed increasingly by statute.

The Annual General Meeting

The Companies Act 1985 provides that a company shall hold an Annual General Meeting of its members. The first Annual General Meeting should be held within 18 months from its formation and thereafter each Annual General Meeting should be held not more than 15 months from the preceding one. The Companies Act do not codify the business which must be transacted at an Annual General Meeting. The business which is usually conducted is:

COMPANIES FORM No. 224

Notice of accounting reference date
(to be delivered within **9 months** of incorporation)

224

Please do not write in this margin.

Pursuant to section 224 of the Companies Act 1985 as inserted by section 3 of the Companies Act 1989

Please complete legibly, preferably in black type, or bold block lettering.

To the Registrar of Companies
(Address overleaf)

Company number

Name of company

*Insert full name of company.

* JOSEPH SHARP (VEGETABLES) LIMITED

gives notice that the date on which the company's accounting reference period is to be treated as coming to an end in each successive year is as shown below:

Important
The accounting reference date to be entered alongside should be completed as in the following examples:

Day   Month

3	0	0	4

5 April
Day   Month

0	5	0	4

30 June
Day   Month

3	0	0	6

31 December
Day   Month

3	1	1	2

†Insert Director, Secretary, Administrator, Administrative Receiver or Receiver (Scotland) as appropriate.

Signed *Joseph Sharp* Designation† *Director* Date 14 Dec 1993

Presentor's name address telephone number and reference (if any):

For official use
D.E.B.

Post room

oyez The Solicitors' Law Stationery Society Ltd., Oyez House, 27 Crimscott Street, London SE1 5TS.

1990 Edition
6.90 F17380
5019191
★ ★ ★

Companies G224

Notes

The address for companies registered in England and Wales or Wales is:

The Registrar of Companies
Companies House
Crown Way
Cardiff
CF4 3UZ

or, for companies registered in Scotland:

The Registrar of Companies
Companies House
100–102 George Street
Edinburgh
EH2 3DJ

COMPANIES FORM No. 88(2)(Rev 1988)

Return of allotments of shares

Pursuant to section 88(2) of the Companies Act 1985 (the Act)

Please do not
write in this
margin

To the Registrar of Companies **(address overleaf)**
(see note 1)

88(2)

(REVISED 1988)

This form replaces forms
PUC2, PUC3 and 88(2)

Please complete
legibly, preferably
in black type, or
bold block lettering

Company number

1487304

1. Name of company

* Insert full name
of company

•	JOSEPH SHARP (VEGETABLES) LIMITED

2. This section must be completed for all allotments

† Distinguish
between
ordinary,
preference, etc.

Description of shares†	Ordinary		
A Number allotted	100		
B Nominal value of each	£ 1	£	£
C Total amount (if any) paid or due and payable on each share (including premium if any)	£ 20	£	£

§ Complete
(a) or (b) as
appropriate

Date(s) on which the shares were allotted

(a) [on __1st February__ 19 _94_]§, or

(b) [from_____ 19 _____ to _____ 19 ____]§

The names and addresses of the allottees and the number of shares allotted to each should be given overleaf

3. If the allotment is wholly or partly other than for cash the following information must be given **(see notes 2 & 3)**

D Extent to which each share is to be treated as paid up. Please use percentage.	100%		
E Consideration for which the shares were allotted_____	Goodwill of the business of Joseph Sharp, retailer.		

Notes

1. This form should be delivered to the Registrar of Companies within one month of the (first) date of allotment.

2. If the allotment is wholly or partly other than for cash, the company must deliver to the Registrar a return containing the information at D & E. The company may deliver this information by completing D & E and the delivery of the information must be accompanied by the duly stamped contract required by section 88(2)(b) of the Act or by the duly stamped prescribed particulars required by section 88(3) (Form No 88(3)).

3. Details of bonus issues should be included only in section 2.

Presentor's name, address, telephone number and reference (if any):

For official use

Post room

Page 1

4. Names and addresses of the allottees

Please do not write in the margin

Please complete legibly, preferably in black type, or bold block lettering

Names and Addresses	Number of shares allotted		
	Ordinary	Preference	Other
Joseph Sharp	99		
51 Paradise Row			
Barset			
Barsetshire BA16 2AL			
Doreen May Sharp			
51 Paradise Row			
Barset			
Barsetshire BA16 2AL	1		
Total	100		

Where the space given on this form is inadequate, continuation sheets should be used and the number of sheets attached should be indicated in the box opposite:

‡ Insert Director, Secretary, Administrator, Administrative Receiver, or Receiver (Scotland) as appropriate

Signed _Joseph Sharp_ Designation‡ _Director_ Date _16ᵗʰ Feb. 1994_

Companies registered in England and Wales or Wales should deliver this form to:–

The Registrar of Companies
Companies House
Crown Way
Maindy
Cardiff
CF4 3UZ

Companies registered in Scotland should deliver this form to:–

The Registrar of Companies
Companies Registration Office
102 George Street
Edinburgh
EH2 3DJ

Page 2

OYEZ The Solicitors' Law Stationery Society Ltd, Oyez House, 7 Spa Road, London SE16 3QQ

Companies G88(2) (Revised 1988)

1988 Edition
10.91 F21109
5019476
★ ★ ★ ★ ★

(i) the presentation of accounts and reports

(ii) the appointment (of reappointment) of auditors

(iii) the declaration of dividends

(iv) consideration of the accounts and the directors' and auditors' reports

(v) the appointment of directors to replace those who are retiring

(vi) the fixing of the auditors' remuneration.

At the Annual Meeting the members of the company may question the directors about their report and their conduct of the company. Under the Companies Act 1989 a private company may elect to dispense with Annual General Meetings.

Extraordinary General Meetings

The Articles of Association will normally specify when an Extraordinary General Meeting may be called and usually give the directors power to call one at any time. The directors must call a meeting if required to do so by the holders of not less than one tenth of the paid-up share capital which carries voting rights.

If the company is public an Extraordinary General Meeting must be called by the directors within 28 days of becoming aware that the net assets of the company have fallen to half or less than half of the called-up share capital.

Statutory books

These documents are kept at the registered office of the company unless otherwise stated. They are:

(i) The Register of Members. This sets out the shareholding of each member and states the class of share which he has.

(ii) The Register of Debenture holders (if the company keeps such a Register).

(iii) The Register of Directors and Secretary. This gives details of the name, address and business occupation of the director as well as of any other directorships held by him.

(iv) The Register of Directors' interest in shares or debentures. A director must notify the company of any registrable interest in the shares or debentures of that company or of any related company. His obligation to notify extends to any interest of his wife or children.

(v) The Register of substantial interests in unrestricted voting capital required to be kept by companies whose share capital is wholly or in part quoted on a recognised Stock Exchange. This, of course, only applies to a public limited company. A substantial interest in this case means one-tenth of the nominal value of the share capital carrying unrestricted voting rights. Certain variations of that interest must be notified for entry on the Register.

(vi) The Register of Charges. This records all charges on company assets, Copies of the documents which create the charges must also be kept there.

(vii) The Minute Book. This contains the minutes of General Meetings.

(viii) The accounts.

(ix) Copies of the directors' contracts of service or written memoranda thereof setting out terms.

Resolutions

It has been seen that members of a company may express their views at a General Meeting (Annual or Extraordinary). They do this by way of resolutions. There are four types of resolution; ordinary, extraordinary, special and elective.

(1) An ordinary resolution is one which is passed by a simple majority of those who choose to attend at the meeting and to exercise their vote.

(2) An extraordinary resolution is one which is passed if three-quarters of those who choose to attend the meeting and vote are in favour. This type of resolution is usually required only for some matters connected with winding up the company, where is to be a variation of shareholders' rights or whenever else the Articles may require it.

(3) A special resolution, too, is passed if three-quarters of those present at the meeting are in favour. The difference between this resolution and the extraordinary resolution is that for this, 21 days' notice must be given of the meeting at which it is to be proposed.

(4) An elective resolution, which requires 21 days' notice and the agreement o all members entitled to attend and vote, can be used by a private company to dispense with certain requirements, *e.g.* holding the Annual General Meeting and the need to make annual appointments of auditors.

Annual return

The annual return is a document which sets out certain specified information giving details of members of the company, the company's share capital, particulars of the director(s) and secretary and details of debentures, charges and mortgages. It must, in general, be sent in every calendar year to the Registrar of Companies within 28 days after the Annual General Meeting and must be made up to the fourteenth day after the same meeting. It is an offence to fail to file the annual return.

CHAPTER 4

PROCEEDINGS IN THE HIGH COURT

Introduction

The unbroken sequence of proceedings in the High Court goes back well over six hundred years, civil wars and revolutions notwithstanding. The High Court now sits in the Royal Courts of Justice in the Strand and also at numerous provincial centres.

The High Court and the County Court—Jurisdiction

Whilst the High Court has its roots far back in history, the modern County Court was created by the County Courts Act 1846 with its own set of rules and practices. The difference between the courts continued until quite recently to be considerable. Each was regulated by separate Codes of Rules and only recently have serious efforts been made to iron out some of the differences. The assimilation of the County Court Rules to those of the High Court was one of the underlying aims of substantial changes made in the County Court Rules 1981. This assimilation is also one of the main objects of the Courts and Legal Services Act 1990 which has been gradually brought into force.

Before July 1, 1991 the County Court had a limited financial jurisdiction. In the most important instances, that is cases in tort and contract, its financial jurisdiction was a maximum of £5,000. In some equity and property matters that jurisdiction was increased to £30,000. Whilst the jurisdiction remains the same in equity and property matters, with effect from July 1991 the County Court now has an unlimited jurisdiction in tort and contract actions. The High Court has always had an unlimited jurisdiction, that is that any action could be started there however small or large the amount unless some specific statute conferred jurisdiction exclusively on the County Court (as for example the Consumer Credit Act 1974 does in general). There is now therefore a total overlap of jurisdictions especially in tort and contract actions.

Plaintiffs' solicitors often saw substantial advantages in litigating in the High Court rather than the County Court. In particular, speed and efficiency of early process and the concept of "party control" whereby a plaintiff, if he was so minded, could both issue and serve his own writ on the same day without the need for assistance from the court's staff in the process; the perceived greater efficiency in enforcement of judgment; and also the provision for interest on judgment debts all made the High Court attractive even where quite modest sums were involved. When deciding where to commence an action in tort or contract however one must now have regard to the High Court and County Court Jurisdiction Order 1991 in effect from July 1, 1991 which aims radically to redistribute business between the two courts. This order makes the following important provisions:

1. That personal injury cases may only be commenced in the High Court where the plaintiff's solicitor is able bona fide to certify that the value of the action is £50,000 or more. A plaintiff's solicitor must now endorse the writ with a certificate in the following terms:

"This writ includes a claim for person injury but may be commenced in the High Court because the value of the action for the purposes of Article 5 of High Court and County Courts Jurisdiction Order 1991 exceeds £50,000." This must also be signed by the plaintiff's solicitor before issue of the writ.

The effect of this is that in personal injury cases value is the only criterion for place of issue of the writ. It matters not that the case has considerable complexities of fact, law or expert evidence or even that it is a test case for a whole series of plaintiffs. If the certificate cannot bona fide be given that the amount involved is more than £50,000 the action must be commenced in the County Court. That is not of course the end of the matter because the rules do provide for the separate later consideration of *place of trial* by reference to certain criteria and it may well be that by reference to those criteria the trial will take place in the High Court.

2. There is no restriction on where other actions may be commenced. Thus a case involving even quite a modest sum might still be brought in the High Court and it is suggested that much routine debt collecting will still commence in the High Court. There is however a sanction for wrongly issuing proceedings in the High Court which should have been issued in the County Court which operates by way of reduction of the winner's costs payable by the loser. There is as yet no case law, guideline or precedent as to how this provision will be interpreted (see below).

3. Place of trial of the action.

When making the decision as to place of trial of an action the court must have regard to Article 7 of the Jurisdiction order. This provides in principle that:

(i) An action which involves a sum of £50,000 or more shall be tried in the High Court unless having regard to certain criteria mentioned below the court considers that the action shall be tried in the County Court.

(ii) Actions involving less than £25,000 will be tried in the County Court unless the court having regard to the same criteria considers that the action should be tried in the High Court.

(iii) Actions involving a sum between these figures may be tried in either court having regard to the said criteria.

4. The relevant criteria for deciding place of trial.

These are set out in Article 7(5) of the Jurisdiction Order and provide that the court shall have regard to:

(i) The financial substance of the action including the value of any counterclaim.

(ii) Whether the action is otherwise important, *e.g.* whether it raises question of importance to persons who are not parties or matters of general public interest (thus the fact for example that it was a test case for hundreds of people similarly affected might be a reason for trying the case in the High Court even if quite a modest amount was involved).

(iii) The complexity of the facts, legal issues, remedies or procedures involved.

(iv) Where the transfer is likely to result in a more speedy trial of the action (although no transfer may be made on this ground alone).

5. <u>The sanction for wrongly commencing an action in the High Court</u>.

If the eventual court of trial concludes that a plaintiff was wrong to have wasted the time of the higher court with an action which really should have been commenced in the County Court, then s.51(8) of the Supreme Court Act 1981 provides that the court of trial can impose a penalty on a successful plaintiff by reducing the costs payable to him by the defendant by any amount up to 25 per cent. This is therefore a straightforward sanction though there is yet no indication of how it will work in practice. The court has a complete discretion in the matter and is not obliged to impose the penalty. It will be borne in mind anyway that there are at least two stages, namely directions for trial, and setting down for trial, where the parties, and the court itself, may consider transferring an action for trial to a different court from that in which it was commenced. Although this does not in itself get round the problem because s.51(8) is intended to punish a plaintiff for *commencing* proceedings in the High Court it would seem that a plaintiff who acts promptly in seeking to have a case transferred which he was wrong, or foolish to have started in the High Court might well escape any sanction.

High Court and County Court—Other Matters

As in the county court, fees are payable at what may be said to be pivotal points in an action: the issue of the writ, setting down for trial, notice of appeal and enforcement of judgment. Small fees are payable by either party on other occasions, throughout the action, particularly on issuing interlocutory summonses.

However, there are basic differences. In the county court, as we saw in Volume 1, each step in the proceedings is filed in the court office, so that the court accumulates a record of the progress of the case. This is used by the judge when the case comes to trial. In the High Court, after the writ is issued and acknowledged, the parties carry on much of the dialogue direct. Of course, the Court must have a record of the procedural directions given by judges, masters, etc., as the case proceeds towards trial, but much of the documentation of a case is only lodged in court when the case is ready for trial.

Another important difference is that the High Court has a more passive role in relation to the conduct of the case. Unlike the County Court, it does not usually call the parties before it at any stage of its own motion. The court does not draw up its own orders, the drafting and service of which are left to the successful party to any particular application. Moreover the High Court employs no bailiff for the service of writs etc. It is always up to the party concerned to serve writs and orders.

The court organisation

The business of the Court is divided into three divisions: Queen's Bench Division (Q.B.D.), Chancery Division (Ch.D.) and Family Division (F.D.). Each Division has its own body of judges and its own specialist on procedural rules. The division of the work of the Court in this way is really a matter of administrative convenience: in law, the jurisdiction of each Division is identical and unrestricted.

Cases may be commenced either in one of the district registries of the High Court or at the Central Office at the Royal Courts of Justice, London. Although Rules of the Supreme Court apply throughout, there are practical differences in the way they are applied in the district registries and in the Central Office. When High Court cases come to trial, in which ever Division, they are tried by a High Court Judge. It is important however to consider the functions of the Officers of the Court before whom earlier stages of a case may come up, that is to say the Judges who deal with all administrative and judicial matters between commencement of the case and trial. In the district registries the control and supervision of all the procedures up to actual trial and after trial has taken place are in the hands of the district judges. They conduct the business of all three Divisions of the Court. In London, on the other hand, the equivalent to the District Judge is called a Master in the Queen's Bench Division, and in the Chancery Division, but a District Judge in the Family Division. In London Masters or District Judges of each Division never sit in the other Divisions.

District Judges and masters exercise considerable judicial powers within the procedural functions allotted to them and within the scope of their authority they, along with the High Court judges, constitute "the court" (Ord. 1, r. 4(2)).

In the Queen's Bench Division, every case proceeding in the Central Office is allocated to a particular master when the first summons is issued. He is then responsible for dealing with nearly all the subsequent procedural steps in the case to the actual trial and after the trial has taken place. Masters sit daily by rota as the "Practice Master" to deal with applications and other matters that can be dealt with without a formal hearing and also to assist litigants and solicitors generally in resolving procedural doubts and difficulties. In most matters the decision of a master is subject to an appeal to a High Court judge in chambers. A master has a general power to refer to a judge for decision any matter he considers should be decided by the judge and there are some matters reserved to the judge in the first instance, *e.g.* contempt of court and contested injunctions.

Chancery masters' duties are both administrative and judicial. They include enquiries to ascertain the beneficiaries entitled to share in estates; arranging sales of property, ordering and supervising the presentation of accounts and so on. They are assisted by Principal Clerks. Masters' Orders are made in chambers and there is a right of appeal to the judge.

Almost invariably, when a case proceeds to trial, an order for the payment of costs is made against one of the parties. The process of obtaining the court's approval of the items to be included and the level of the charges to be made is called "taxation." It is carried out in London by taxing masters, who are appointed from among solicitors. Outside London, it is done by the district judges. The procedure on taxation is dealt with below (p. 210).

The High Court sits in four terms separated by periods of vacation. The vacations are at Christmas, Easter and late Spring Bank holidays and in addition there is the so called "long vacation" which is now the month of August. During the vacations only vacation judges sit to deal with urgent business. District judges and Masters are available during the vacations except that the court hours are shorter and in the long vacation special leave is needed to obtain a hearing date for certain routine summonses, although again, urgent matters can be dealt with.

The jurisdiction

Whilst we have said the jurisdiction of the High Court, unlike that of the county court, is unrestricted, that must be understood as applying within the geographical territories in which the royal writ runs. This is England and Wales and Berwick-upon-Tweed. It does not extend to Scotland (which of course has its own system of law) and the Isle of Man, the Channel Islands or Northern Ireland.

This still leaves the question of serving a writ on a person or body who is outside these geographical limits. It is often possible to serve a High Court writ outside England and Wales but usually it is necessary to demonstrate some positive relationship with the cause of action, *e.g.* that the action concerns breach of a contract made within England and Wales, or concerns land within the jurisdiction.

The Rules

The system of regulation by which litigation in the High Court is conducted, the Rules of the Supreme Court (R.S.C.), are set out in *The Supreme Court Practice*, the *White Book*. This has three volumes, which every litigation practitioner has at his elbow. As with the County Court Rules (C.C.R.), they are divided into a series of Orders which are subdivided into rules. They are accompanied in the *White Book* by copious notes containing a wealth of advice derived from judicial decisions, Masters' Practice Notes and so on.

In Vol. 1, in which the Rules of the Supreme Court are set out, each page is headed with the Order and rule number dealt with. Thus, Ord. 18, r. 12: Order 18, rule 12. Each rule is followed by the notes in numbered paragraphs. These are shortly referred to, for example, as follows: 18/12/37. This is, of course, Note 37 under rule 12 of Order 18. Volume 2 of the *White Book*, which contains the Forms prescribed by the Rules of the Supreme Court and also relevant Acts and Orders has a continuous series of reference numbers in the margin. Apart from the clear layout and page reference system, the book has an excellent index contained in Volume 3, all of which go far to take away the dread its combined 3,500 or so pages would otherwise inspire. As the *White Book* is not published every year, care must be taken to ensure that the latest half-yearly supplement is available and to check for changes since the date of publication. Subscribers also now receive a further publication "The Supreme Court Practice News" published 10 times a year.

An additional useful feature is that now, as a special supplement, the whole of the County Court Rules are published as part of the Supreme Court Practice in a separate small volume. This greatly facilitates comparison of the relevant rules where necessary.

As the object of the Rules is to facilitate the presentation of a claim or defence and not to discipline the parties, non-compliance does not nullify what has been done by or on behalf of a party: it is treated as an irregularity capable of being corrected, even though the party at fault may have to pay the costs "thrown away," *i.e.* the abortive costs, his own and his opponent's, incurred through his failure or mistake. This applies, for instance, where a plaintiff chooses the wrong process in commencing proceedings, *e.g.* a writ instead of an originating summons.

Whilst a party is hardly ever *unsuited* (*i.e.* dismissed from the proceedings) for procedural errors, the court can at any stage strike out a particular pleading or require it to be amended. This happens, for instance, where a writ discloses no reasonable cause of action or defence, where a pleading is scandalous or frivolous or where it is otherwise an abuse of the process of the court.

However, there are a few instances where the rules impose a rigid time limit for taking a particular step. In this case, the party who fails to act in time may be seriously disadvantaged or may find it impossible to go on. This happens, for instance, where a party fails to obtain the leave of the court to extend the four month period allowed for the service of a writ before that period has expired. If in the meantime the cause of action has become statute barred, there is usually no possibility of starting afresh by issuing another writ.

As in other chapters of this book we will proceed by illustrating the practical steps taken by a firm of solicitors in a particular debt action in the High Court and then in a personal injuries action to demonstrate how the basic procedures apply in these two kinds of cases which represent the most common ones in the Queen's Bench Division.

A claim for goods sold and delivered

Samuel Richardson v. *Daniel Defoe Limited*

Samuel Richardson carries on business at 184 High Street Barset as a general merchant. In 1992 Daniel Defoe Limited purchased goods from him at the total price of £17,000. Unfortunately, the accounts rendered for these goods have not been paid and in response to polite letters requesting payment the reason given is that the Company has a cash flow problem. It is suggested that if the supplier will only be patient a little while longer the problem will resolve itself and payment will be made. At length Mr. Richardson, anticipating that if payment is further delayed he will be in the same difficulty, writes, threatening that if payment is not received within 10 days he will consult his solicitors and ask them to take legal action. There is no reply. Consequently, Mr. Richardson makes an appointment with Mr. Anthony Adverse, a partner of Messrs. Makepiece & Streiff, whose office is near by.

Mr. W. White, the legal executive who manages the litigation department of Messrs. Makepiece, is given a note of the interview, copies of the invoices and the file of correspondence. The client's instructions are to take whatever action is necessary to recover the debt. As the debt is £17,000 it is clear that the County Court would have jurisdiction. This is however the very kind of case where, notwithstanding that, many solicitors would choose to start the action in the High Court, in the main because in such cases the plaintiff has greater control over the speed of the early stage of proceedings and because, if, as the plaintiff will hope, the case ends very early without the need for a full trial, the court is most unlikely to impose any sanction for having started the action in the High Court. If, contrary to the plaintiff's view, the case does become seriously defended and likely to go on for a full trial, then it is inevitable that it will subsequently be transferred to the County Court for that trial in any event. Accordingly in such cases most plaintiffs will still opt to start in the High Court. Mr. White finds that the goods were ordered by the manager of the Company's shop at 10 High Street, Barchester. The Company's letter heading gives the address of the registered office: Island House, Swiss Cottage, NW6. The writ will have to be served on the Company at its registered office.

On the same day, Mr. White writes to the local manager, with a copy to the Company at its registered office, summarising the course of events and demanding payment within seven days, in default of which a writ will be issued. The importance of this "letter before action" has been explained in Volume 1 (p. 297). He makes a note in his diary for June 18, 1993, the date on which the seven days will expire, to proceed with the issue of the writ if payment is not received.

When the writ is issued the name of the company and its address must exactly agree with the particulars in the Register of Companies. Accordingly Mr. White ascertains from the company agents which his firm employs the precise registered particulars of the defendant company. When received these confirm the accuracy of the letter heading. No communication having been received by June 17, Mr. White is keen to demonstrate to his opponents that he is not bluffing and he puts in hand the issue of the writ.

Every writ must be accompanied or followed by a Statement of Claim summarising the allegations on which the plaintiff relies to establish the defendant's liability. In Mr. Richardson's action, following the normal practice where the claim is for a debt or liquidated demand, the Statement of Claim will be set out in the space provided on page 2 of the writ form.

From the file of papers provided by Mr. Richardson, Mr. White knows that invoices were provided with delivery of goods and statements of account have been sent repeatedly since. In these circumstances only a short statement of the total debt need be inserted in the writ, with the addition that such details have been supplied. Mr. White drafts the Statement of Claim accordingly and passes it to his trainee assistant Joan to prepare the writ for issue in the district registry.

Interest

It is now necessary if a plaintiff is to be awarded interest by the Court for him to claim it in his pleadings. A right to interest arises under statute, namely section 35A of the Supreme Court Act 1981. It is important to distinguish between the cases where interest is sought in a damages case, *e.g.* a personal injuries case; and a debt case.

Damages

Where the plaintiff seeks an unliquidated sum such as in a personal injuries case all he need do is insert at the end of his pleadings . . . "and the Plaintiff claims interest pursuant to a s.35A Supreme Court Act 1981 at such rate and for such period as the court shall think fit." In this case it is impossible for the plaintiff to work out the interest due to him because of course the court itself will have to assess damages. Guidelines are available as to the rates at which a court should award interest in such cases and at the time of writing the guidelines are that on any element of the plaintiff's claim relating to pain, suffering and loss of amenities interest should be awarded at the rate of two per cent. per annum from the date of service of the writ to the date of judgment; and that in the case of special damages interest should be awarded at the rate of half the rate currently prevailing on the special account rates in force for the period. The special account rate is the rate of interest available on the court's own investment fund. Damages for future loss of earnings carry no award of interest which is naturally fair since they have not yet been incurred.

Debt cases

In cases where the plaintiff is claiming a specified sum then interest may arise in two different ways. First, it may be that where there has been non-payment of some sum due under the contract that the contract itself contains a provision for the rate of interest in the event of non-payment. In that case a claim to the interest must be pleaded in the way hereafter described, the rate being that set out in the contract. The interest claimed will be both as a lump sum due up to the date of commencement or proceedings and at a daily rate thereafter. If however the contract contained no provision for the payment of interest then a claim to interest can still be made. The plaintiff can in fact claim any rate of interest which he thinks proper and arguable and in the case of substantial commercial transactions a very high rate of interest might well be sought, *e.g.* 20 per cent. In such a case however there is no point in working out the amount due as a lump sum and daily rate since there will have to be an assessment of interest by the court. However, there is provision in the rules that if the the plaintiff is willing to restrict his claim to interest at the same annual rate as that currently prevailing on judgment debts (currently 8 per cent.) then a plaintiff may plead his claim for interest and compute it exactly by way of a lump sum and a continuing daily rate as previously described in contractual interest claims.

It both these latter cases the point of working out a daily rate is that at any given moment the defendant knows precisely what his liability is and can offer to settle the claim in full inclusive of interest.

To simplify things in the present case we will assume that the contract between the plaintiff and the defendant specified that in the event of the sums not being paid within 7 days of the invoice being delivered interest will run at 20 per cent. until the date of payment. As will be seen from the specimen of the Statement of Claim endorsed on the writ illustrated at p. 160 a computation of the amount due up to the date of issuing the writ and a daily rate is provided.

It will be noted that there is after the Statement of Claim what is called a "fixed costs" endorsement. The amount of costs allowable can be found in tables within the Supreme Court Practice and is related to the amount claimed. The purpose of this endorsement is to enable the defendant, if he is so minded, to settle the entire matter once and for all within 14 days of receipt of the writ. If he pays the amount direct to the plaintiff for the claim and interest on the claim (which he can compute as previously explained) and the amount of the fixed costs claimed then his liability to the plaintiff ceases then and there. In an ordinary case the plaintiff will not then be able to go on and claim any further or greater sum for costs from him.

The district registry being some 20 miles away in Barchester, the writ will be issued by post. As there is only one defendant to be served it is to be prepared in triplicate. Using the composite writ form A1 she makes out the original typescript. In doing this, she is careful to make the entries with clarity and precision, filling in the blanks and deleting words not applicable. As the claim is for a liquidated sum only, she must complete the paragraph on page 2 giving the mount of fixed costs to be added to the debt to discharge the defendant's liability if payment is made within 14 days of service of the writ. She also completes the endorsement alongside showing that the cause of action arose in the Barchester district. As carbon copies are not accepted by the court, she makes two photo-copies and checks them for legibility. On the front of one of the copies she endorses in the margin the firm's name, leaving space for signature on behalf of the firm. This indicates who in the firm is dealing with the case and it is this copy that will be retained by the court. The three copies are then given to Mr. White who checks the typescript and signs the Statement of Claim on all three copies in the firm name. He adds his personal signature to the marginal endorsement on the one copy. Joan prepares a brief letter to the Chief Clerk, High Court District Registry, Barchester: "Please issue the enclosed Writ of Summons." With the letter she sends:

1. The three completed writ forms.
2. The firm's cheque for the court fee of £70 made payable to H.M. Paymaster General.
3. Stamped, addressed envelope for the return of the sealed writs.

On receipt, the District Registry stamp the date and time of receipt on the documents and check them to see that they are complete and otherwise in order. The year, letter and number of the action are then assigned and entered on the writs. The two writ forms not signed in the margin are impressed with the red seal of the court and one of these is stamped "ORIGINAL." These, are posted back to Messrs. Makepiece. The third copy, signed by Mr. White, is impressed with the issuing fee and is kept in the Registry as the court's record. The writ as issued is as shown on pp. 159–160.

This being a writ directed to a registered company, service is by post. Joan addresses a short letter to the defendants saying: "We enclose, by way of service, writ of summons and form for acknowledgement of service." With it she encloses one sealed writ (not the "original") and the acknowledgement of service form, E22 which she has prepared. This being posted on June 24 service is deemed to be effected on a limited company in the ordinary course of post which means that if something is posted first class it is deemed to be received on the second working day thereafter, and if second class on the fourth working day thereafter. Naturally Joan posts it first class. Joan takes note that the last day for receipt of the completed acknowledgment by the court (14 days, including the day of service) will be July 12. She enters this in Mr. White's diary, as being the first day on which final judgment can be entered if the acknowledgement is not filed in time.

COURT FEES ONLY

Writ indorsed
with Statement
of Claim
[Liquidated
Demand]
(O.6, r. 1)

IN THE HIGH COURT OF JUSTICE

Queen's Bench Division

[BARCHESTER   **District Registry]**

19 93 .— R .—**No.**3026

Between

SAMUEL RICHARDSON   Plaintiff

AND

DANIEL DEFOE LTD   Defendant

(1) Insert name.

To the Defendant (¹)   DANIEL DEFOE LTD

(2) Insert address.

of (²)   ISLAND HOUSE, SWISS COTTAGE, LONDON N.W. 6.

This Writ of Summons has been issued against you by the above-named Plaintiff in respect of the claim set out on the back.

Within 14 days after the service of this Writ on you, counting the day of service, you must either satisfy the claim or return to the Court Office mentioned below the accompanying **Acknowledgment of Service** stating therein whether you intend to contest these proceedings.

If you fail to satisfy the claim or to return the Acknowledgment within the time stated, or if you return the Acknowledgment without stating therein an intention to contest the proceedings, the Plaintiff may proceed with the action and judgment may be entered against you forthwith without further notice.

(3) Complete
and delete as
necessary.

Issued from the (³) [Central Office] [Admiralty and Commercial Registry]
[BARCHESTER   District Registry] of the High Court
this   18th   day of   JUNE   19 93

NOTE: —This Writ may not be served later than 4 calendar months *(or, if leave is required to effect service out of the jurisdiction, 6 months)* beginning with that date unless renewed by order of the Court.

IMPORTANT

Directions for Acknowledgment of Service are given with the accompanying form.

Statement of Claim

The Plaintiff's claim is for the sum of £19,543.01 being the price of goods sold and delivered to the Defendants by the Plaintiff together with interest thereon pursuant to a contract.

Particulars.

11th September 1990   To the Price of tents and   £17,000
                        camping equipment.

And the Plaintiff claims:

(1) The said sum of £17,000
(2) Interest pursuant to clause 4 of a contract made between the Plaintiff and the Defendants dated 8 September 1992 at the rate of 20% per annum from 18th September 1992 until issue herein equivalent to a sum of £2,543.01.
(3) Interest as above at the rate of £9.31 daily from the date hereof until judgment earlier payment.

(Signed)   *Mul, J Still*

If, within the time for returning the Acknowledgment of Service, the Defendant pay s the amount claimed and £ 150.25 for costs and, if the Plaintiff obtains an order for substituted service, the additional sum of £ 43 , further proceedings will be stayed. The money must be paid to the Plaintiff , his Solicitor or Agent.

(1) If this Writ was issued out of a District Registry, this indorsement as to place where the cause of action arose should be completed.

(2) Delete as necessary.

(3) Insert name of place.

(4) For phraseology of this indorsement where the Plaintiff sues in person, see *Supreme Court Practice*, vol. 2, para 1.

(¹) [(²) [The cause] [One of the causes] of action in respect of which the Plaintiff claim s relief in this action arose wholly or in part at (³)   Barset in the district of the District Registry named overleaf.]

(⁴) **This Writ** was issued by   Makepiece and Streiff
of   Bank Chambers, High Street, Barset

[Agent for
of   ]

Solicitor   for the said Plaintiff whose address   (²) [is] [are] 184 High Street Barset in the County of Barchester.

Solicitor's Reference   WW   Tel. No: 00765 4321

Although the registered office of the defendants is in London, their place of business is where the goods were delivered, 10 High Street, Barchester, and the writ and form E22 are forwarded by their Head Office to the local manager there. He passes them to Messrs. Rime & Reason, at their Barchester office, with their file of invoices and correspondence, for necessary action. The manager explains that they have reached the limit of their bank credit so that it is vital to the Company to "buy time." If they can have a respite for some four weeks there is every hope that their financial position will be relieved to the extent that they can offer a payment. Messrs. Rime tell their clients that, to hold the position as long as possible, they will indicate an intention to defend, although their instructions do not allow any scope for substantiating a defence.

The defendants have the full 14 days from (but including) the date of receipt of the writ in which to deliver their completed acknowledgement to the court. Since the statement of claim was endorsed on the writ in this case the defendants, having delivered their acknowledgement to the court, will have a further 14 days (*i.e.* a total of 28 days from the date of receipt of the writ) in which to deliver their defence direct to the plaintiff. If therefore the "Yes" box in paragraph two of the form of acknowledgement is ticked, the defendants will not be in default of delivering their defence until this later date (*i.e.* 28 days from receipt of the writ) and accordingly the next day after that would be the earliest date on which Messrs. Makepiece will be able to enter judgment in default of defence. This then is the longest respite for which the defendants can hope.

However, Messrs. Rime are well aware that when the plaintiff's solicitors receive the acknowledgement they may well not be content to wait to see if a defence is delivered. There is, as we shall see, another tactic open to them. At this stage Messrs. Rime are concerned to delay all possible steps on behalf of the plaintiff. They therefore defer delivering the completed acknowledgement to the court until just before the 14 days expires. On July 9, the form E22 is completed and delivered to the district registry by hand. There, after scrutiny for accuracy and completeness, the form is stamped with the date of receipt and entered in the Cause Card Index, on which the record is kept. Photo-copies are made of the stamped document and these are sent by post to both firms of solicitors (see p. 163).

Messrs. Makepiece receive the copy acknowledgement on July 12, and Mr. White telephones Mr. Richardson to tell him of the defendants' stated intention to defend. Mr. Richardson is understandably annoyed at what would appear to be an attempt to evade their responsibility. At no time before the issue of the writ have the defendants raised any dispute or complaint about the goods delivered or questioned their obligation to pay for them.

Mr. White tells him that in his view it is a delaying tactic and one which is a frequently used device by defendants against which there is no real sanction. He advises that an application be made to the court immediately for what is called "summary judgment" under Order 14. Joan is asked to prepare a summons under Order 14 and an affidavit of the plaintiff in support. She prepares these documents (see pp. 165–166) and arranges on the telephone an appointment for Mr. Richardson to attend at the office of another firm of Barchester solicitors, Messrs. Seal and Servitt to have the affidavit sworn. When the sworn affidavit is returned by Mr. Richardson two copies of the summons together with the original affidavit and the court fee of £10 are sent by post to the District Registry. The covering letter requests a date for the hearing as soon as possible and states that the hearing may be expected to last 20 minutes. Some four days later the firm receive back one copy of the summons sealed by the court (the affidavit is retained) and the date for the appointment is marked as July 30 at 2.00 p.m. and marked by the court with the estimated length of hearing of 20 minutes. Messrs. Makepiece are now able to serve a copy of this summons and the affidavit on Messrs. Rime. Under the rules this summons must be served no later than 10 clear days before the hearing date.

Acknowledgment
of Service of Writ
of Summons
Queen's Bench)

IN THE HIGH COURT OF JUSTICE
Queen's Bench Division
[**District Registry]**

19 93 .— .—No.3026

*The adjacent
heading should
be completed by
the Plaintiff*

Between

SAMUEL RICHARDSON   Plaintiff

AND

DANIEL DEFOE LTD   Defendant

If you intend to instruct a Solicitor to act for you, give him this form IMMEDIATELY. Please complete in black ink.

IMPORTANT Read the accompanying directions and notes for guidance carefully before completing this form. If any information required is omitted or given wrongly, THIS FORM MAY HAVE TO BE RETURNED. Delay may result in judgment being entered against a Defendant whereby he or his Solicitor may have to pay the costs of applying to set it aside.

*See Notes 1, 3, 4
and 5*

1   State the full name of the Defendant by whom or on whose behalf the service of the Writ is being acknowledged.   DANIEL DEFOE LTD

2   State whether the Defendant intends to contest the proceedings (*tick appropriate box*) ☑   yes   ☐   no

See Direction 3

3   If the claim against the Defendant is for a debt or liquidated demand, AND he does not intend to contest the proceedings, state if the Defendant intends to apply for a stay of execution against any judgment entered by the Plaintiff (*tick box*)   ☐   yes

See Direction 4

4   If the Writ of Summons was issued out of a District Registry and
      (*a*)   the Defendant's residence, place of business or registered office (if a limited company) is NOT within the district of that District Registry AND
      (*b*)   there is no indorsement on the Writ that the Plaintiff's cause of action arose wholly or in part within that district,
      state if the Defendant applies for the transfer of the action (*tick box*) ☐ yes

If YES, state—   ☐   to the Royal Courts of Justice, London:
(*tick appropriate box*)   OR

**State which
Registry*

       ☐   to the*   District Registry

Service of the Writ is acknowledged accordingly

*†Where words
appear between
square brackets,
delete if
inapplicable
Insert "Defendant
in Person" if
appropriate*

(*Signed*)   *Rim J Reason*

† [Solicitor] [Agent for]   RIME AND REASON   ]

Address for service (*See notes overleaf*)   INVICTA HOUSE,
                                      MARKET STREET, BARSET.

Please complete overleaf

If the case were to be seriously defended rather than merely an attempt being made to delay judgment for as long as possible, Messrs. Rime would now have to prepare an affidavit for their client's manager to swear which would have to be served not less than three days before the hearing date of the summons. This would have to state as concisely as possible what the defence is, not in terms of a pleading but setting out the facts on which it is said the defence would be based. At the hearing the court would then decide whether there was any triable issue raised by the facts as disclosed by the two affidavits. If it felt that the case was clear then judgment would be given for the plaintiff with costs against the defendant and the case would be over there and then. If on the other hand the court thought that some triable defence was disclosed by the affidavit the court would give "leave to defend" and would then also give directions for a defence to be served and any other directions required. This does not mean in any sense that the court is accepting that the defendant will win at trial. It is merely deciding that the summary judgment procedure is not suitable because some serious issue has been shown and should be tried after all the normal interlocutory steps by a judge in open court. Leave to defend might be given unconditionally where matters are clear, but if the court thinks that the "defence" disclosed is thin or shadowy it may give "conditional leave to defend" usually on the basis that the defendant demonstrates his good faith by paying some or all of the disputed amount into court funds within a specified period. This would be appropriate perhaps in a case such as the present where the court might well suspect that the defendant has no serious defence but is merely unable to pay the amount required and is seeking to gain time by his tactics.

The procedure for summary judgment must not be abused. If it appears at the hearing that the plaintiff knew that the defendant had a defence the summons will be dismissed with costs against the plaintiff.

Order 14 is also available for unliquidated claims. In such a case if the court thinks there is no defence on the issue of liability it can order judgment to be entered for "damages to be assessed." The district judge or master will then assess the precise sum to be awarded at a later date. The procedure can also be used for claims for possession of land. It is not available, however, in certain cases for example where defamation is alleged. Such issues must generally be determined by a jury.

In the present case Joan receives an acknowledgement of receipt of the copy summons and copy affidavit from Messrs. Rime. At the hearing Messrs. Rime do not attend and Mr. White has no difficulty in obtaining judgment. He proves service of the documents by producing the letter to the district judge. The judgment is final, that is it deals with all the relief sought in the action both in terms of the debt owed and interest on the debt. Having obtained this judgment Mr. White can advise Mr. Richardson on the steps he may take to enforce it if the defendant still does not pay the amount due within the time fixed by the court.

Summons under
Order 14 for Whole
Claim *(District
Registry)*

IN THE HIGH COURT OF JUSTICE

Queen's Bench Division

1993.— R.—3026

District Registry

Between

SAMUEL RICHARDSON   Plaintiff

AND

DANIEL DEFOE LTD   Defendant

(1) Fill in address.

Let all Parties concerned attend the District Judge at the Office of the District Registry situate at(1) High Street, Barchester

on Friday the 30th   day of   July   1993, at
2 o'clock in the after noon on the hearing of an application on the part of the Plaintiff for final judgment in this action against(2) The Defendant

(2) The Defendant
(or if against one or
some of several
Defendants insert
names).

(3) Or as the case
may be, setting out
the nature of the
claim.

for the (3) amount claimed in the statement of claim with interest, if any, and costs.

Take Notice that a party intending to oppose this application or to apply for a stay of execution should send to the opposite party or his solicitor, to reach him not less than three days before the date above-mentioned, a copy of any affidavit intended to be used.

Dated the   13th   day of   July   1993.

To MESSRS RIME AND REASON
INVICTA HOUSE
MARKET STREET
BARSET

Solicitor or Agent for the Defendant of

This Summons was taken out by
MAKEPIECE AND STREIFF
of BANK CHAMBERS,
HIGH STREET, BARSET
Solicitor for the Plaintiff
[Agent for

]

~~Solicitor for the Plaintiff~~

1993 - R - No 3026

In the High Court of Justice

Queen's Bench Division

Barchester District Registry

Between   Samuel Richardson   **Plaintiff**

and

Daniel Defoe Ltd   **Defendant**

Affidavit in support of Application for Summary
Judgment under O.14

I Samuel Richardson of 184 High Street Barset in the County
of Barsetshire the abovenamed Plaintiff MAKE OATH AND SAY AS
FOLLOWS:-

1.   The Defendant Daniel Defoe Ltd is and was at the commencement
of this action truly indebted to me in the sum of £19,543.01 for
the price of goods sold to the Defendant and interest thereon
pursuant to contract. The particulars of the said claim appear
by indorsement on the writ of summons in this action.

2.   It is within my own knowledge that the said debt was incurred
and is still due as aforesaid.

3.   I verily believe that there is no defence to this action.

S. Richardson

Sworn at Pilgrim's Way Barset
in the County of Barsetshire
this 13th day of July 1993

Before Me   *A Seal*

A Practising Solicitor

This affidavit is filed on behalf of the Plaintiff

An action for personal injuries caused by negligence

Beaumont v. *Fletcher*

The story begins with Mr. Francis Beaumont calling on Mr. Amity of Makepiece and Streiff.

	MAKE & STREIFF		
	ATTENDANCE NOTE		
INTERVIEW/TEL.CON		DATE:	4th May 1993
WITH:	F. Beaumont	OF:	4A Gardeners Walk, Barset
TAKEN BY:	C A	TIME:	2.00–3.35 pm

Names: Francis Beaumont: Age, 46 years. Born, 2.2.47

I am a coachdriver, employed by Topgear Coaches Ltd. of High Cross, Barset. I have been with them 10 years. I have a black Ford Granada F915 THJ.

On 7th March I was driving along the road from Barset to Fairmarket. I was on my own in the car. I reached the crossroads with the road from Dimwhittle to Damchurch at Crawleigh. It was about 2.45 p.m.

The junction is just past the Bell Inn, which I passed on my left. At the junction, which is a blind approach from that side because of the pub, I was suddenly aware of a van approaching the junction from my nearside on the road from Dimwhittle. The driver did not seem to have taken any notice of the junction and came slap into my rear nearside door and wing. I braked hard and my car came to rest on the opposite carriageway. It had slewed right round and was facing in the Barest direction. The Barset-Fairmarket road is the major road. There are white lines and give way signs in the minor road. I use that road regularly and know it very well. My speed would have been about 40–45 m.p.h. I was severely jolted by the impact and shaken. I got out and saw the driver of the van. He came over and asked if I was alright. I said "yes, I think so" although I was shaking. He asked if I needed help, I said I did not know if the car was driveable. We looked at the damage. The offside rear was badly bashed in and he helped me to pull the rim of the wing away from contact with the rear wheel. I got in and ran the engine. I drove the car forward a little and into the kerb. The brakes seemed to be in order and I thought the car was driveable. I went over to his car. It was an Austin furniture removals type van. The main impact had been taken on the van's bumper bar, which was buckled. There was also some damage to the front of the wings. It was a heavy vehicle and the damage was not anything like as extensive as the damage to mine. It was a plain grey van. I did not notice any firms name printed on it. He did not say who owns the vehicle. It had been turned about by the impact and was facing in the Fairmarket direction on the nearside of the road.

I took particulars. His registration: G478 UND. His insurance certificate: COM455/F3371925. Insurers: Country and County. I did not notice the name of the policy holder. He gave me his name: John Fletcher, 2 Endbutt Lane, Damchurch. He did not offer any explanation of his failure to stop at the white line. I was too shaky to think of discussing whose fault it was.

There was no one else about. It was just after Sunday lunch. No other car stopped. Police were not called.

He asked me if I was sure I was not injured. I said I ached a bit. He offered to take me back to Barset and have a check-up at the hospital. I said I felt well enough to drive myself. I then drove back home.

Later the same day I was walking round at home and the back pain was becoming gradually more intense. Suddenly in the kitchen I fainted. When I came round I was in hospital, my wife having called an ambulance. I was X rayed by the House Registrar. I do not know his name. He told me that I had a very bad whiplash injury to my neck and the possible risk of complications in the lower back. In addition I had slight concussion. I stayed in hospital for two days for further X rays and tests. I went back to my own doctor, Dr. A Heeler and he said that he had been in touch with the hospital and it was quite clear that I must not do any driving because I had to rest and preferably be in a flat position. He recommended that I only get out of bed in the evenings for a couple of hours and that is what I have been doing.

Unfortunately my employers, Top Gear Coaches Ltd. are a small concern and were unable to keep my job open for me because they have to have a driver for each of their four coaches otherwise they themselves will go out of business. They have no other work in the nature of office work or other light duties that they could have transferred me to either especially as the date of my being able to work, if at all, is uncertain. I am very worried about my future because there is large scale unemployment in our area. I asked my brother, who is a long distance lorry driver, to make enquiries through the Union and at the job centre about driving vacancies and he tells me that at present the industry is very depressed and that there are scores of unemployed long distance and public service vehicle drivers on the books of the local job centre and no vacancies have come up in the last few months.

I am still in great pain from my back and neck and am awaiting an appointment at the hospital with the orthopaedic consultant. I can only go out if my wife drives me and even then I can only stand to be out for no more than a couple of hours due to the back pain caused by being in an upright position.

My own doctor tells me that the injury is complicated because of arthritis. He says that whilst but for this accident I would have had many years more coach driving, this injury means that it will probably be unwise for me to go back to coach driving at all.

Although I would have been unable to drive after the accident my wife had to hire a car because she also uses our car to get to and from work. I live with my wife and our daughter Rosemary aged 15 years. The car repairs are likely to be about £2,000.

Note: Not eligible for legal aid at present as capital too high. Will send £1,000 on account of costs generally.

Mr. Amity passes the file to Mr. White, the legal executive in the firm's litigation department. On the facts Mr. White can see that the client has a good claim and he wastes no time before writing a letter before action.

<u>Makepiece and Streiff Solicitors</u>

Clement Amity	Bank Chambers,
Anthony Adverse	Barset.
Our Ref: CA/WW/AB	Tel. 00765 4321
	4th May 1993.

J. Fletcher Esq.,
2, Endbutt Lane,
Damchurch.

<u>Mr. F. Beaumont Accident 7th March 1993</u>

We are instructed by Mr. Beaumont to make a claim against you for damages caused by your negligent driving on the above date. Just after lunchtime on 7th March last you were driving a van along the road from Dimwhittle to Damchurch at Crawleigh. At the junction with the road from Barset to Fairmarket you failed to award precedence to our client who was driving his Ford Granada car. You continued over the junction when it was unsafe to do so.

Our client's vehicle was badly damaged and he suffered serious whiplash injuries to his neck. We are instructed to commence proceedings against you in the High Court for damages and we ask you to pass this letter to your insurers without delay.

Yours faithfully,

Makepiece and Streiff (signed)

A few days later a letter arrives as follows:–

Country and County Insurance Company PLC

Our Ref:	B/2719/H/LW	
Your Ref:	CA/WW/AB	

Messrs. Makepiece and Streiff,
Bank Chambers,
Barset.

Claims Dept.,
27, Oxford Street,
Middletown,
Surrey, SU1 3BZ.

13th May 1993

Dear Sirs,

Our insured: J. Fletcher Accident: 7.3.93

Your letter of 4th May to our insured has been passed to us. It is quite clear that your client was to blame for this accident by entering the junction when our insured was already there. All liability is denied. We have nominated Messrs. Marx & Co., Red House Square, Oxford to act on our behalf if you are determined to proceed.

Yours faithfully,

Leslie Walker

(for) Country & County Insurance plc

Registered Office: As above.

Registered in England
No. 1782641

Mr. White can see that negotiations will prove fruitless and that to correspond with the insurers or their solicitors would be a waste of time. Although a negotiated settlement of personal injury claims is the method by which most cases are eventually resolved it is very much in Mr. Beaumont's interest to have proceedings begun without delay. Interest on any judgment later obtained in respect of special damages, *i.e.* out of pocket items) runs from the date of the cause of action but interest on most items of general damages, *i.e.* compensation for the injuries, only runs from the date of service of proceedings.

An additional reason for getting proceedings going quickly is that from any settlement arrived at, or judgment obtained in court, a plaintiff in a personal injury claim has to reimburse the Department of Social Security's Compensation Recovery Unit for all the benefits which he has received from the date of the accident until the date of settlement or judgment. These benefits are notified by the Department of Social Security to the defendants and they have an obligation to deduct them from any damages or compensation to be paid over to the plaintiff. Thus the earlier an action is completed the smaller will be the deduction from the damages or compensation figure payable to reimburse the Department of Social Security for benefits received.

Before issuing proceedings Mr. White has to consider two other matters. The first of these is that it will be necessary to serve with the statement of claim a copy of a medical report substantiating all the plaintiff's injuries. This can cause considerable delays in commencing proceedings because in some parts of the country it may take some months to get an appointment with a suitable expert. Fortunately for the present case Mr. White is however able to get a very early appointment for Mr. Beaumont to see Mr. E. Setter FRCS, an orthopaedic surgeon, due to a cancellation in Mr. Setter's list of appointments. There will thus be no delay caused by the need to get a suitable medical report.

The second matter that Mr. White has to consider is whether to start the action in the High Court or the County Court. As we have seen in the introduction, a case involving damages for personal injuries can only be commenced in the High Court if the solicitor for the plaintiff is able personally to certify that the case involves a sum of £50,000 or more. It is often difficult to put a very precise value on a claim, especially in circumstances such as the present. However so long as a solicitor acts in good faith there would be unlikely to be any sanction if the eventual award of damages did not in fact exceed £50,00. In the present case the plaintiff appears to have had a whiplash and back injury and mild concussion. In themselves these would certainly not attract an award of £50,000 or more. However it seems on the present facts that the damage flowing from the injury might be such as to mean that, due to local circumstances in the employment market, Mr. Beaumont might not work again for many years, if at all. If he is in fact unable to do long distance driving in future the prospects for future employment, in the current economic climate, look bleak. After finding out that Mr. Beaumont, with bonuses has earned about £300 per week take home pay in the recent past, Mr. White feels able to certify in good faith that the claim in total is likely to involve more than £50,000 and he therefore decides to commence proceedings in the High Court.

Out of courtesy Mr. White informs Messrs. Marx & Co. that proceedings will be commenced if they are not prepared to confirm within seven days that they are willing to pay damages in full. There is no reply and Joan prepares for issue and service three copies of a writ of summons together with one copy of the completed form of acknowledgement of service. Meanwhile Mr. Beaumont has sent in the repair bill and car hire account and authorised issue of a writ if negotiations proved pointless.

The acknowledgement of service is in the same form as that used in the debt recovery action. The writ of summons is different however in that it only contains a brief statement of the nature of the claim. This will have to be substantially expanded by the later service of a separate statement of claim pleading the case fully. No fixed costs are mentioned because this would not be appropriate in a claim for unliquidated damages and there is no attempt to quantify the claim for interest.

The writ of summons is issued in exactly the same manner as in the "Richardson" action. Joan takes three copies to the court office. Two copies of the writ are sealed and returned. Joan pays the court fee on issue of £70.

The methods of service available are also exactly the same so Mr. White decides to effect services by post. If there was some urgency in the effecting of service he would have instructed a process server to effect personal service. At the same time as Mr. White gave instructions to Joan to issue the writ, he wrote to Country & County Insurance Company plc as follows:

"We give notice in accordance with the provisions of section 152 of the Road Traffic Act that proceedings against your insured John Fletcher will be commenced in the High Court of Justice."

By giving such notice Mr. White reserves the right to proceed against the insurers to enforce any judgment obtained against Mr. Fletcher for damages for the personal injury and loss of earnings occasioned thereby as well as for property damage.

By virtue of sections 143 and 145 of the Road Traffic Act 1988 a motorist is obliged to be insured against liability, for personal injury, consequential loss and property damage up to a value of £250,000 arising out of a road traffic accident. Section 152 of the 1988 Act provides that an insurer covering such risk is obliged to meet any unsatisfied judgment in respect of these items notwithstanding that the insurer might in the normal law of insurance otherwise be entitled to repudiate or avoid the policy (for example because of non-disclosure of past driving convictions by the insured person at the time when he completed a proposal form for the insurance). This ensures that a person who is injured by the negligence of the driver, or who suffers property damage, will be paid damages by the insurance company concerned without being prejudiced by any matters which arise only as between the insured person and his insurer. Notice of intention to commence proceedings must be given to the insurers concerned either before the issue of the writ, or no later than seven days thereafter in order that section 152 can be relied upon. At the end of the case, after they have paid what is known as the "Road Traffic Act" liability, the insurers would be entitled to the benefit of the judgment so that they could then take enforcement proceedings to recover the money paid out against their insured if the facts were such that they were entitled to repudiate the policy as between themselves and their insured.

Following service of the writ of summons upon him, Mr. Fletcher passed it to his insurers who, in turn, pass it to their solicitors Messrs. Marx & Co. of Red House Square, Oxford. These solicitors will represent Mr. Fletcher but will deal with the action in accordance with instructions received from the insurers as provided by the contract of insurance.

Marx & Co. do not have an office in Barchester. Their Legal Executive Jane Hovent, who specialises in "defendant's" litigation, is allocated the action. The acknowledgement of service, indicating an intention to defend the action, is completed and sent by post to Barchester District Registry. A letter to that effect is sent to Messrs. Makepiece & Streiff. The District Registry clerk photocopies the acknowledgement of service and a sealed copy is sent to each of the firms of solicitors involved.

Miss Hovent makes certain that the completed form of acknowledgement of service will be received at the District Registry within the time
allowed for filing (within 14 days of service including the day of service)
because failure to comply can result in "interlocutory" judgment being
entered in default. Interlocutory judgment means that the case is over
so far as liability is concerned though there will obviously need to be a
later hearing to assess the plaintiff's damages since the present case he is
suing for unliquidated sum. As discussed in relation to the previous case
study, if an action concerns a liquidated sum, *i.e.* one that does not need
to be assessed by the court, then final judgment can be obtained at this
stage if no acknowledgement of service is returned to the court in time.

Writ of
Summons
[Unliquidated
Demand]
(O.6,r.1)

IN THE HIGH COURT OF JUSTICE

Queen's Bench Division

19 93 — B. —No. 4106

[BARCHESTER   **District Registry]**

Between

FRANCIS BEAUMONT   Plaintiff

AND

JOHN FLETCHER   Defendant

(1) Insert name.   **To the Defendant (¹)**   JOHN FLETCHER

(2) Insert address.   of (²)   2 ENDBUTT LANE, DAMCHURCH, OXFORDSHIRE

This Writ of Summons has been issued against you by the above-named Plaintiff in respect of the claim set out on the back.

Within 14 days after the service of this Writ on you, counting the day of service, you must either satisfy the claim or return to the Court Office mentioned below the accompanying **Acknowledgment of Service** stating therein whether you intend to contest these proceedings.

If you fail to satisfy the claim or to return the Acknowledgment within the time stated, or if you return the Acknowledgment without stating therein an intention to contest the proceedings, the Plaintiff may proceed with the action and judgment may be entered against you forthwith without further notice.

(3) Complete and delete as necessary.

Issued from the (³) [Central Office] [Admiralty and Commercial Registry] [BARCHESTER   District Registry] of the High Court this 18th day of June 1993.

NOTE:—This Writ may not be served later than 4 calendar months *(or, if leave is required to effect service out of the jurisdiction, 6 months)* beginning with that date unless renewed by order of the Court.

IMPORTANT

Directions for Acknowledgment of Service are given with the accompanying form.

The Plaintiff's claim is for damages for personal injury and
losses arising from a traffic accident which occurred at
Crawleigh Barchester on 7th March 1993 caused by the negligence
of the Defendant.

This writ includes a claim for personal injury but may be commenced
in the High Court because the value of the action for the purposes
of Article 5 of the High Court and County Courts Jurisdiction Order
1991 exceeds £50,000.

Malcolm J Streiff

---

(1) If this Writ
was issued out of
a District Registry,
this indorsement
as to place where
the action arose
should be
completed.

(2) Delete as
necessary.

(3) Insert name of
place.

(4) For phrase-
ology of this
indorsement where
the Plaintiff sues in
person, see
*Supreme Court
Practice*, vol. 2,
para 1.

(¹) [(²) [The cause] [One~of~the~causes] of action in respect of which the Plaintiff
claim s   relief in this action arose wholly or in part at (³)   Crawleigh
in the district of the District Registry named overleaf.]

(⁴)**This Writ** was issued by   Makepiece and Streiff

of   Bank Chambers, High Street, Barset, Oxfordshire.

[Agent~xxxxx~for~xx   ]

of

Solicitor   for the said Plaintiff   whose address   (²) [is] [are]

    4a Gardener's Walk, Barset, Oxfordshire.

Solicitor's Reference   WW   Tel. No: 00765 4321

oyez   The Solicitors' Law Stationery Society Ltd., Oyez House, 27 Crimscott Street, London SE1 5TS   4.90 F16761
                         High Court A1   5044019
                                                                               * * * *

Mr. White had anticipated that liability for the accident would not be admitted and had carried out sufficient investigation to enable counsel to be instructed to settle the plaintiff's statement of claim. He took proofs of evidence from Mr. Beaumont and the witnesses of the accident, and arranged for a medico-legal report to be obtained from Mr. Setter, FRCS, who has considerable experience in the preparation of reports and the giving of evidence in accident cases. Joan also obtained documentary evidence in support of the claim for special damages. She wrote to Mr. Beaumont's employers for details of his earnings over the last six months and asked what his work prospects would be if his condition did not improve and he could not return to coach driving. She also wrote off to Mr. Beaumont's trade union and to the local job centre for further evidence about the state of the local employment market for long distance drivers. She also obtained Mr. Beaumont's National Insurance Number. The purpose of this is that that number, together with his date of birth must be supplied to the defendants early in the case. When the defendants have this information they will in their turn write to the Compensation Recovery Unit of the Department of Social Security quoting the particular details of the plaintiff. The reason, as we have seen, is that if the defendants wish to offer settlement of the action whether informally, or by payment into court (see later) or even if, should no settlement be possible, where the plaintiff is awarded damages by the court at trial, the defendants need to know the precise amount paid out by the state to the plaintiff in benefits since the accident happened. The defendants then have a duty to remit to the Department of Social Security a sum equivalent to those benefits from any damages agreed upon or awarded to the plaintiff. The purpose of this is so that the plaintiff is not doubly compensated, and that public funds do not bear any loss arising out of the accident. She then prepared instructions to counsel Mr. A. Lawman to settle the statement of claim which, in order to comply with the rules, should be served within 14 days of the date when the acknowledgement of service was filed. In fact it is usually prudent to have counsel settle this pleading in draft even before issuing the writ. Counsel does not concern himself with details of the special damages at this stage which are computed by the solicitor for insertion in counsel's draft. The final version of the Statement of Claim is illustrated as follows.

In the High Court of Justice   1993–B–No.4106
Queen's Bench Division
Barchester District Registry
(Writ issued 18th June 1993)

Between:

Francis Beaumont   Plaintiff

and

John Fletcher   Defendant

STATEMENT OF CLAIM

1.   At all material times the Plaintiff was the owner and driver of a Ford Granada saloon motor car registered number F915 THJ and the Defendant the driver of an Austin motor van registered number G478 UND.

2.   On 7th March 1993 the Plaintiff was driving his motor car along the Barset to Fairmarket road at its junction with the road to Damchurch at Crawleigh in the County of Oxon. The Defendant drove the said motor van on to the junction from the road to Damchurch and into collision with the Plaintiff's said motor car.

3.   As a result of the matters aforesaid the Plaintiff's said motor car was damaged and the Plaintiff has suffered personal injury loss and damage and inconvenience whilst without the use of his said motor car during the period that it was undergoing repair.

4.   The said personal injury, loss, damage and inconvenience was caused by the negligence of the Defendant in the driving management and control of the said motor van.

PARTICULARS OF NEGLIGENCE

The Defendant was negligent in that:
(a)   he failed to keep any or any proper lookout
(b)   he drove at a speed which was excessive in the circumstances
(c)   he failed to observe and/or to heed the traffic sign controlling the said Damchurch Road
(d)   he drove from a minor road on to a major road when by reason of the presence of the Plaintiff's motor car it was unsafe to do so
(e)   he failed to accord precedence to the Plaintiff's motor car which was on the major road
(f)   he failed to stop, slow down, alter course or otherwise to take action so as to avoid colliding with the Plaintiff's motor car.

PARTICULARS OF INJURY

The plaintiff who was born on the 2nd February 1947 suffered a whiplash injury to his neck and lower back together with shock and general shaking up. The impact occasioned aggravation of a pre-existing dormant arthritic condition of the spine. As a result of the injury the plaintiff is unlikely to be able to work again as a long distance coach driver. Full particulars are supplied in the report of Mr E Setter, served herewith.

PARTICULARS OF SPECIAL DAMAGE

Cost of repairs to motor car	£2,100
Hire of replacement car during period of repairs (7 weeks at £200 per week)	1,400
Loss of earnings 8 March 1993–25 June 1993 (16 weeks at £300 per week) and continuing	4,800
Total special damage to date	8,300

5.   The plaintiff is entitled to interest on damages pursuant to s.35A of the Supreme Court Act.

AND the plaintiff claims:—

(i) Damages
(ii) Interest as aforesaid pursuant to section 35A of the Supreme Court Act 1981 at such rate and for such period as the court thinks just.

I. Lawman

Served this 29th day of June 1993 by Makepiece & Streiff of Bank Chambers, High St., Barset, solicitors for the plaintiff.

The instructions to be sent to counsel are typed out on brief paper. The brief contains the heading of the action giving details copied from the writ; lists the enclosures which in this case would be a copy of the writ, the plaintiff's proof of evidence, and the medical report, and then explains the enclosures to counsel. A well drafted set of instructions to counsel will draw counsel's attention to salient points of fact and evidence and law and explain the issues on which he is to advise or in this case say what he is to do, namely draft the pleading. In fact in a routine case where there is little other factual information than the plaintiff's own proof of evidence it is not usually necessary to do much more than instruct counsel to refer to the enclosed documents and draft the pleading.

When drafting the statement of claim counsel will have in mind that this pleading is intended to state;

(a) how the action arises
(b) what relief or remedy is being sought
(c) why it is contended that the defendant is liable to the plaintiff for the relief claimed.

Consequently care must be taken to ensure that the pleading fairly states the case intended to be made out so that the defendant will not be taken by surprise at the trial. Thus for example so far as the allegations of negligence are concerned, these should cover everything that could be alleged at the trial. The plaintiff will not usually be permitted to bring evidence about or base his case upon any allegation not properly pleaded. For example the plaintiff has pleaded six different ways in which the defendant was negligent. He would not be entitled at the trial to suggest that there was any other instance of negligence not covered by these particulars, for example that the defendant failed to heed a warning sounded on the horn by the plaintiff.

Mr. White makes a diary entry to remind counsel's clerk for the return of the settled pleading if there appears to be delay. Once counsel's draft is received it is checked by Mr. White before being engrossed for service by post upon the defendant's solicitor. A diary entry is made of the date when the defence is due. It is also necessary for the plaintiff's solicitor to serve with the statement of claim a medical report substantiating all the injuries of which it is proposed to adduce evidence at trial. Accordingly, Mr. White ensures that a copy of Mr. Setter's report is available for service with the statement of claim. In addition a full schedule of special damages should be served within the statement of claim or as a separate document annexed to it and this schedule should set out all matters of loss and loss of earnings together with details of loss of future earnings which the plaintiff is likely to sustain. In fact where an action is commenced promptly after the accident it is often the case that neither the medical report, nor the schedule of special damages can be very definite about the plaintiff's future prospects. For that reason solicitors sometimes agreed to defer service of these further documents until some later stage. In other cases only lip service is paid to the need to serve a medical report by obtaining, not a full report from a medico-legal specialist, but simply a copy of the casualty officer's report from the hospital where the plaintiff was first treated.

Miss Hovent upon receipt of the statement of claim makes a note as to the date when the defence falls due. This is 14 days after the date of service and if time is not extended and the defence is not served the plaintiff's solicitor would be entitled to enter interlocutory judgment and later have the damages assessed. No similar automatic sanction can be applied to a plaintiff who fails to serve the statement of claim within the 14 days period of time that the court rules provide for service of that pleading, but the defendants could apply to strike the case out for want of prosecution. Miss Hovent requests and is granted facilities for medical examination of Mr. Beaumont. She also puts in hand the making of certain factual enquiries about how the accident came to happen and attempts to trace an eye witness who is believed to have observed the accident from the garden of a nearby house.

Although the defence should be served within 14 days of receipt of the statement of claim there is provision under Order 3 for the parties to agree extensions of time for this or any other step between themselves. It is normally considered courteous for the plaintiff to give the defendant at least one reasonable extension to draft and serve the defence. If the defendant were not to obtain such an extension from the plaintiff voluntarily there is provision to apply to the court by way of what is called a "time summons" for the court itself to grant extension of time.

The defendant's solicitors are granted two successive extensions of 14 days each further time by the plaintiff but have still not served their defence and are told that if any further extension is required they must make application to the court which is exactly what they do.

Joe, the trainee legal executive with Marx & Co., prepares the time summons. He provides a top copy for the court together with a further two copies—one to retain and the other to serve. He has other business in Barchester and attends personally at the court office to issue the summons. He could have arranged for agents to issue, or if he had sufficient time issued the summons by post. Time summonses are usually urgent and treated as such by the court. Because the issue of such a summons does not stay an action, the rules provide for a summons to extend or abridge time to be heard on the next day following the day of service. In most other cases a summons must be served not less than two clear days before the day of the hearing.

The summons is shown over.

In the High Court of Justice   1993–B–No.4106
Queen's Bench Division
Barchester District Registry

Between:

Francis Beaumont	Plaintiff
and	
John Fletcher	Defendant

LET ALL PARTIES CONCERNED attend before the District Judge in Chambers, Crown Buildings, Guildhall Street, Barchester on Monday the 9th day of August 1993 at the hour of 10 o'clock in the forenoon on the hearing of an application on the part of the above-named Defendant FOR AN ORDER that he does have 21 days further time for service of his defence herein.

AND that the costs of this application be provided for

Dated this 5th day of August 1993

This summons was taken out by Marx & Co.,
of Red House Square, Solicitors for the Defendant.

To the District Registrar
and to the above-named
Plaintiff and to his
Solicitors, Messrs. Makepiece & Streiff.

On the appointed day for the time summons Mr. White and Miss Hovent appear before District Judge Cross in Chambers. Miss Hovent explains her application which arises out of the problems in tracing the eye-witness which has meant she has only been able to deliver instructions to counsel to settle her defence some seven days ago. She understands from counsel's clerk that the defence will be sent to her within the next four or five days and she asks for a further brief extension of time. Mr. White in his reply does not accept that the defendant's solicitors were without sufficient information to enable the defence to be drafted some time before.

The District Judge, whilst acknowledging that the defendant had probably been given sufficient time in which to serve a defence, nevertheless, as frequently happens, decides to grant a final 14 days extension. He does, however, let it be known that in his opinion the defendants had already been granted sufficient time by awarding the costs of the application to be the plaintiff's "in any event." This means that whatever may be the result of the action the Plaintiff will recover the costs of this application. The District Judge endorses the court copy of the summons accordingly.

The draft defence is received from counsel within the further time granted by the court and a top copy is prepared typed on judicature paper and served on the plaintiff. A copy of the defence appears below.

The defence contains the defendant's answer to the allegations of the plaintiff as set out in the statement of claim. If the plaintiff has made an assertion which is not disputed it will be *admitted* in the defence. If the defendant wishes to put the plaintiff to strict proof of any matter the defence will state the same to be "*not admitted.*" If the defence contains a *denial* of an allegation, the plaintiff is put on notice that the defendant intends to adduce evidence at the trial to prove the contrary.

In the action with which we have been concerned, the defence does not raise any new issue which could defeat the plaintiff's action. If it had, the plaintiff would need to serve a further pleading called a reply which, as the term implies, will contain the plaintiff's answer to the new issue which has been raised. Should a reply become necessary it should be delivered within 14 days of receipt of the defence.

Fourteen days after service of the last pleading the time arrives when the pleadings are deemed to be closed. During that period the parties may reconsider the pleadings which they have served and if considered necessary may amend the same once. Any further amendment or an amendment which becomes necessary after close of pleadings can only be made with the leave of the Court. Such leave is obtained by issuing a summons for hearing before the District Judge. If an amended pleading is served which affects the opposing party's case so that he in turn wishes to amend his pleadings, the amended pleading in reply to the earlier amendment must be served within 14 days and this does not affect the date for the close of pleadings.

In the High Court of Justice   1993–B–4106
Queen's Bench Division
Barchester District Registry

Between:

Francis Beaumont   Plaintiff

and

John Fletcher   Defendant

DEFENCE

1.   Paragraph 1 of the Statement of Claim is admitted.

2.   The Defendant denies that he is guilty of the alleged or any negligence as alleged in paragraph 4 of the Statement of Claim or at all. Each and every allegation contained in the said paragraph and in the particulars thereto is denied as specifically as if the same were herein set out and traversed seriatim.

3.   The personal injury, loss, damage and inconvenience alleged are not admitted. If, which is not admitted, the Plaintiff suffered any thereof the same were caused solely by or contributed to by the negligence of the Plaintiff.

<u>Particulars of Negligence</u>
The Plaintiff was negligent in that:

(i) he failed to keep any or any proper lookout
(ii) he drove at a speed which in the circumstances was excessive
(iii) he failed to give any warning of his approach
(iv) he drove onto the said junction when by reason of the Defendant's van already being established thereon, it was unsafe to do so
(v) he failed to stop slow down alter course or otherwise to take action so as to avoid colliding with the Defendant's motor van.

4. Save as hereinbefore expressly appears none of the allegations contained in the Statement of Claim is admitted.

B. REDDY

Served this 23rd day of August 1993 by
Marx & Co. of Red House Square, Oxford,
Solicitors for the Defendant

Notes on pleadings—further and better particulars

The purpose of pleadings in an action is to establish the nature of the dispute between the parties so that the court will be made aware of the real issues upon which it will be called to adjudicate. At the same time each of the parties will be made aware of the issues which they will have to deal with and so be able to gather together such evidence as will be necessary so to do. The issues should be stated with sufficient clarity so that neither party is taken by surprise at the trial.

If a party's case is loosely pleaded so that a number of options are left open the opposing party should seek to reduce the options by making a request for *further and better particulars*.

To prevent a defendant using this procedure for the purpose of delay, further and better particulars of a statement of claim will only be ordered to be served prior to delivery of defence if such are necessary to enable the defendant to draft his defence. If this is so, time for delivery of defence will be extended for a period of time after the "particulars" have been served. If this is not so then the particulars will be ordered to be served within a period which is not affected by delivery of defence.

A request for further and better particulars of the items of claim, however, might well be allowed prior to service of defence where a defendant is minded to make a payment into court (dealt with in the following section). This occurs because a defendant has a right to be made aware of the extent of his liability, so far as is possible, so that he may take steps to meet the same at the earliest opportunity without incurring unnecessary costs.

An example of a request for further and better particulars might have arisen if for example in the statement of claim in the present case the plaintiff had pleaded that "the defendant failed to observe the provisions of the Highway Code." As the Highway Code is a lengthy document containing many items of guidance on proper driving, such an allegation would have left the defendant considerably in the dark as to what was being alleged against him. In an attempt to ascertain the precise nature of the allegation and indeed in an attempt to cut the plaintiff down to one particular version of the facts at the trial, the defendant would have served a request for further and better particulars in the terms probably, *e.g.* "of the allegation 'drove contrary to the Highway Code' state precisely which provision of the Highway Code it is alleged that the defendant failed to observe."

A request for further and better particulars is not a pleading but it should be drafted like one with the full heading. The request should first be sent with a letter but if the request is ignored or refused an application by summons is then made to the District Judge in chambers. On such an application the District Judge will consider whether a request is fair and whether the pleading as presently drafted does genuinely leave one party in ignorance of the full case against him and if he considers it necessary for the proper conduct of the action will make the order that the other party gives the further and better particulars sought.

Payment into court

Francis Beaumont v. *John Fletcher*—continued

Although a defence to Beaumont's action has been served denying liability, the facts giving rise to the action leave Miss Hovent in no doubt that at least some liability will be established against Fletcher.

Having completed her enquiries into the issues of liability and quantum (damages) and had the benefit of counsel's advice thereon she advises Country and County Insurance plc that the plaintiff is likely to be awarded up to £35,000 damages. The Insurers accept this advice and instruct Marx & Co. to endeavour to negotiate a settlement on the best terms up to that sum and that if a negotiated settlement is not possible a payment into court should be made.

Miss Hovent telephones Mr. White and discusses the matter with him and makes an offer of £30,000 plus costs. The discussion is "without prejudice" which means that it is privileged and cannot be referred to at the trial. Miss Hovent confirms the offer by letter which is headed "without prejudice."

Mr. White considers this offer to be totally inadequate. The provable special damages alone as at the date of the Statement of Claim were £8,300 and of course Mr. Beaumont has been suffering a continuing loss of earnings of £300 per week, although Mr. White appreciates that eventually the amount of benefits which Mr. Beaumont has been receiving will be withheld from any compensation by the defendants for onward transmission to the Department of Social Security. Mr. White is however also aware that there may be some doubts about liability and contributory negligence and it is not entirely impossible that if the judge preferred the evidence of the defendant that Mr. Beaumont could get nothing at all. Hitherto, Mr. Beaumont has been financing his own litigation which he is in a position to do because a year or so before the accident his mother died leaving him a very substantial legacy. Nonetheless, the costs of losing a contested High Court case at trial are very substantial indeed and Mr. White knows therefore that since the outcome of litigation is rarely certain serious consideration must be given to all offers received. He is therefore bound to take instructions from Mr. Beaumont.

At the interview Mr. Beaumont asks Mr. White what he thinks his claim is worth. Mr. White tells him that there are very grave difficulties in valuing the claim in particular because of the possibility that Mr. Beaumont might have had only a few years coach driving left due to the fact that he already had an arthritic condition. Taking all the imponderables into account, and bearing in mind a discussion about the case which Mr. White has already had with his counsel, Mr. Lawman, Mr. White suggests that for early settlement he would consider a payment of £60,000 a reasonable settlement, and he reminds Mr. Beaumont that from this sum the defendants would be entitled to deduct the benefits received between accident and settlement for onward transmission to the Department of Social Security. Mr. Beaumont accepts that advice. Accordingly Mr. White is instructed to reject the present offer and to say that £60,000 would be the minimum sum that would be acceptable plus interest thereon. He writes to Messrs. Marx & Co. in a letter marked "without prejudice" to that effect.

The introduction of a demand for interest at this stage might seem to be inappropriate when interest only becomes recoverable where there has been a judgment. However, Mr. White knows that if a settlement is not negotiated Marx & Co. will make a payment into court.

Order 22, rule 1(8) provides that if a payment into court is to provide a safeguard in respect of costs incurred since the date when it was made, not only must the amount in court be sufficient to cover the award of damages but also such interest thereon as would be recoverable on a judgment as at the date of the payment into court. In these circumstances although the right to interest does not strictly occur until there is a judgment it is an aspect which has to be taken into consideration when advising as to the reasonableness of an offer in settlement.

Miss Hovent, taking the view that a settlement within the limit of her authority will not be possible, advises that a payment into court be made representing a gross sum of £35,000 plus appropriate interest. For the purpose of this example it is assumed that the interest would amount to £500 and thus the payment into court would in principle be the gross sum of £35,500. Before making this payment however Miss Hovent writes to the Compensation Recovery Unit of the Department of Social Security to obtain a certificate of the total benefits hitherto paid to Mr. Beaumont. When she receives details of that figure she deducts that figure from the £35,500 and pays into court the balance. She will give notice to Mr. Beaumont's solicitors that the sum she has paid into court is deemed to be increased by the amount of benefits that have been withheld by her so that the true amount "on offer" is £35,500.

Payment into court is made by sending a cheque made payable to H.M. Paymaster General together with a form of lodgment to the Supreme Court Funds Office giving details of the name of the case and the party by whom the payment in is made. A receipt is then returned to Miss Hovent by the Supreme Court Funds Office. Thereupon she gives notice of payment in to Messrs. Makepiece and Streiff who must acknowledge safe receipt within three days.

When he receives the notice of payment in Mr. White is aware of the total amount on offer. He has no idea however how this amount is broken down as between general damages for pain and suffering, special damages, general damages for future loss of earnings, and interest, and the defendants are under no obligation to indicate what their breakdown is. The precise breakdown does not in any event matter very much in a case such as the present because the amount in court will not necessarily represent an offer of the full value of the claim since, in the present instance there are so many imponderables as to liability, the possibility of contributory negligence in particular, and the difficult problems of quantification of the plaintiff's claim.

Notes on payment into/out of court

The making of the payment into court provides a defendant with a means of placing a plaintiff "on risk" where the defendant accepts that it is likely that the plaintiff might succeed in establishing some liability on the part of the defendant and will thereby be entitled to some damages. The first time a plaintiff has to give serious consideration to the consequences of declining an offer is once the sum offered has been paid into court. This represents a sort of legal gamble. Where there has been a payment into court the plaintiff must be advised that whilst the court has a discretion as to the award of costs in every case, it is almost certain that if at the trial he recovers no greater sum than the amount paid in (that sum being calculated by including interest appropriate to the award as would have been recoverable up to the date of payment in) he will only recover his costs up to the date of the payment into court from the defendant and will be responsible for the defendant's costs thereafter. It is also important in personal injury cases for plaintiff's solicitors to bear in mind the benefit points mentioned above namely that the amount of benefits which have been withheld from payment into court have to be considered when seeing whether a total offer should or should not be accepted.

Such costs would be set off against the damages and costs awarded to him, the plaintiff. The actual sum recovered by the plaintiff would however include interest on the full amount awarded right up to the date of judgment. The consequences of this could well be drastic. By far the heavier costs in litigation are incurred close to trial and at the trial itself and therefore if a well calculated payment into court is made sufficiently early in the case, by reason of the fact that the plaintiff will have to pay the defendant's costs after the payment into court and of course will have to bear his own costs also from that day (since nobody else will pay them) the benefit of winning the case and obtaining an award of damages could well be totally wiped out. The trial judge must not have knowledge of the fact that there has been a payment into court in the action being tried until after he has dealt with all issues of liability and quantum. The payment into court may then become relevant to the award of costs. Needless to say, a copy of the notice of payment into court must not be included with the "pleadings" lodged with the court when the action is set down for trial.

If the plaintiff does not obtain judgment for more than the amount of the payment in at trial (taking interest and benefits into account as previously described) he is regarded as having lost the case on liability from that point. This means that almost invariably an order will be made as explained above, that the plaintiff pays the defendant's costs from the date of the payment in and of course bears his own costs also from that time. This provides defendants with a means of putting tactical pressure upon the plaintiff from an early stage in the case since the plaintiff will be aware of the possibly drastic consequences of failing to "beat" the payment in.

Where the plaintiff is claiming in respect of a number of causes of action a payment into court may be made to cover them all. However, the plaintiff may apply on summons to the District Judge for the sum paid in to be apportioned between the various causes.

When money is paid into court in respect of an action by an infant the procedure is rather different. An application must be made to the court for leave to accept the money offered. At the hearing before him the District Judge will consider all matters of liability and quantum and rule on whether the sum offered should be accepted on behalf of the infant. If he feels that the amount offered is satisfactory then the amount will usually be left in court until the infant attains its majority. Any application to withdraw part of the fund for the welfare of the child would be made to the court.

When a plaintiff receives a notice of payment into court, in principle he has 21 days in which to decide whether to accept. If he decides to accept then a notice will be served upon the defendant's solicitors and lodged at court and an appropriate form supplied for the Supreme Court Funds Office. That form will then be forwarded to the funds office and a cheque will be drawn from the money in court and sent to the plaintiff's solicitors.

It a plaintiff decides to accept the payment into court after the expiry of the 21 day period for acceptance he must apply to the court for leave to accept out of time. Leave will usually be given subject to the plaintiff's costs being restricted to those incurred prior to the date of the payment in and the defendant's costs (if any) from such date being paid by the plaintiff.

An amount paid into court can be increased at any time without leave. Thus if for example early in a case a defendant had paid into court the sum of say £10,000 plus interest and this was not accepted by the plaintiff, then in order to put increasing pressure on the plaintiff as trial approached, the defendant might pay in say a further £2,000 plus the extra accrued interest to date. The plaintiff would then be on a risk if the trial judge awarded a sum of £12,000 or less at trial. Naturally the full 21 days for consideration of the increased offer runs from the date of the second payment in and the plaintiff therefore has that further period in which to decide whether to withdraw the full £12,000 from court.

Having decided against accepting the payment into court Beaumont's action continues to the next stage. This stage is known as "automatic directions." The purpose of the direction stage in an action is to enable the parties before proceeding to the actual trial to pause, take stock of the situation, ensure that all proper evidence has been gathered, and that all proper interlocutory applications have been made. In actions not concerning personal injuries an application is made to the court at this stage on what is called a "summons for directions." At this hearing the District Judge considers the case and gives directions for how the matter should proceed towards trial and what steps should be taken by each party in the interests of obtaining an expeditious and economical hearing. In personal injury cases however there are now "automatic directions." These automatic directions merely represent what was ordered any way in routine personal injury cases. It gives the parties an opportunity to save the time and expense of a court hearing and to carry out by agreement between themselves the necessary steps for preparing the case for trial. The automatic directions come into effect when the pleadings are deemed to be closed. The automatic directions are as follows; and apply to all personal injury cases except Admiralty and medical negligence cases:

Automatic directions in personal injury actions

1. Each party shall give discovery of documents within 14 days and inspection of documents seven days thereafter, but where the action arises out of a road accident discovery is limited to disclosure by the Plaintiff of any documents relating to special damages. A road accident means an accident on land due to a collision or apprehended collision involving a vehicle;
2. Where any party intends to place reliance at the trial on expert evidence he shall within 14 weeks disclose the substance of that evidence to the other parties in the form of a written report which shall be agreed if possible;
3. Unless such reports are agreed the parties shall be at liberty to call as expert witnesses those witnesses the substance of whose evidence has been disclosed in accordance with the preceding sub-paragraph except that the number of expert witnesses shall be limited in any case to two medical experts and one expert of any other kind;
4. If a party intends to place reliance on any other oral evidence he shall, within 14 weeks of close of pleadings, serve on the other parties written statements of all such oral evidence which he intends to adduce;
5. Photographs, a sketch plan and the contents of any police accident report book shall be receivable in evidence at the trial and shall be agreed if possible;
6. The action shall be tried in London if the action is proceeding in London but if the action is proceeding in a District Registry then it shall be tried at the trial centre for the time being designated for the District Registry;
7. The action shall be tried by judge alone as a case of substance or difficulty (Category B) and shall be set down within six months;
8. The court shall be notified upon setting down of the estimated length of trial.

These directions are only meant to represent what are routine. If either party required additional or different directions an application to the court might be made on a summons for directions just as if the case were not one which concerned personal injuries. Such other directions might relate, *e.g.* to amendments of pleadings, or the recording of unreasonable refusals to admit relevant matters which are in issue on the pleadings and which might result in costs at the trial being awarded against the party acting unreasonably so far as the admitting of these matters is concerned.

It is customary for the plaintiff's solicitors at the close of pleadings to enquire of the defendant's solicitors whether any directions other than automatic directions will be required and if so then a summons for directions will be issued such as is required in any other type of action. Such a summons is made by taking to the court two copies of a pre-printed form obtained from a law stationers on which the directions most commonly sought are printed together with a substantial blank for any further or extra directions required to be put in by the parties seeking them.

In our present case Mr. White would be of the opinion that automatic directions would suffice. If however he was of the opinion that some extra direction should be sought he would issue a summons for direction for that purpose. If upon receipt of that summons Miss Hovent wished for additional directions to be given she would in her turn serve a notice on the plaintiff and on the court setting out the directions she was seeking no later than seven days before the date fixed for the hearing.

Discovery of documents

As will have been observed the automatic directions refer to the question of discovery of documents. The moment has arrived when for the first time the defendant becomes entitled as of right to be furnished with the list of documents in the possession, custody or power of the plaintiff. The extent of the documents which will have to be disclosed depends upon the type of action. As will be observed from the wording of the automatic directions, where the personal injury action involves a road accident discovery is limited to documents relating to special damage. In the present case therefore the documents which are relevant would be details of the loss of pay and of any benefits received.

It is therefore at a relatively late stage in the action when Fletcher is entitled to view confirmatory documentation of the items of claim for special damages for which he is being held liable. Automatic directions are in this form because it is usually considered that in a road accident case as the parties will not previously have been in any correspondence or presumably even known to each other before the accident there will not be very much in the way of documents which the defendant will have relevant to the case. On the other hand in, say, a commercial contract action there may be dozens or even thousands of documents in the possession of the parties which are relevant to the action. In the present case therefore Fletcher will not have to supply a list of his documents for inspection unless a specific order for this purpose has been made in the action. An example of a case where this might be appropriate is where perhaps the plaintiff suspected that the condition of the defendant's vehicle might have contributed to the accident. He might therefore think that seeing, say, the vehicle's maintenance records might substantially assist him with proving liability. Even though automatic directions make no provision for disclosure of documents by the defendant this would be a case where the plaintiff might think it appropriate to seek discovery which he would do by issuing a summons specifically for that purpose, either for discovery alone or as apart of a more general application for directions if for instance there were other things he wanted which were not covered by the automatic directions.

In the present case therefore Mr. Beaumont's list of documents might be served somewhat informally as follows because there are so few documents:

In the High Court of Justice   1993–B–No.4106
Queen's Bench Division
Barchester District Registry

Between:

                        Francis Beaumont   Plaintiff

                              and

                        John Fletcher   Defendant

LIST OF DOCUMENTS OF PLAINTIFF

PURSUANT TO O25r8(1) (a)

1.	ESTIMATE BODGE & CO (ENGINEERS) LTD	7th April 1993
2.	ACCOUNT BODGE & CO (ENGINEERS) LTD	25th May 1993
3.	ACCOUNT COZY CAR HIRE CO.	25th May 1993
4.	ENGINEER'S REPORT AUSTIN CARR & CO.	25th May 1993
5.	LETTER PLAINTIFF'S EMPLOYERS TO PLAINTIFF'S SOLICITORS	1st June 1993
6.	LIST OF PRE-ACCIDENT EARNINGS	
7.	LETTER FROM BARCHESTER JOB CENTRE	8th June 1993
8.	LETTER FROM AMALGAMATED UNION OF COACH DRIVERS	10th June 1993

Served this 1st day of September 1993 by
Makepiece & Streiff, of Bank Chambers, High Street, Barset,
Solicitors for the Plaintiff

Upon receipt of the plaintiff's list of documents the defendant's solicitors have a right to attend at the plaintiff's solicitor's office to inspect the documents and to make copies. There is now provision permitting a party to insist on copy documents being supplied rather than attending for physical inspection, and it is customary for copies of the documents that exist, in this type of action, to be supplied on request with an undertaking to pay reasonable copying charges.

If Beaumont's action had arisen out of say, an accident at his place of work, discovery would be a more lengthy process and both parties would give discovery by list of all documents relating to the matters in question which are or have been in their possession, custody or power.

The list already illustrated sets out documents of which the opposing party is entitled to make copies. If a full list of documents is required it must contain details of all documents which have existed or are in existence irrespective of whether privilege is claimed. Because the opposing party is not entitled to inspect privileged items the list is divided into two schedules and the first schedule into two parts.

"Privilege" is a complicated legal concept but in essence it means documents falling within certain classes which the court allows the party to treat as so confidential that their *contents* need not be disclosed to the opposing party by giving him inspection of them. The *existence* of these documents must however be disclosed. The mere fact that a document is harmful to a party's case will not suffice to make it privileged. Indeed often documents which are crucial to liability will need in consequence of discovery honestly carried out to be shown to the opposing party. Privilege only attaches in certain limited circumstances, chiefly to documents which arise out of the obtaining of legal advice, *e.g.* communications between solicitor and client. In cases where litigation is involved witness statements and other documents obtained from third persons by a party or his legal advisers are also subject to privilege and therefore one need not give inspection of, for instance, one's own witnesses' proofs of evidence.

The first schedule part one contains documents in respect of which privilege is not claimed. It will include documents such as those set out in the short form list previously illustrated but other documents will be added, *e.g.* correspondence between the solicitors for the parties, the pleadings in the action, public documents that are available to the parties such as a police report, magistrates court depositions and reports by H.M. Inspectors of Factories.

The second part of schedule one lists the privileged documents which should include correspondence with one's own client and witnesses, proofs of evidence, instructions to counsel and counsel's drafts and opinions and "without prejudice" correspondence if the issues contained therein remain to be resolved. It is possible for a party to challenge a claim of privilege and to have the matter determined by summons to the District Judge.

The second schedule illustrates clearly the intention of the courts to ensure that discovery is complete because one now has to list those documents which the parties have had but no longer possess at the time of preparing the list. Such documents not only have to be listed but information given as to when they were last possessed and what has become of them. Frequently the documents listed under this head are limited to the originals of the copy correspondence listed elsewhere. It would be stated that they were last in the party's possession on the dates that they were posted and are now in the possession of the persons to whom they were addressed. Although it is usually true to say that inspection of documents takes place at the address for service of the party supplying the list, different provisions can apply if they are business documents in constant use. Certified extracts of these documents may be required as an alternative to inspection at the place where the documents are normally kept and in use.

The formal list is shown at pp. 191–193 by way of illustration.

If Fletcher was minded to challenge the completeness of Beaumont's list, it would be customary for the solicitors concerned to write pointing out the apparent deficiency. If this did not have the desired effect, an application would be made for discovery of specific documents and such an application would have to be supported by an affidavit setting out the grounds for the assertion that relevant documents had not been disclosed. As an alternative Beaumont might be ordered to serve an affidavit verifying his list.

In some exceptional cases it is possible to obtain discovery before an action is brought. This procedure only applies to potential actions for personal injuries or death and the power to order discovery is discretionary. A good example would be in the case of a medical negligence claim where a party might wish to see hospital records to see whether a claim for damages for medical negligence might lie. In such a case generally the criterion that a District Judge applies when deciding on such an application is whether or not sight of the document is crucial to helping the potential plaintiff to decide whether to sue at all.

There is also now a power where a writ has been issued to order discovery against a person who is not a party to an action but who has documents which are relevant to that action in his possession.

Security for costs

It is highly unlikely that in the *Beaumont* v. *Fletcher* type of action this question will arise.

Nevertheless, it is necessary to have in mind circumstances where security for a defendant's costs *may* be granted and to realise that no automatic right to security exists even though it is clear that the costs of a successful defence to an action will be irrecoverable. The most likely situation where security will be awarded is when the plaintiff ordinarily resides out of the jurisdiction of the court and has no substantial assets within the jurisdiction. There would also be reasonable prospects of security being ordered if it could be shown that the plaintiff has given a wrong address on the writ of summons or has moved his address to evade the consequences of the litigation. Likewise, where the plaintiff is a limited company and there is good evidence to lead the court to believe that the company would be unable to pay the successful defendant's costs. Although this might suggest that impecuniosity will always provide grounds for an order being made, it is not so. For example, a plaintiff with the benefit of a legal aid certificate will not have an order for security for costs made against him.

List of
Documents
(O.24 r.5)

IN THE HIGH COURT OF JUSTICE   19⁹³.— B.—**No.** 4106

QUEEN'S BENCH   **Division**

BARCHESTER DISTRICT REGISTRY

Between

FRANCIS BEAUMONT   Plaintiff

AND

JOHN FLETCHER   Defendant

LIST OF DOCUMENTS

The following is a list of the documents relating to the matters in question in this action which are or have been in the possession, custody or power of the above-named(¹)   Plaintiff

(1) Plaintiffs (or Defendant(s)) A.B.

and which is served in compliance with Order 24, rule 2 [~~xxxxxxxxxxxxxxxx~~ ~~day of~~   , 19xx].

(2) Plaintiff(s) or Defendant(s).

1. The (²) Plaintiff   has in his possession, custody or power the documents relating to the matters in question in this action enumerated in Schedule 1 hereto.

(3) State ground of objection.

2. The (²) Plaintiff   object s to produce the documents enumerated in Part 2 of the said Schedule 1 on the ground that (³)   the same are privileged

3. The (²) Plaintiff   has had, but ha s not now, in   his possession, custody or power the documents relating to the matters in question in this action enumerated in Schedule 2 hereto.

4. Of the documents in the said Schedule 2, those numbered   in that Schedule were last in the (⁴) Plaintiff's possession, custody or power on (⁵) the dates when   ~~and the remainder on~~(⁶) the same were (⁶) posted and are now in the possession of the addressees.

(4) Plaintiff's or Defendant's.
(5) State when.
(6) Here state what has become of the said documents and in whose possession they now are.

5. Neither the (²) Plaintiff nor   his Solicitor   nor any other person on his behalf, has   now, or ever had, in their possession, custody or power any document of any description whatever relating to any matter in question in this action, other than the documents enumerated in Schedules 1 and 2 hereto.

SCHEDULE 1.—Part 1.

(Here enumerate in a convenient order the documents (or bundles of documents, if of the same nature, such as invoices) in the possession, custody or power of the party in question which he does not object to produce, with a short description of each document or bundle sufficient to identify it.)

Description of Document	Date
1. Estimate Bodge & Co (Engineers) Ltd	8th March 1993
2. Account Bodge & Co (Engineers) Ltd	25th May 1993
3. Account Cozy Car Hire Co.	25th May 1993
4. Engineer's Report Austin Cain & Co	25th May 1993
5. Letter Plaintiff's Employers to Plaintiff's Solicitors.	15th May 1993
6. List of pre-accident earnings	15th May 1993
7. Medical Report of Mr B Setter, FRCS	22nd June 1993
8. Letter from Barchester Job Centre	8th June 1993
9. Letter from Amalgamated Union of Coach Drivers	10th June 1993
10. Correspondence common to the parties	various
11. Pleadings.	

SCHEDULE 1.—Part 2.

(Here enumerate as aforesaid the documents in the possession, custody or power of the party in question which he objects to produce.)

Description of Document	Date
Correspondence between the Plaintiff and his Insurers and his Solicitors. Instructions to Counsel and Counsel's drafts and opinions. Statements of evidence and other documents prepared for the purpose of pursuing the Plaintiff's action. 'Without Prejudice' correspondence.	

SCHEDULE 2.

(Here enumerate as aforesaid the documents which have been, but at the date of service of the list are not, in the possession, custody or power of the party in question.)

The originals of the copy correspondence listed in Part 1 of Schedule 1.	various.

Dated the   2nd day   day of   September   , 19 93 .

NOTICE TO INSPECT

Take notice that the documents in the above list, other than those listed in Part 2 of Schedule 1 [and Schedule 2], may be inspected at [the office of the Solicitor of the above-named (7)   Plaintiff

(7) Plaintiff(s) *or* Defendant(s) *(insert address) or as may be.*

on the   ANY WEEKDAY   day of   , 19 , between the hours of 10. am   and 4 p.m.

(8) Defendant(s) *(or Plaintiff(s) C.D.*

To the (8) Defendant   Served the   2nd   day of September 19 93 . by   Makepiece & Streiff of   Bank Chambers, High Street, barset.

and his Solicitor   Solicitor for the Plaintiff.

An application for security for costs is made by summons to the District Judge and has to be supported by an affidavit setting out the grounds upon which it is being made. If an order is made it should provide for the amount ordered to be brought into court within a specified period. The action will be stayed until the order is complied with and if it is not, application could be made for the action to be dismissed.

Transfer from High Court to county court

As indicated in the introduction, one matter which will be considered during a case is the question of court of trial, no matter where the action was commenced. In general the position is as follows:

1. Actions of any kind which involve a sum of less than £25,000 will be tried in the County Court unless there are special features which render an action more suitable for trial in the High Court notwithstanding the amount involved is modest.

2. Actions involving sums of £50,000 or more will in general be tried in the High Court unless again, by reference to certain criteria which will be discussed below, the action is a very simple and straightforward one notwithstanding the amount involved.

3. Between the figures of £25,000 and £50,000 the place for court of trial will be decided by reference to certain criteria.

The criteria to be considered (and which appear in Article 7(5) of the High Court and County Court Jurisdiction Order 1991) are as follows:

(a) The financial substance of the action, including the value of any counterclaim.

(b) Whether the action is otherwise important and, in particular, whether it raises questions of importance to persons who are not parties or questions of general public interest.

(c) The complexity of the facts, legal issues, remedies or procedures involved and

(d) Whether transfer is likely to result in a more speedy trial of the action (however transfer shall not be made on this ground alone).

Beaumont v. *Fletcher—about to be set down for trial*

It is at this stage of setting down for trial when there is an important difference between the practice in London and that in a District Registry. In District Registry cases setting down for trial involves the plaintiff lodging two bundles of documents, the contents of which are described below. In addition, however, the plaintiff has to lodge a statement certifying readiness for trial. This document must certify whether the orders made on the summons for directions (if any) have been complied with and in particular whether medical or expert reports have been agreed and if not how many medical or expert witnesses will be called; whether plans and photographs have been agreed; and up to date estimate of the length of trial; the names, addressed and telephone numbers of the solicitors and counsel involved in the case.

When these documents are lodged the action joins the list of cases awaiting trial. It is at that time possible, in order to take the uncertainty out of listing to apply to the court for a fixed date of hearing. This is sometimes appropriate if it is important that certain counsel be available, or if there are numerous expert witnesses whose availability must be made certain some considerable time in advance of the trial.

Frequently problems occur, not because of any lack of consideration by the court but because the judges have to divide their time between criminal and civil trials. There is considerable judicial and political pressure upon the judges to ensure that persons awaiting trial in custody in criminal matters are dealt with as speedily as possible. This results in preference being given to the criminal list at the Crown Courts and sometimes even fixed dates in civil matters are not honoured.

The documents which comprise each of the two bundles which are lodged at the District Registry on an action being set down are as follows:

(a) Writ of summons.

(b) Notices of issue of Legal Aid Certificates and amendments thereto.

(c) The pleadings including request for and further and better particulars thereof and also including any orders made for the giving of such particulars.

(d) Any orders made on the hearing of a summons for directions.

(e) A statement of the value of the action form PF 204.

One of the bundles is for the use of the trial judge. The other bundle is retained by the court as the official record. Upon this bundle the names, addresses and telephone numbers of the solicitors for each of the parties must be endorsed and it will be stamped to show that the setting down fee has been paid.

When the documents are lodged in an automatic directions case there is of course no order for directions, although an estimate must be given as to the likely length of the trial. At that time the question of transfer to the County Court will also be reviewed in the light of the statement of value of the case as certified. After setting the action down for trial Mr. White will write to Messrs. Marxs & Co. informing them that the action has been set down.

In Mr. Beaumont's action where automatic directions applied, Mr. White had six months in which to set the action down for trial. There is, of course, no need to use the whole period and if both parties had been ready then the action could have been set down very much earlier than the end of the six month time limit provided for in automatic directions. If by any chance a plaintiff lets matters go beyond the time period within which he should have set the case down for trial he no longer needs to apply to the court for leave to set down out of time but may go ahead and set it down anyway. It is then up to the other party to make objection in any form he thinks appropriate, *e.g.* by applying to dismiss the action for want of prosecution.

Additional notes on setting down in London

Because of the volume of work there are, in London, seven lists into which an action may be set down, as follows:

(a) Jury list.
(b) Non Jury list, also known as the general list.
(c) Short cause list, to which cases are allocated that are likely to take less than two hours.
(d) Commercial list.
(e) Revenue list.
(f) Motions for judgment list.
(g) Special paper list.

If Beaumont's action had been proceeding in London, with a likely estimated hearing of possibly two days it would have been set down in the non Jury list.

To achieve this, the two bundles of documents would either be delivered or posted to the Head Clerk, Crown Office and Associates Department, Royal Courts of Justice, Strand. Applications to fix a date for the hearing are made to the Clerk of the Lists and if agreement cannot be reached it will be dealt with by the judge in charge of the list.

The action proceeds

Unless there is likely to be a considerable delay before the action is to be heard, both Mr. White and Miss Hovent will start their preparations for the trial as soon as it has been set down for trial.

If the case is of any complexity it will be important to take counsel's advice on evidence. Counsel will have conduct of the trial and it is generally considered that since he is the expert in the field of evidence he should give advice as to how the matters which remain in contention are to be proved. He may advise for example that a notice to admit certain facts be served on the defendant or that Civil Evidence Act notices be served in an attempt to introduce the evidence of certain witnesses without calling them, or that of say five eye-witnesses who all say more or less the same thing only two need to be called and so on. Counsel's advice on evidence should be followed as expeditiously as possible and all proper notices served. It is at this stage also that a conference with counsel might sometimes be thought desirable. At this conference counsel may well wish to see the plaintiff personally to advise him on the progress of the case and on consideration of any late offers of settlement which may come forward. Counsel may wish to test the client's version of events by questioning him closely about what occurred. Counsel may not as a rule see any other witnesses of fact in his chambers but the Bar's rules of etiquette do permit him to confer with expert witnesses and thus if there is, say, a serious difficulty about the medical evidence or about accountant's evidence concerning future loss of earnings, counsel may attempt to clarify matters by asking for a conference with the expert witnesses concerned.

Letters will be written to the witnesses to ascertain their availability. Mr. White will instruct a surveyor to prepare a scale plan of the junction and this, together with any photographs will be submitted to Marx & Co. for agreement. An attempt will be made to agree the special damage and medical evidence subject to liability.

Under the rules a plaintiff is now required just before trial to serve on the defendant a schedule showing precisely the special damages claimed and how they are computed. This is particularly relevant in a case where a continuing loss of earnings is claimed to ensure that all figures are brought exactly up to date before trial so that a great deal of judicial time is not wasted by the need to demonstrate to the judge complicated computations of relatively small sums. The defendant is then required to give notice of any particular features of the computation to which he objects so that the true differences between the parties, if any, on the computation of special damages can be highlighted. Agreement is often possible even in the most bitterly contested case. Such agreement will naturally be subject to liability or it may also be subject to the plaintiff demonstrating in principle that a certain type of claimed loss is due. In other words the plaintiff may need to prove to the judge that he is entitled to claim for, say, the expenses of a relative who visits him to carry out part-time nursing, but that once the judge accepts that such are properly claimable the defendant will then agree that the rate claimed is reasonable.

The court bundle

It is very important that the court should have all relevant documents before it at least a couple of days before the trial so that the judge can read and familiarise himself with the necessary papers. To this end there is a new requirement that the plaintiff and defendant should co-operate to agree a "court bundle" comprising the important documents which they have mutually disclosed upon discovery. These should be prepared in a properly paginated and indexed form for ease of reference during the court proceedings. This bundle must be lodged at court at least two days before the trial and in addition the plaintiff must lodge a set of those witness statements which have been exchanged and experts' reports which have been disclosed together with an indication of whether the contents of such documents are agreed. In this way the judge will be full informed about relevant and outstanding issues before the trial commences. It is thus important to ensure that medical evidence is updated close to trial and the reports exchanged between the parties in order to ensure if possible that medical evidence is agreed. If the reports are agreed, there is then of course no need to call the witnesses at trial so there will be a consequent saving in time and expense. The same applies not only to other expert witnesses, but now to witnesses of fact whose statements must also be exchanged before trial. Obviously if either experts or witnesses of fact are not in agreement, the judge must not be left to make up his mind on the basis of written documents and the expert, or witness of fact, must be called to give oral evidence.

It is also important to ensure the attendance of the witnesses at the trial and it is not wise to assume that promises to attend will be honoured. In these circumstances both Mr. White and Miss Hovent will give instructions for subpoenae to be issued and served. The subpoena is a command to the witness to attend at a place which is specified on a date to be determined to give evidence on the part of the party serving the same. If the witness is required only to give oral evidence the subpoena served is called a *subpoena ad testificandum*. A witness required to produce documents will be served with a *subpoena duces tecum* and this specifies the documents required to be produced. If in Beaumont's action the police had been called to the scene the officer would be likely to be instructed to bring with him on the hearing, "your note book, original statements, sketch plans and all other documents relating to a traffic accident which occurred at the junction of the Barset to Fairmarket road with the road to Damchurch at Crawleigh, Oxfordshire, on March 7, 1993." It will be noted that specific documents which the officer should have and will be required to be produced are specifically referred to and this is coupled with a general description in the hope that thereby all relevant documents will be made available. Obviously a party cannot be heard to complain about a witness' failure to produce documents if they were not detailed on the subpoena.

Subpoenas are issued free of charge either at the place where the action has been proceeding or at the District Registry for the Crown Court where the trial is to take place. A praecipe is required together with the form of subpoena. If it is *duces tecum* it will contain the witness' name and address with a separate form required for each witness.

A *subpoena ad testificandum* may be issued in blank for up to three unnamed witnesses. In the margin of such a form there will appear the words "limited to three witnesses" or as the case may be. On issuing the subpoenas the praecipe is left with the court and the subpoena sealed and returned. A copy of the subpoena has to be served upon the witness within 12 weeks of its issue and at least four days prior to the date of the witness' attendance at court. Personal service of the subpoena is absolutely necessary and there is no provision in the rules for service by any other method. At the time of service conduct money of a sum sufficient to meet the expenses of the witness proceeding to and from the place of the hearing has to be tendered. It is customary to arrange for the witness to sign a receipt on the rear of the sealed copy of the subpoena in the following terms: "Received one subpoena together with £15 conduct money." The receipt will be dated as well as signed. Whilst there is no obligation upon a witness to sign such a receipt, in most cases they are quite willing to do so. It is of great assistance to all concerned if the person effecting service obtains details of holidays and other commitments of the witness together with a telephone number where he may be contacted during business houses. Problems associated with the general uncertainty of the actual date of trial should be explained so that he appreciates that late notification is not necessarily the fault of the solicitors involved. After service it is useful to keep the witness informed of any factors which may have some bearing upon the trial date. If a witness is kept in the picture little difficulty is generally experienced in retaining his co-operation.

A subpoena can be served upon a witness anywhere in the United Kingdom and his failure to attend when required at the trial is a contempt of court. It should be noted that there is no property in a witness and therefore a witness can be interviewed by either party and make statements to whomever he chooses. It is not infrequent that a witness is *subpoenaed* by both parties.

Beaumont v. *Fletcher*—continued

After an action has been set down for trial by lodging the two bundles of necessary documents and, outside London, the statement certifying readiness for trial, the action will begin to move up the lists.

If a fixed date of trial has not been obtained the action will eventually appear in a warned list giving some three weeks notice of the week when the action is likely to be tried. It will then appear in the weekly list either as a fixture for a particular day or as a reserved case either for a day or generally for the week. This practice creates many difficulties for the busy practitioner and for witnesses who are kept "on call" even when there is little reasonable prospect of the action coming on for trial during the week for which it is warned.

Although the solicitors are responsible for watching the list, counsel's clerks are more in touch with the progress of the list and they keep the solicitors involved posted as to the progress in the list of actions awaiting trial, especially as they are anxious to be able to plan the work load of members of the Chambers for whom they work. Once an action appears in the warned list it is reasonable to deliver the brief to counsel.

There is a tendency for plaintiff's solicitors to deliver their brief at the earliest opportunity and for some defendants solicitors to delay delivery until the last moment in order to save the payment of fees if the action settles before coming on for hearing. The practice of delivering briefs at the last moment is obviously undesirable. Not only is it unreasonable to expect counsel to have to read the brief in a matter of any complexity for the first time on the evening before the hearing but it does not provide any safeguard in the event of counsel discovering a problem which has hitherto been overlooked. If an action is settled after delivery of briefs but prior to the hearing, it may be possible to negotiate a reduced fee with counsel's clerk.

Counsel's brief must be drafted thoroughly and with great care. It should contain copies of all relevant documents in the appropriate order and should then go on to rehearse the outstanding issues of fact, evidence, and law containing the comments of the person who drafts the brief on these matters. Care must be taken to ensure that counsel is supplied not only with such documents as proofs of evidence but also with correspondence between the parties and in short anything which might bear on an issue which may arise during the trial. It must be remembered that counsel's knowledge of the case is limited to the instructions contained in his brief and the accompanying documents, and that even if counsel has settled pleadings or advised in the case before it cannot be assumed that he will have any detailed recollection of it in view of the volume of work with which busy counsel deal.

The Hearing of Beaumont v. *Fletcher*

Once the date of the hearing is known both Mr. White and Miss Hovent will make their final preparations for the trial. Assuming that briefs have been delivered, it is likely that this will entail making arrangements for a conference with counsel at the Civil Crown Court on the morning of the hearing, and contacting the witnesses. It is obviously more satisfactory if one has the means of obtaining confirmation from the witnesses that the message has been received and no problem has arisen to prevent their attendance. If the case is such that counsel will be making reference to some case law, counsel's clerk is likely to inform the Judge's clerk of the references of the cases to be referred to so that the Judge will have copies of the reports for his own use.

It has been agreed that the medical reports on Mr. Beaumont by the specialists instructed by both sides should constitute the medical evidence so the originals of all the reports are made ready to hand to the Judge by Mr. Lawman when he opens the plaintiff's case. Mr. Lawman will also have been told of the amount at which the special damage has been agreed and this is also made known to the Judge during counsel's opening speech.

The manner in which the trial is conducted is the same in the High Court as in the County Court. The order in which the parties call their evidence, the rules of evidence and the order of speeches is no different.

At the conclusion of the trial, after all the evidence has been called and both counsel have made their closing speeches, Mr. Justice Scratchett, who has a reputation for meanness in his assessment of personal injury damages proves to be true to form. He awards general damages to cover pain and suffering and loss of amenity and loss of future earnings in a sum of £53,000 which was rather less than Mr. White had hoped for given that Mr. Beaumont is still suffering considerable pain, and that his prospects of further employment are uncertain. In addition Mr. Justice Scratchett awards the agreed special damages in respect of car repairs, car hire and the provable loss of earnings to the date of trial in the sum of £11,100. As will be observed, this award is nonetheless considerably more than the amount paid into court. No doubt when making the payment into court Miss Hovent was anticipating that the judge might reduce damages because of a finding of contributory negligence against Mr. Beaumont. However, the judge made no such finding and his award is on the basis of full liability against Mr. Fletcher. No difficulty therefore arises in the present case. In cases of complexity, however, where some items of a claim may carry interest at differential rates or for differing periods, and the defendant has declined in his notice of payment in to specify precisely the amount paid in for interest it may be necessary to carry out some rapid and complicated calculations with pocket calculators to see whether the amount awarded by the judge has beaten the payment into court or not. A further complication will be the question of benefits to be deducted from damages, which has been discussed earlier. In the present case since the plaintiff has beaten the payment into court he recovers his costs. Mr. Justice Scratchett will therefore direct that there be judgment for the plaintiff for £64,100 plus interest with costs to be payable by the defendant to the plaintiff on the standard basis. He would further direct that the sum paid into court be paid out to the plaintiff in part satisfaction of this claim and that the interest on this sum which will have been earned in the court's account should be paid to the defendant's solicitors. The defendant's solicitors may on the other hand suggest to the judge that this sum of interest which is theirs should be paid out to the plaintiff anyway in further part satisfaction of the balance due from them. The amount of benefits to be retained by the defendant for onward transmission to the Compensation Recovery Unit of the Department of Social Security will also be mentioned so that the final balance due from the defendant is precisely computed.

If Mr. Justice Scratchett had in fact awarded the plaintiff say only £34,000 then the plaintiff would have failed to beat payment in. In that case the judge would have directed that the plaintiff only receive his costs up to the date of the payment in and that thereafter the costs of the defendant be paid by the plaintiff. As this latter amount would clearly be very substantial the judge might well direct that the whole, or a proportion (say £10,000), of the amount awarded by him remain in the court funds until the extent of the plaintiff's liability for the costs of the defendant be known. Any surplus over the amount awarded by the judge would naturally be returned to the defendants. After the trial the important step to be taken by one of the parties is to draw up the judgment so as to give effect to the Judge's order.

The plaintiff, where he succeeds, or the defendant if he succeeds wholly in the action, will obtain from the Associate his certificate. This document sets out the period of time during which the Court was engaged upon the trial, and the directions of the Judge. If exhibits were used at the trial the Associate will also provide a certificate listing these for use, if necessary, in the Court of Appeal. Mr. White arranges for Joan to pick up the certificate together with two bundles of documents, deposited with the Court when the action was set down.

Mr. White draws the judgment and Joan takes to the District Registry, where the action was set down for trial, two copies of the judgment and the Associate's certificate. One copy of the judgment and the Associate's certificate are retained by the Court and the remaining copy of the judgment is sealed and returned to Joan. Mr. White serves a copy of this by sending the same by post to Messrs. Marx & Co. The judgment is illustrated below.

If the action was heard in London the Associate would send his certificate directly to the Judgment Department, so that the successful party's solicitor draws the judgment from the endorsement by counsel on his brief, or from his own notes, and takes two copies together with the original sealed writ to the Judgment Department for the judgment to be entered and sealed.

Judgment after
Trial before Judge
without Jury
(O. 42, r. 1)

IN THE HIGH COURT OF JUSTICE   19 93 . — B . —No. 4106

Queen's Bench Division

Between

FRANCIS BEAUMONT   Plaintiff

AND

JOHN FLETCHER   Defendant

Dated and entered the   4th   day of   MARCH   19 92.

THIS ACTION having been tried before the Honourable Mr. Justice   SCRATCHETT

(1) "the Royal Courts of Justice or as may be

without a jury, at(¹)   CIVIL CROWN COURT

, and the said Mr. Justice   SCRATCHETT

having on the   31st   day of   MARCH   1994 ,

(2) "Plaintiff" or "Defendant"

ordered that judgment as hereinafter provided be entered for the(²)   PLAINTIFF

XXXXXXXXXXXXXXXXXXXXXXXXXXXXXXXXXXXXXXXXXXXXXXXXXXXXXXXXXXXXXXXXXXXXX

XXXXXXXXX

(3) "the Defendant do pay the Plaintiff £
and his costs of action to be taxed" or "the Plaintiff do pay the Defendant his costs of defence to be taxed" or as may be according to the judge's order.

IT IS ADJUDGED that(³)   THE DEFENDENT DO PAY THE PLAINTIFF £64,100 AND
INTEREST IN THE SUM OF £3811.21p MAKING A TOTAL OF £67,911.21p
and his costs of the action to be taxed.

(4) or as may be according to the judge's direction.

XXXXXXXXXXXXXXXXXXXXXXXXXXXXXXXXXXXXXXXXXXXXXXXXXXXXXXXXXXXXXXXXXXXXX
XXXXXXXXXXXXXXXXXXXXXXXXXXXXXXXXXXXXXXXXXXXXXXXXXXXXXXXXXXXXXXXXXXXXX
XXXXXXXXXXXXXXXXXXXXXXXXXXXXXXXXXXXXXXXXXXXXXXXXXXXX

The above costs have been taxed and allowed at £   as appears by a

taxing officer's certificate dated the   day of   19

Makepiece and Streiff
Barset.

Solicitor

Enforcement of judgment

Mr. Beaumont will experience no problem in recovering the sum due to him under the judgment over and above the amount paid into court because Fletcher was covered by a valid policy of insurance, and as we have seen before because of the operation of section 152 of the Road Traffic Act 1988 his insurers are bound to honour the award. In fact even if Fletcher had had no insurance at all then under an arrangement existing with a body called the Motor Insurers Bureau (who are a syndicate of major motor insurance companies) a person who is a victim of the negligence of an uninsured driver is able to recover from the M.I.B. an amount equivalent to common law damages for personal injury and property damage who will pay any judgment obtained through the courts against the uninsured driver. There is a similar agreement in relation to drivers who are untraced (*i.e.* hit and run drivers). In this case, however, since no action through the court is possible the M.I.B. will make an offer and if this is unacceptable there is then a process of arbitration before one of a panel of Queen's Counsel who will fix the award. In the case of untraced drivers unfortunately the award will be limited to personal injury damages and consequential loss and no payment for property damage is possible.

Sadly in cases other than road traffic accidents not all plaintiffs are so fortunate and consideration may well have to be given as to ways and means of enforcing the judgment. Although the procedure may be somewhat different all but one of the methods available for enforcing a a judgment in the County Court are also available in the High Court. The exception is the application for attachment of earnings and even this method can be made available by transferring the judgment to the County Court for the district in which the judgment debtor resides. Because of the difficulties of enforcing judgment it is always wise, particularly in straightforward debt collecting cases to advise a plaintiff to spend some money, *e.g.* on an enquiry agents report, before the issue of proceedings to ascertain that the defendant is worth suing at all. Few things are as frustrating for the layman as to have gone to the expense and trouble of obtaining a judgment against an individual only to be told for the first time by his solicitor that one cannot get blood out of a stone and that if the defendant has no money then it may be very difficult ever to obtain payment of the sum due.

Oral examination

Sometimes the problem arises as to which of the methods of enforcement would be most likely to achieve the desired result. The judgment creditor's solicitor faced with this dilemma might decide either to instruct an enquiry agent to endeavour to ascertain the debtor's means or to make an application to the Court for the debtor to be examined as to his means. An order for the debtor's attendance is obtained *ex parte* by the filing of an affidavit so requesting and confirming the judgment. The order which gives the appointment for the examination has to be served personally and at the time of service a sum of money sufficient to cover the debtor's travelling expenses to and from the place of the examination has to be tendered. In order to be able to apply for the debtor to be committed to prison should he fail to attend upon the hearing, it is necessary for the copy order served to be endorsed with a "penal" notice. The effect of this notice is to warn the debtor that disobedience of the order will be a contempt of court and that he may be committed to prison. The examination will be heard in chambers, and the practice now is to order that the examination takes place in the offices of the County Court nearest to the debtor's home. This does not however mean that the case has been made a County Court case. It is simply that the place of the oral examination is there. The judgment remains a High Court judgment. At the hearing the judgment creditor may be represented either by a solicitor, or legal executive. The judgment debtor will give his evidence on oath and will then have to undergo cross examination about his means.

Execution of a Judgment

The first method to consider is the enforcement of a money judgment by a writ of *fieri facias* (known as a *fi. fa.*). This is obtained by preparing a form of a request to the court to issue the writ of *fi. fa.* Two copies of the actual writ are also taken to the court office. The writ is sealed and a sealed copy returned to the person issuing it who pays a small fee.

The writ is sent to the Under Sheriff for the County in which the debtor has goods to be seized together with the Sheriff's fee. The Under Sheriff passes the writ to his Officer who executes the same. The Officer is empowered to take possession of sufficient goods to cover the amount for which the writ is issued plus the Sheriff's charges and the costs arising from the sale of the goods.

When the Sheriff's Officer attends upon the judgment debtor in order to execute the writ it is likely that the debtor will be informed of his rights to make an application under Order 47, rule 1 to stay the execution. The Sheriff's Officer will have taken possession of goods with a likely sale value to cover all aspects of the execution. He will, however, assume what is known as "walking possession", to give the debtor an opportunity of raising funds to cover the amount due or to make the application for a stay provided the debtor enters into an undertaking not to part with possession of the goods seized. This arrangement results in the goods remaining at the debtor's premises until either the debt is cleared, the writ stayed, or it becomes apparent that there is no alternative to the removal and sale of the goods seized. On occasions problems arise when someone other than the judgment debtor lays claim to the goods seized by the Sheriff's Officer. If the judgment creditor wishes to dispute the claim the Sheriff will issue an *interpleader summons*, the purpose of which is to enable the court to determine the respective rights of the claimants. Whilst the interpleader proceedings are in progress the Sheriff's Officer retains possession over the goods seized in execution.

A judgment creditor can find that to make an unsuccessful challenge to such a claim will prove to be expensive. As a general rule it might be said that unless the claimant is the debtor's wife, who may find if difficult to prove ownership, the risks associated with challenging the claim are too great to accept without some evidence that will be available to disprove the claim.

Although the writ of *fi. fa.* is the method of executing a judgment which one is most frequently likely to use, there is a number of other methods available for enforcing judgments. Each is designed to cater for a particular type of asset.

Garnishee proceedings

If a judgment creditor is able to obtain details of any debts owing to the judgment debtor he will be able to obtain an order which will require the person owing money to the judgment debtor to pay the same direct to the judgment creditor. Although this might appear to be creating problems with the introduction of yet another "debtor" this in reality need not be so.

Because it is important for the judgment creditor to be able to act swiftly to restrain the judgment debtor from withdrawing his funds or obtaining settlement of debts owing to him, the judgment creditor first of all obtains an order nisi. Such an order is obtained *ex parte* (*i.e.* without warning the judgment debtor in advance) from the District Judge, or Master, by lodging with the court an affidavit identifying the judgment and the amount unpaid and the grounds for asserting that the proposed garnishee is indebted to the judgment debtor. It is also necessary to confirm that the garnishee is within the jurisdiction of the court.

A good example is that of a bank. If there is a credit balance on a current or savings account then a bank is in a position of debtor to its customers so that banks are often the target of these kind of proceedings. Similarly, if the judgment debtor is in business of any kind he is likely to be owed money in his turn by customers and it may be possible to attach these debts before they ever reach the judgment debtor by the procedure which is now described.

The garnishee order nisi requires the garnishee to show cause as to why he should not pay over the money which he really owes to the judgment debtor direct to the judgment creditor. The order nisi has to be served personally upon the garnishee and also upon the judgment debtor. Naturally one serves the order first on the garnishee to "freeze" the money in his hands before the judgment debtor has any idea of what is afoot. The order nisi prohibits the garnishee from parting with monies owed to the judgment debtor. At least 15 days notice of the appointment for further consideration must be given to the garnishee and at least seven days notice to the judgment debtor. At the hearing the Master or District Judge will consider whether to make the order absolute (that is, final). If he decides to do so then he will usually award the costs of the application. The garnishee will then be required to pay the money directly over to the judgment creditor less any costs that have been awarded to the garnishee. By complying with the court order the garnishee is protected from any action that the judgment debtor may have wished to take in respect of the debt which the garnishee owed the judgment debtor.

Charging order

The procedure in obtaining such an order is similar to that for garnishee proceedings. The order, which is made under the Charging Orders Act 1979 is made *ex parte* on the filing of an affidavit.

The purpose of the order is to impose a charge on any land or interest in land or security owned by the judgment debtor. The affidavit (i) identifies the judgment (ii) identifies the judgment debtor (iii) specifies the land or security to be charged (iv) verifying that the land or security is the judgment debtor's and stating the source of information and grounds for belief.

The order nisi has to be served upon the debtor giving him seven days' notice of the appointment for further consideration. Once the order is made absolute and registered it inhibits any dealing with the property by the judgment debtor. The order should be registered under the Land Charges Act (or at the Land Registry if the title is registered) as an "order affecting land."

The judgment creditor may then apply to enforce the charge by seeking an order for sale. The application for sale has to be made under the provisions of Order 88 of the Rules of the Supreme Court.

Writ of possession

Where the judgment or order provides for the giving of possession of land this may be enforced by the issue of a writ of possession which is executed by the Sheriff for the county in which the land is situated. Unless the possession arises out of a mortgage action to which R.S.C., Order 88 applies, leave of the court is required before the writ of possession may be issued. Leave will only be granted to enforce a final judgment or order for possession. Sometimes the judgment for possession also provides for payment of a sum of money—perhaps for arrears of rent. In such cases it would be proper to issue a writ of *fi. fa.* at the same time as the writ of possession so that the Sheriff may execute them together.

Writ of delivery

Where the judgment is that certain goods be delivered without allowing the judgment debtor to pay the value of them in the alternative, (*e.g.* where the plaintiff wanted the return of the specific goods because they had some personal value to him) then a writ of delivery may be issued by the court. This writ is executed by the Sheriff who will seize the goods in question and deliver them to the plaintiff. If the judgment provides that either the goods should be delivered or their assessed value paid then a writ which provides for those alternatives is issued for execution by the Sheriff who may either seize the goods in question or, if there is difficulty in this, seize other goods and auction them to raise the money owing.

Committal

Committal to prison is the ultimate sanction that the court can apply for disobedience of its order and judgments. Such provision might apply in cases of judgments to deliver goods where the defendant refuses to comply. It is not usually obtainable however for non-payment of a money judgment.

If in any situation thoughts are given to the making of an application for committal, care must be taken to ensure that the order or judgment lays down an exact time within which the defendant must comply.

The order or judgment must be indorsed with a penal notice, which is a notice warning the defendant that disobedience may result in imprisonment, and be served personally. Before an order of committal is made the defendant will be provided with an opportunity to appear before a High Court Judge to show cause as to why he should not be committed. The most certain method of avoiding committal being ordered is to comply with the order or judgment, before appearance before the judge.

Attachment of earnings

Although this is not a "High Court" method of enforcing a money judgment it can be applied to High Court judgments. The procedure on attachment of earnings was dealt with in Chapter 6 of *Introduction to Legal Practice* (Volume 1). In respect of a High Court judgment it is necessary to obtain a certified copy of the judgment to be filed with the application and an affidavit confirming the judgment and the amount owing thereunder, in the County Court for the district in which the judgment debtor resides.

A Note on Interlocutory Applications

Apart from a time summons or the summons for direction three special forms of interlocutory application have become very important in practice during the last few years. These are:

(i) Applications for interim payments.
(ii) *Mareva* injunctions.
(iii) *Anton Piller* orders.

Application for interim payment

Order 29, rule 10 allows the plaintiff to apply to the court by summons for an interim payment to be made by the defendant. This may be done at any time after the date for the return of the acknowledgement of service has passed. When first introduced in 1970 this procedure was limited to applications in personal injury actions but it was later extended to all types of case.

The application must be supported by an affidavit verifying the amount of damages and providing any supporting documentary evidence. The summons must be served at least 10 clear days before the hearing. It must either be shown that the defendant has admitted liability (which is uncommon) or that judgment has been obtained for damages to be assessed (not very common). Alternatively—and most applications will be made on this ground—it is enough to show that at the trial the plaintiff would recover substantial damages, taking into account any reduction that might be made for contributory negligence. But the court can only award a reasonable proportion of the damages it thinks the plaintiff would be likely to recover. In this way any allegation of contributory negligence can be taken into account. In a personal injuries claim an interim payment can only be ordered where the defendant is insured, is a public authority or has the means to make the payment. The judge at trial must not be told of any interim payment until the trial is over.

This procedure still tends to be used principally in personal injury actions. It is particularly appropriate where the question of liability is not seriously in doubt but the medical prognosis is not yet clear.

It is a particularly useful tactical weapon because it enables one to obtain money for a plaintiff who may be under serious financial pressure due to having been disabled from work by the accident itself. Such plaintiffs might well have been very susceptible to accepting an early payment into court of an amount considerably less than they might have hoped to obtain at trial because of such financial pressures.

Arguably the plaintiff's solicitors would have been likely to try such an application in the case of *Beaumont* v. *Fletcher*. Although, as we know Mr. Fletcher was not in desperate financial need due to a legacy which he had recently received, it is often thought a good tactical manoeuvre to keep the initiative with the plaintiff. Unfortunately some District Judges are more cautious than others when deciding on such applications and if there seems to be a really serious doubt on liability (as the defendants contended there was in the case of *Beaumont* v. *Fletcher*) it may be that no interim payment would have been awarded. However, even in that case, unless the District Judge concluded that the application was so doomed to failure that it should never have been brought, probably the order for costs made would have been "costs in the cause" the effect of which would be that the eventual winner of the trial would obtain the costs of the interim payment application also and thus nothing would have been lost. Certainly in personal injury litigation many plaintiffs' solicitors routinely apply for interim payments to demonstrate how certain they feel that success will be.

It is essential when drafting the affidavit in support of an application for an interim payment to specify any particular need that the plaintiff has of the money, *e.g.* to pay debts incurred by his being now disabled, to obtain private medical treatment etc. The availability of interim payments means that it may well be possible to negotiate an early voluntary interim payment from the defendant's insurance company where liability is unlikely to be seriously disputed.

Mareva injunctions

The High Court has always had power to grant interlocutory injunctions. This is often used in cases of nuisance, breach of copyright and similar cases. The court has very wide powers to grant an injunction "in all cases in which it appears to be just and convenient to do so" (Supreme Court Act 1981, s.37). It must tread a careful path between pre-empting the final outcome of the case and denying the plaintiff immediate relief where this is obviously needed. The basic rule the courts now follow is to see whether there is a serious issue to be tried. If so the test then applied is to ask where the balance of convenience lies. This involves asking whether the defendant could meet any eventual award of damages and, if not, whether the defendant might succeed at the trial. In all cases the plaintiff will have to undertake to pay damages if it later appears that the injunction should not have been granted. Whether the plaintiff could afford to pay any such damages is also relevant.

One special form of interlocutory injunction has been introduced to deal with a growing problem. If the plaintiff succeeds in a commercial or debt case there is often a risk that the defendant will not be able to meet the judgment. During the action assets may have been disposed of or transferred abroad. This may not always be with the intention of defeating any judgment obtained but the effect will often be precisely that. In *Mareva Compania Naviera S.A.* v. *International Bulk Carriers S.A.* [1980] All E.R. 213 the courts broke new ground by creating a special remedy in such a case. It is now possible to obtain a *Mareva* injunction after issue of a writ which will prevent the defendant from disposing of any assets in the United Kingdom or abroad pending the trial. The plaintiff must make a full and frank disclosure of the nature of the action and of all the information that is available showing the risk of the defendant removing or disposing of assets prior to the trial. It is also necessary to show that such removal would defeat the plaintiff's claim and that is that there are no other assets in this country from which it could be paid. It is a most formidable aid to the plaintiff in a suitable case.

Anton Piller orders

In some cases a defendant may destroy or dispose of vital documents, papers, video tapes or other matters in which the plaintiff has an interest. For example a defendant may have "pirated" the plaintiff's films and, when served with a writ claiming heavy damages may sell the illicit copies very cheaply or simply destroy them so as to conceal the evidence. In *Anton Piller K.G.* v. *Manufacturing Processes Ltd.* [1976] Ch. 55 it was held that a court may, when sitting *in camera* (behind closed doors) order a defendant to hand over all such material to the plaintiff.

It may even allow the plaintiff to enter the defendant's premises and search for illegally held goods and papers.

This is a very severe remedy. It will only be available if the plaintiff shows that there is a grave danger of the defendant destroying or concealing the items and that the plaintiff will thereby suffer great harm. Again it is an example of the judges developing a remedy to meet a need.

A note on costs (R.S.C., Order 62)

Although the power to award costs is discretionary the general rule is that "costs follow the event" so that the party who loses will have to pay the winning party's costs. The question of costs when the plaintiff fails to beat a payment into court has already been dealt with. Costs must be taxed if not agreed. In this context "taxed" means assessed. This means that a detailed bill has to be drawn up and submitted to the court for adjudication. The basis of taxation between the parties is now known as the "standard" basis of taxation and is in the following terms:

> "There shall be allowed a reasonable amount in respect of all costs reasonably incurred and any doubts which the taxing officer may have as to whether the costs were reasonably incurred or were reasonable in amount should be resolved in favour of the paying party."

This is the basis that will be employed in a routine case. It would not allow extravagant or needless costs to be recovered, *e.g.* employing the services of an expensive Queen's Counsel when junior counsel or even a solicitor would have been able to appear on the type of application concerned. As well as being the basis on which a loser will have to pay a winner's costs in litigation it is also the basis where costs are to be paid from the legal aid fund to a legally aided litigant's solicitors.

In addition there is another basis of taxation called the "indemnity basis" which will provide more or less for the complete recovery of costs incurred. It is anticipated that this order will not be made in routine cases but only where there is something oppressive in the conduct of the losing party or for instance where a trustee has brought litigation on behalf of a trust fund and is entitled to recover the costs for so doing from the fund.

Finally there is the "solicitor and client" basis of taxation. A privately instructed solicitor is entitled to payment on this basis from his own client which covers not only essential costs but all other costs expressly or impliedly authorised by the client. This basis is applied where a client challenges his solicitor's own bill and is the way in which the District Judge who carries out the taxation approaches consideration of the reasonableness of the solicitor's bill. It would only in very exceptional circumstances be ordered as the basis of taxation by which one party pays another party's costs in litigation.

Finally, in interlocutory proceedings costs are usually awarded as "costs in the cause." This means that whoever finally wins the case recovers those costs and means that there is no prejudgment of the issue of who is likely to be eventually awarded costs. Alternatively, however,

if the court wishes to express its disapproval of one or other party's conduct of the interlocutory proceedings it may award costs to the other
party "in any event." This means that the costs of that part of the proceedings culminating in that interlocutory application were recoverable
from the other party even if that other party wins the action as a whole.
Such an order indicates the court's disapproval of the conduct of the
party concerned. It is usually made where the party is wilfully in default
of some rule or has failed to take some necessary step in procedure or to
behave reasonably which has necessitated the application to the court.

CHAPTER 5

FAMILY PRACTICE

PROCEEDINGS IN THE DIVORCE COUNTY COURT

Introduction

Since the reforms that came into effect in 1971, the sole ground for divorce has been that the marriage has irretrievably broken down. To establish that this has occurred a husband or wife suing for divorce (the petitioner) has to satisfy the court of at least one of five facts. These are now set out in the forefront of the Matrimonial Causes Act 1973, section 1(2), and in view of their importance in any divorce proceedings, they are set out here:

(a) that the respondent has committed adultery and the petitioner finds it intolerable to live with the respondent;

(b) that the respondent has behaved in such a way that the petitioner cannot reasonably be expected to live with the respondent;

(c) that the respondent has deserted the petitioner for a continuous period of at least two years immediately preceding the presentation of the petition;

(d) that the parties to the marriage have lived apart for a continuous period of at least two years immediately preceding the presentation of the petition and the respondent consents to a decree being granted;

(e) that the parties to the marriage have lived apart for a continuous period of at least five years immediately preceding the presentation of the petition.

In the great majority of cases there is no dispute about the breakdown and it is now rare for the application for the decree of divorce itself to be opposed. Where there are children, there are often disputes about their care and maintenance and in nearly all cases there are differences about financial and property matters. These can now be dealt with as the case proceeds. Child maintenance for the majority of children is now dealt with by the Child Support Agency, rather than the courts.

A divorce is described as defended only if the decree itself is opposed. In such cases the petition will be heard in either the High Court or now, since February 1986 when Part V of the Matrimonial and Family Proceedings Act 1984 came into force, in the County Court. We shall be concerned here mainly with the procedure for undefended petitions in a divorce county court, of which Barset County Court is one.

We shall consider two undefended divorce suits handled by Messrs. Makepiece & Streiff. The first will illustrate the procedure in the most straightforward type of case where the parties have agreed on a divorce, they have no children and, since they both have good jobs, neither of them wishes to claim maintenance from the other. The second case will illustrate the more complex situation where children are involved and there is a claim for maintenance.

AN UNDEFENDED DIVORCE

Mary Baker v. *John Baker*

Phillip Friendly, Messrs. Makepiece's assistant solicitor deals with most of their matrimonial work. In this, he has the assistance of Mr. White, their litigation legal executive. At Mr. Friendly's request Mr. White interviews a Mrs. Baker, who comes to consult the firm about a divorce.

MAKEPIECE & STREIFF

ATTENDANCE NOTE

INTERVIEW/~~TEL. CALL.~~   DATE: 7.1.94

WITH: Mrs. Baker   OF: 7 Larks Grove, Barset

TAKEN BY: WW   TIME: 2.50–3.45

Full names: Mary Baker. Teacher. Married
John Baker 3rd May 1989. Now of 3 Stable Way, Barset.
Salesman. No children.

After marriage lived in rented property at 16 Castle Street, Barset, until separation. Marriage unhappy from start. Many rows about trivial things. Never really compatible. Agreed to live apart on 1st June 1991 and never lived together since then. Went to live at respective present addresses. Have agreed to divide furniture between them. No possibility of reconciliation.
   Her earnings exceed limits for green form legal aid so she will pay herself. NB Claim half of costs from her husband in petition.
   She has written to ask him if he will agree to a divorce and he says he will. She does not want maintenance, and no other property.
   Told her that her marriage certificate must be filed at court with other documents. Asked her to post it on.

After receiving Mrs. Baker's marriage certificate through the post Mr. White gives it with the interview record to his assistant Joan, asking her to make a file for county court proceedings, make out the petition (D8) based on separation for two years and consent: ground (d); also to prepare the Certificate with regard to Reconciliation (MCR3/D560), based on Mrs. Baker's statement that there is no possibility of this. Joan checks with the firm's file register to obtain the next serial file number and enters the case in that register. She then opens a new file under that number. She prepares the petition (pp. 215–217) and Certificate (p. 218) making a copy of each for the file and an extra copy of the petition as the court requires one to serve on the respondent as well as the copy for the court record. (Where there is more than one party to be served the court requires a signed copy of the petition for each.)
   The documents are checked and approved by Mr. White who signs

the certificate and two copies of the petition in the firm name. He instructs Joan to post them to the chief clerk of the court with the marriage certificate and a cheque made payable to the Paymaster General for the court fee.

Before completing this form, read carefully the attached **Notes for Guidance.**

In the   BARSET   **County Court***   * Delete as
                                                       appropriate

~~In the Divorce Registry*~~ XXX   **No.**

(1)   On the   3rd   day of   May   19   89   the petitioner

                        MARY BAKER   was lawfully married to

                        JOHN BAKER   (hereinafter called "the

respondent") at   ST. PATRICKS CHURCH BARSET IN THE COUNTY OF BARSETSHIRE

(2)   The petitioner and respondent last lived together as husband and wife at
               16 CASTLE STREET BARSET

(3)   The petitioner is domiciled in England and Wales, and is by occupation a

       TEACHER   and resides at   7 LARKS GROVE BARSET   AFORESAID

                                       and the respondent

is by occupation a   SALESMAN

                   and resides at   3 STABLE WAY BARSET AFORESAID

(4)   There are no children of the family now living ~~except~~ X

(5)   No other child, now living, has been born to the petitioner/~~respondent~~ during the marriage ~~(so~~
~~far as is known to the petitioner) except~~ X

D.8.

(6)   There are or have been no other proceedings in any court in England and Wales or elsewhere with reference to the marriage (or to any child of the family) or between the petitioner and respondent with reference to any property of either or both of them ᴇxᴄᴇᴘx X

(7)   There are no proceedings continuing in any country outside England or Wales which are in respect of the marriage or are capable of affecting its validity or subsistence ᴇxᴄᴇᴘx

(8)   (Tᴄis paragraph should be completed only if the petition is based on five years' separation.) XXXXX No agreement or arrangement has been made or is proposed to be made between the parties XXXXX for the support of the petitioner/respondent (and any child of the family) except XXX

(9)   The said marriage has broken down irretrievably.

(10)   The parties to the marriage have lived apart for a continuous period of at least 2 years immediately preceding the presentation of this petition and the respondent consents to a decree being granted.

(11) Particulars

On or about the 1st day of June 1991 the parties agreed to live apart and have not lived together since then.

Prayer

The petitioner therefore prays

(1) The suit

That the said marriage be dissolved

(2) Costs

That the   Respondent   may be ordered to pay half the costs of this suit

(3) Ancillary relief

That the petitioner may be granted the following ancillary relief:

(a)   an order for maintenance pending suit

a periodical payments order

a secured provision order

a lump sum order

a property adjustment order

(b)   ~~For the children~~

~~a periodical payments order~~ x

~~a secured provision order~~ x

~~a lump sum order~~ x x

(4)   ~~Children~~ x x

Signed

The names and addresses of the persons to be served with this petition are:—

Respondent:—   JOHN BAKER   3 STABLE WAY BARSET

Co-Respondent (adultery case only):—

The Petitioner's address for service is:—   MAKEPIECE & STREIFF   BANK CHAMBERS BARSET

Dated this   11th   day of   January   19 94

Address all communications for the court to: The Chief Clerk, County Court,

The Court }
office at }

is open from 10 a.m. to 4 p.m. (4.30 p.m. at the Divorce Registry) on Mondays to Fridays.

Certificate with regard to Reconciliation

Form 3   Case No
                          IN THE BARSET COUNTY COURT
Between   Mary Baker   Petitioner
and   John Baker   Respondent
~~and~~   ~~Co-respondent~~

I̶/We Makepiece & Streiff
the solicitors acting for the Petitioner in the above cause do hereby certify
that I̶/we have/~~have not~~ discussed with the Petitioner the possibility of a reconciliation and that I̶/we ~~have~~/have not given to the Petitioner the names and
addresses of persons qualified to help effect a reconciliation.
                              Dated this 11th day of January 1994

                                                         (Signed)

                                         Solicitors for the Petitioner
                                                             D 560

On receipt of the documents, the chief clerk allocates a reference
number which begins with the last two digits of the year, followed by D
for divorce and the serial number of the case, thus: 94 D 386. The chief
clerk acknowledges receipt (form D88) and posts to the respondent the
petition, sealed with the court seal, a rubber stamp. With the petition he
sends a Notice of Proceedings (form D8(3) p. 219) with a detachable fly-
leaf on which the respondent can acknowledge service. This is form
D10(3)—the version appropriate to a petition based on two years' separation and consent (p. 221). The respondent duly returns this to the
court, completed. The chief clerk makes photocopy and forwards it to
Messrs. Makepiece.

In the   BARSET COUNTY COURT   **County Court**

                                      No. of matter   94 D386

Between .... MARY BAKER .... Petitioner

and .... JOHN BAKER .... Respondent

~~and~~ .... ~~Co-respondent~~

Notice of Proceedings

A petition for divorce has been presented to this Court. A sealed copy of it and a copy of the petitioner's Statement of Arrangements for the child(ren) are delivered with this notice.

1.   You must complete and detach the acknowledgment of service and send it so as to reach the Court within 8 days after you receive this notice, inclusive of the day of receipt. Delay in returning the form may add to the costs.

2.   If you intend to instruct a solicitor to act for you, you should at once give him all the documents which have been served on you, so that he may send the acknowledgment to the Court on your behalf. If you do not intend to instruct a solicitor, you should nevertheless give an address for service in the acknowledgment so that any documents affecting your interests which are sent to you will in fact reach you. Changes of address should be notified to the Court.

Notes on Questions in the Acknowledgment of Service

3.   If you answer Yes to **Question 4** you **must**, within 29 days after you receive this notice, inclusive of the day of receipt, file in the Court office an answer to the   petition together with a copy for every other party to the proceedings.

4.   Before you answer Yes to **Question 5** you should understand that:

    (a)   If the petitioner satisfies the Court that the petitioner and you have been living apart for two years immediately before the presentation of the petition and that you consent to a decree, the Court will grant one unless it considers that the marriage has not broken down irretrievably;

    (b)   A decree absolute of divorce will end your marriage so that:

        (i)   any right you may have to a pension which depends on the marriage continuing will be affected;

        (ii)   you will not be able to claim a State widow's pension when the petitioner dies;

        (iii)   any rights of occupation you may have in the matrimonial home under the Matrimonial Homes Act 1983 will cease unless the Court has ordered otherwise before the decree is granted;

    (c)   Once the Court grants a decree absolute or decree of judicial separation, you will lose your right to inherit from the petitioner if he or she dies without having made a will, and if the petitioner has made a will a decree absolute of divorce will deprive you of any right which you may have under that will to act as executor or to take any gift under the will, unless a contrary intention appears in the will.

    (d)   A decree may have other consequences in your case depending on your particular circumstances and if you are in any doubt about these you would be well advised to consult a solicitor.

5.   If after consenting you wish to withdraw your consent you must immediately inform the Court and give notice to the solicitor.

6.   If you answer Yes to **Question 6** you must before the decree is made absolute, make application to the Court by filing and serving on the petitioner a notice in Form D64, which may be obtained from the Court.

7.   (a)   If you do not wish to defend the case but object to the claim for costs, you should answer Yes to **Question 7** in the acknowledgment. You must state the grounds on which you object. An objection cannot be entertained unless the grounds are given which, if established, would form a valid reason for not paying the costs. If such grounds are given, you will be notified of a date on which you must attend before the Judge if you wish to pursue the objection.

    (b)   If you do not object to the claim for costs but simply wish to be heard on the amount to be allowed, you should answer No to **Question 7.**

    (c)   If you are ordered to pay costs, the amount will be assessed by the Court unless it is agreed between the petitioner and yourself or fixed at a prescribed sum. If costs are to be assessed, you will be sent a copy of the petitioner's bill of costs and will have the right to be heard about the amount before it is finally settled.

Notice of Proceedings - Respondent Spouse
MATRIMONIAL CAUSES ACT 1973
Section 1(2)(a)(b)(c)

F. P. Rule 2.6(6) (Form M5)

                                                             D8(3)

8.   (a)   Please answer Question 8.
          If your answer to Question 8(c) is Yes please make sure that you sign the form at 10(A).

          If your answer to Question 8(d) is Yes you must make an application on form CHA 10(D).
          You can get this form from the court office.
          If you wish to apply for any of these orders or any other order which may be available to you under Part I or II of
          the Children Act 1989 you are advised to see a solicitor.

     (b)   It will be open to you to apply for any of these orders to be made or varied later even if you do not do so now.

9.   If you wish to contest the petitioner's financial or property claim, you will have an opportunity of doing so when you receive a
notice stating that the petitioner intends to proceed with the claim. You will then be required to file an affidavit giving particulars of
your property and income and be notified of the date when the claim is to be heard.

10.   If you wish to make some financial or property claim on your own account, you will have to make a separate application. If
you are in doubt as to the consequences of divorce on your financial position, you should obtain legal advice from a solicitor.

Dated   14 JANUARY 1994

Address all communications to the "Chief Clerk" **and quote the above case number**   THE REGISTRAR, COUNTY COURT
                                                                                          BARSET
The Court Office at   20 RIVER STREET, BARSET

is open from 10 a.m. till 4 p.m. on Mondays to Fridays only.

D8(3)

In the   BARSET

County Court

No. of matter   94D386

Between .... MARY BAKER .... Petitioner

and .... JOHN BAKER .... Respondent

and .... ~~Co-respondent~~   (SEAL)

- If you intend to instruct a solicitor to act for you, give him this form immediately
- Read carefully the Notice of Proceedings before answering the following questions
- Please complete using black ink

1.	Have you received the petition for divorce delivered with this form?	Yes
2.	On which date and at what address did you receive it? at	On the 14th day of January 19 94 3 Stable Way Barset
3.	Are you the person named as the Respondent in the petition?	Yes
4.	Do you intend to defend the case?	No
5.	Do you consent to a decree being granted?	Yes
6.	In the event of a decree nisi being granted on the basis of two years' separation coupled with the respondent's consent, do you intend to apply to the Court for it to consider your financial position as it will be after the divorce?	No
7.	Even if you do not intend to defend the case do you object to paying the costs of the proceedings? If so, on what grounds?	I have no objection to paying my share
8. (a)	Have you received a copy of the Statement of Arrangements for the child(ren)?	
(b)	What was the date of the Statement of Arrangements? (the date beside the Petitioner's signature at Part 3)	
(c)	Do you agree with the proposals in that Statement of Arrangements? **Notes** If **NO** you may file a written statement of your views on the present and the proposed arrangements for the children. It would help if you sent that statement to the court office with this form. You can get a form from the court office.	
(d)	Do you intend to make an application on your own account for a Residence Order, Contact Order, Specific Issue Order or a Prohibited Steps Order?	
9.	(In the case of proceedings relating to a polygamous marriage). If you have any wife/husband in addition to the petitioner who is not mentioned in the petition, what is the name and address of each such wife/husband and the date and place of your marriage to her/him?	

D10(3)

10(a).   **You must complete this part if**

•   you answered **Yes** to Question 5

or

•   you answered **Yes** to Question 8(c)

or

•   you do **not** have a solicitor acting for you

Signed: ꝑ Baker   Date: 15 January 1994

Address for service:*   3 STABLE WAY BARSET BARSETSHIRE

*Note: If you are acting on your own you should also put your place of residence,
or if you do not reside in England or Wales the address of a place in
England or Wales to which documents may be sent to you.
If you subsequently wish to change your address for service,
you must notify the Court.

10(b).   I am / We are acting for the Respondent in this matter.

Signed: Solicitor(s) for the Respondent

Date:

Address for service:

Note: If your client answered **Yes** to Question 5 or Question 8(c)
your client must sign and date at 10(a)

Address all communications for the Court to the Chief Clerk **and quote the above case number**
The Court Office at   20 RIVER STREET BARSET

is open from 10 am to 4pm on Mondays to Fridays only

Acknowledgment of Service - Respondent spouse

F.P. Rule 2.9(5) (Form M6)

D10(3)

Dd 8252445 65M 9/91 Ed(2931471)

On receiving the respondent's Acknowledgment of Service, Messrs. Makepiece write to their client:

MAKEPIECE & STREIFF

Solicitors

Clement Amity
Anthony Adverse

Bank Chambers
Barset

Tel: 00765 4321

Our Ref: PF/WW/OBE

Mrs. M. Baker,
7 Larks Grove,
Barset.

21st January 1994.

Dear Mrs. Baker,

Your Divorce Petition

I have now received from the court a copy of your husband's Acknowledgment of Service on him of the petition. This confirms what you told me, that he consents to the divorce and will not defend the petition. This makes it possible to obtain a decree without a court hearing provided the District Judge issues a certificate that he is satisfied with your case.

To satisfy him of this you will need to provide an affidavit, i.e. written evidence given on oath. I enclose the form of affidavit appropriate to your case, to which is attached the Acknowledgment of Service which your husband has signed. Please check that the affidavit is accurate. You will need to sign it before a solicitor or a court officer.

Unfortunately, it is not permitted for the affidavit to be sworn before solicitors acting in this matter. You may take it to another firm of solicitors, in which case there will be a small charge. There are also facilities for the swearing of documents at the Court Offices in River Street, where no charge is made. I shall be glad to have the sworn document back at your early convenience.

When he issues his certificate, the District Judge will fix the day when the decree nisi can be pronounced by the judge in open court.

Your faithfully,

(Signed)

Makepiece & Streiff

Mr. White photocopies the affidavit and prepares a Request for Direction for Trial (Form D84) (p. 224). This he posts with the original affidavit to the chief clerk. As, on consideration, the District Judge is satisfied that the petitioner has sufficiently proved the contents of the petition and that the respondent has given his consent and indicated that he will not oppose the grant of the decree, he authorises entry of the cause in the Special Procedure List and certifies that the petitioner is entitled to a decree.

Affidavit by petitioner in support of petition under
Section 1(2)(d) of Matrimonial Causes Act 1973

Family Proceedings
Rule 2.24(3) (Form M7)

No. of matter   94D386

In the   BARSET   County Court

Between   MARY BAKER   Petitioner

and   JOHN BAKER   Respondent

Question	Answer
About the Divorce petition 1. Have you read the petition filed in this case?	Yes
2. Do you wish to alter or add to any statement in the petition? If so, state the alterations or additions.	No
3. Subject to these alterations and additions (if any), is everything stated in your petition true? If any statement is not within your own knowledge, indicate this and say whether it is true to the best of your information and belief.	Yes
4. State the date on which you and the respondent separated.	1st June 1991
5. State briefly the reason or main reason for the separation.	My marriage had been unhappy for some time and we agreed to live apart.
6. State the date when, and the circumstances in which, you came to the conclusion that the marriage was in fact at an end.	On the 1st June 1991 when we separated.

7. State as far as you know the various addresses at which you and the respondent have respectively lived since the date given in the answer to Question 4, and the periods of residence at each address.

	Petitioner's Address		Respondent's Address
From 1 June 91 to Present date	7 LARKS GROVE BARSET BARSETSHIRE	From 1 June 91 to Present date	3 STABLE WAY BARSET BARSETSHIRE

8. Since the date given in the answer to Question 4, have you ever lived with the respondent in the same household?

    If so, state the addresses and the period or periods, giving dates.

    No

About the children of the family

9. Have you read the Statement of Arrangements xxxxxxxxxxxxxxxxxxxxxxxxxxxxxxx filed in this case? xxxxxxxxxxxxxxxxxxxxxxx

10. Do you wish to alter anything in the Statement x of Arrangements or add to it? xxxx

    If so, state the alterations or additions xx

11. Subject to these alterations and addition(s) (if any) is everything stated in your petition [and Statement of Arrangements for the child(ren)] true and correct to the best of your knowledge and belief?

    Yes

I,　　　MARY BAKER　　　　　　　　　　　　　　　　(full name)

of　　　7 LARKS GROVE BARSET BARSETSHIRE　　　(full residential address)

　　　　TEACHER　　　　　　　　　　　　　　　　　(occupation)

make oath and say as follows:

1.　　　I am the petitioner in this cause.

2.　　　The answers to Questions 1 to 11 are true.

(1) Insert name of the respondent exactly as it appears on the acknowledgment of service signed by him/her.

3.　　　I identify the signature .... J BAKER .... (1)
　　　　appearing on the copy acknowledgment of service now produced to me and marked "A" as the signature of my husband/wife, the respondent in this cause.

(2) Insert the Respondent's name if the Respondent has already signed a Statement of Arrangements.

4.　　(2) I identify the signature XXXXXXXXXXXXXXXXXXXXXXXXXXXXXXXXXXXXXXXXXXXXXXX
　　　　appearing on Part XX of the Statement of Arrangements now produced to me XX
　　　　and marked "B" as the signature of the respondent XXXXXXXXXX

(3) Exhibit any other document on which the petitioner wishes to rely.

5.　　(3)

(4) If the petitioner seeks a judicial separation, amend accordingly.

6.　　　I ask the Court to grant a decree dissolving my marriage with the respondent (4) on the grounds stated in my petition [and to order the respondent to pay one half of the costs of this suit]. (5)

(5) Delete if costs are not sought.

Sworn at　　　　BARSET COUNTY COURT 20 RIVER STREET BARSET
in the County of　　BARSETSHIRE　　　　　　　)............... M Baker
this　2nd　　　day of February　　, 19 94

Before me, ... J Downes

(6) Delete as the case may be.

A Commissioner for Oaths x
Officer of a Court appointed
by the Judge to take Affidavits. (6)

D80D

In the   BARSET   **County Court**

		No of matter 94D386
Between	MARY BAKER	Petitioner
and	JOHN BAKER	Respondent
~~and~~		~~Co-respondent~~

Application for directions for trial (Special Procedure)   *F.P. Rules 2.24*

The petitioner   MARY BAKER   applies to the District Judge for directions

for the trial of this undefended cause by entering it in the Special Procedure List.

The petitioner's affidavit of evidence is lodged with this application.

Signed   *M Baker*   [~~Solicitor for~~] the petitioner

Dated   2 FEBRUARY 1994

If you write to the Court please address your letters to "The Chief Clerk" and quote the **No. of the matter** at the top of this form.

The Court Office is at   20 RIVER STREET,
                            BARSET

and is open from 10am to 4pm on Monday to Friday.

Printed in the UK by HMSO 808219 Dd 8252452 9 91 C1700 PP

D84

Having arranged with the chief clerk a date on which the district judge or judge will formally pronounce the decree nisi, the District Judge completes the Directions for Trial at the foot of Form D84, copies of which are despatched by the chief clerk to Messrs. Makepiece and the respondent (p. 227). When the registrar's Directions come to hand Messrs. Makepiece write to their client:

MAKEPIECE & STREIFF

Solicitors

Clement Amity
Anthony Adverse

Bank Chambers
Barset

Tel: 00765 4321

8th February 1994.

Mrs. M. Baker,
7 Larks Grove,
Barset.

Dear Mrs. Baker,

Your Divorce Petition

I am pleased to tell you that the Court has indicated that your petition is approved and that you are entitled to a decree nisi. This will be formally granted by the Judge on Thursday 24th March. However, you do not have to go to court and I will write to confirm that the decree has been pronounced.

I should point out that the decree nisi does not in itself terminate the marriage. It is, as you know followed after an interval of 6 weeks by the decree absolute which is the effective dissolution and legally makes you once again a single person. In view of the irrevocable character of this step, I would ask you to confirm that you wish me to apply for the decree absolute, which should be obtained early in May.

Your faithfully,

(Signed)

Makepiece & Streiff

On receiving the letter, Mrs. Baker telephones to acknowledge receipt and to say that the quicker the decree absolute is received the better she will be pleased. Mr. White puts a note of the telephone call on the file.

On March 29th, Mr. White receives in the post a copy of the decree nisi pronounced on the 24th together with a certificate confirming that there are no children of the family to whom s.41 of the Matrimonial Causes Act 1973 applies (Form D84B).

Mr. White retains the decree nisi in the case file and enters May 6th, as the earliest date on which the decree nisi can be made absolute.

On that day, Joan at his request prepares the Notice of Application for Decree Nisi to be made Absolute (Form D36, p. 230). This is signed by Mrs. Baker and posted to the chief clerk. By return of post Mr. White receives the Certificate making Decree Nisi Absolute (Form D37, p. 231) which he sends to Mrs. Baker to report the completion of the proceedings. He encloses the firm's account for their fees, showing that Mrs. Baker is expected to pay only one-half of the bill, the remainder being met by the respondent under the court order.

Jurisdiction for matrimonial causes

The law relating to proceedings for divorce has undergone significant change since 1984 when the Matrimonial and Family Proceedings Act of that year was enacted. Section 1 of that Act provides that divorce proceedings cannot be commenced within the first year of marriage. Formerly the restricted period was the first three years of marriage although applications could be made to the court for leave to present a Petition within the first three-year period in cases of "exceptional depravity" on the part of the Respondent or "exceptional hardship" on the part of the Petitioner. In contrast the present one-year bar is absolute and there is no provision for a person to seek leave to issue proceedings for divorce however grave their position or the conduct of their partner may be. The court simply does not have jurisdiction.

Matrimonial causes, including divorce, nullity, judicial separation must be commenced either in a divorce county court or the Divorce Registry, Somerset House, Strand, London, which for the purpose acts as a divorce county court registry.

In the London area only one or two county courts in the outer areas have been designated divorce county courts by the Lord Chancellor. Outside London, nearly all county courts are so designated and nearly all of these are also designated as courts of trial. Much of the courtwork in matrimonial matters is carried out by District Judges. Older text books may refer to a court Registrar and students should note that a Registrar and a District Judge are the same person.

Undefended matrimonial causes are dealt with throughout in the divorce county court, although in cases proceeding in the Divorce Registry at Somerset House the decree is pronounced at the Royal Courts of Justice. When a cause becomes defended, it will proceed in the County Court except in cases of difficulty when it may be transferred by the District Judge to the High Court.

As the jurisdiction of each divorce county court is unrestricted in area, proceedings can be commenced in the court most convenient to the petitioner.

The rules governing the procedure for divorce are the Matrimonial Causes Rules 1977, as amended ("M.C.R."). Although proceedings are commenced in a divorce county court, these rules are not set out in the County Court Practice (the *Green Book*), but rather in the Supreme Court Practice (the *White Book*), and also in the main practitioner's work on divorce, namely *Rayden on Divorce*. The main Acts of Parliament dealing with divorce, the Matrimonial Causes Act 1973, and the Matrimonial and Family Proceedings Act 1984 are also found in those texts.

Notice of Application for Decree Nisi to be made Absolute

	IN THE	BARSET	COUNTY COURT*
			DIVORCE REGISTRY*

Rule 65

*Complete
and/or delete as
appropriate
If proceeding in a
District Registry,
delete both head
ings and insert In
the High Court of
Justice, Family
Division (Divorce),
          District
Registry

No. of matter   94D386

Between .... MARY BAKER .... Petitioner

and .... JOHN BAKER .... Respondent

and .... Co-Respondent

TAKE NOTICE that the Petitioner   MARY BAKER

applies for the decree nisi pronounced in his (her) favour on the   24th

day of   March   1994 , to be made absolute.

Dated this   6th   day of   May   1994

Signed ...... M. Baker ....
Solicitors for Petitioner
of ....
....

Address all communications for the Court to: The Chief Clerk, County Court* ....

....
(or to the Divorce Registry, Somerset House, Strand, London WC2R 1LP) quoting the number in the top right-hand corner of this form.
The Court Office is open from 10 a.m. till 4 p.m. (4.30 p.m. at the Divorce Registry) on Mondays to Fridays only.

IN THE   BARSET   COUNTY COURT

No. of matter   94D386

Between .... MARY BAKER .... Petitioner

                                JOHN BAKER

and .... Respondent

~~and~~ .... ~~Respondent~~

Referring to the decree made in this cause on the

24th   day of   March   1993 , whereby it was decreed that

the marriage solemnised on the   3rd   day of   May   19 89,

at   St Patricks Church Barset in the County of Barsetshire

between   MARY BAKER

                                the Petitioner

and   JOHN BAKER

                                the Respondent

be dissolved unless sufficient cause be shown to the Court within six weeks from the making thereof why the said decree should not be made absolute, and no such cause having been shown, it is hereby certified that the said decree was on the 6th day of May 19 94 made final and absolute and that the said marriage was thereby dissolved.

Dated   6th May 1994

Stuart Fairweather
District Judge.

Note: Divorce affects inheritance under a will. Where a will has already been made by either party to the marriage then, by virtue of section 18A of the Wills Act 1837, from the date on which the decree was made absolute:—

(a)   any appointment of the former spouse as executor or trustee is treated as if omitted and;

(b)   any gift in the will to the former spouses lapses;
        unless a contrary intention appears in the will.

Address all communications to the Chief Clerk AND QUOTE THE ABOVE CASE NUMBER

THE COURT OFFICE AT   20 RIVER STREET   BARSET

is open from 10 a.m. till 4 p.m. on Mondays to Fridays only

Certificate making Decree Nisi Absolute (Divorce)

MATRIMONIAL CAUSES RULES
Rule 67(2)

MCR 340090/1/8917822 133m 1/85 MCI   D37

Most of the forms used in divorce proceedings can be obtained without charge from the Court itself. They are also available from law publishers, which provide their own series numberings.

In divorce the law does justice evenhandedly between the sexes and all remedies can be applied for by either party to the marriage. In these notes to avoid being pedantic the petition is assumed to be brought by the wife, but the reader will understand that "she" always stands for "she or he" and vice versa.

The petition

Every divorce suit is commenced by petition in accordance with rule 8(1) Matrimonial Causes Rules (M.C.R.). It is filed by the spouse seeking the divorce (the "petitioner") and served on the other spouse (the "respondent"). The first eight paragraphs of a petition deal principally with the details concerning the marriage and the children of the family. The wording of paragraph one of a petition must follow precisely the wording used on the marriage certificate, since it is this paragraph which specifies the marriage which the court is being asked to dissolve. Thus the place of marriage should be fully stated including the County in which it took place. Also the full names of the parties should be given, including their surnames. In Paragraph 2 the full address of the place where the parties last lived together as husband and wife should be provided including the County.

Paragraph 3 is drafted to meet the case of the great majority of petitioners, whose permanent home is England and Wales and who are accordingly domiciled in this country. The Notes make it plain that persons who do not qualify in this way may still apply if they have been habitually resident here for at least a year before the filing of the petition. In those cases, Clause 3 is altered to show residence for that period. For this purpose, short periods of absence, *e.g.* for business or holidays, are disregarded. The occupation of both parties must also be given in Paragraph 3.

In paragraph 4, "child of the family" includes not just children of the marriage, natural or adoptive, but also any other child (not being a foster child) who has been treated as a child of the family.

Paragraph nine will always allege that the marriage has broken down irretrievably since this is the sole ground for divorce. However, as mentioned earlier, irretrievable breakdown can be established only by proving one or more of the five facts set out above (p. 212). Accordingly, paragraph ten goes on to specify which one or more of those five facts will be relied upon by the petitioner to establish irretrievable breakdown. Paragraph 11 then gives brief details of the incidents which have occurred during the marriage which are alleged by the petitioner as showing that one of the five facts has occurred.

The petitioner concludes with a prayer. This simply sets out all the orders which the petitioner is asking the court to make. Of course in a divorce petition the prayer will always begin with a request that the marriage should be dissolved. In addition, the prayer may go on to ask for various orders relating to children, maintenance, matrimonial property and costs. Whether or not all or any of these additional orders will be requested will depend upon the circumstances of each petitioner.

In cases such as Mrs. Baker's, where the petition is based on two years' separation coupled with the consent of the respondent to a decree, it is quite common for the prayer to ask that the respondent should be ordered to pay only half the costs. In this way, the costs of the divorce are borne equally by each party.

The date at the end of the petition, which will normally be the date on which it is filed is important. Where the petitioner is relying on two years' separation coupled with the respondent's consent, or on two years' desertion, or on five years' separation as the basis for the divorce, then these periods of time must have elapsed before the petition is filed. In computing such periods, a period or periods totalling not more than six months' cohabitation after the initial separation are disregarded. Cohabitation for a period or periods in excess of six months will automatically break the continuity of the separation.

Commencement of proceedings

To commence divorce proceedings the completed divorce petition should be filed at the court office of the chosen county court or at the Divorce Registry with the appropriate supporting documents required by the M.C.R. 1977. Since the court requires the petitioner to provide an original petition plus one copy for each party to be served at least one copy must be made for the respondent. In a case where adultery or a number of instances of adultery are alleged a copy or copies will be required for each co-respondent named. Documents supporting the petition which must be filed with it include the marriage certificate (or duplicate or copy if the original is unavailable) and a Statement of Arrangements for Children (Form M4) if appropriate. If there are children under 16 years or between 16 and 18 years receiving instruction at an educational establishment or training for a trade or profession then this form will be required. In addition, if the solicitor is acting for the petitioner he or she must file a certificate (Form 3) stating whether or not he has discussed the possibility of a reconciliation with the petitioner and given her names and addresses of persons qualified to help effect a reconciliation.

Service of the petition

Once the petition and supporting documents are received by the court and a file number allocated to the petition it must be served on the respondent. The rules for the service of the petition are not dissimilar from those for the service of a summons in the county court.

Provided there is no difficulty in relation to the address of the respondent or any other person to be served, service is normally by the court by post. An officer of the court who posts a petition to any party must indorse on a copy of the Notice of Proceedings the date of posting and the address to which it was sent. This is accepted as evidence of the post-ing (M.C.R., r. 121(1)). The court will send to the petitioner a photo-copy of any Acknowledgment of Service received, whether filed within the period of eight days specified in the form or later. After the expiry of 14 days from service, if no acknowledgment has been received in the meantime the petitioner (or his solicitor) will receive from the court a notification of non-service. The petitioner or solicitor may then request personal service by the court bailiff on payment of the fee and filing a further copy of the petition and any other documents, or have a further copy sealed by the court for service by a process server. Service by the bailiff will be proved by his indorsement of service; in the case of a pro-cess server, an affidavit of service is required. This must state the means of knowledge by which the respondent was identified. Personal service by the petitioner is prohibited (M.C.R., r. 14(3)). However, when no acknowledgment of the postal service is received, but the petitioner knows to her personal knowledge that it has been received, she may apply *ex parte* on affidavit for service to be deemed effective (M.C.R., r. 14(2)). In appropriate circumstances an order for substituted service can be obtained, *e.g.* by advertisement. Where the respondent or other opposing party's whereabouts are unknown because, for example, one petitioner has lost touch with the respondent and cannot provide an address for him, application can be made in the same manner for service to be dispensed with (r. 14(11)). There are arrangements in being with the DSS whereby when the petitioner is applying for financial relief and other means of tracing the spouse have failed, the district judge, on application by the petitioner, will apply to the DSS for the information. The Department will usually need to be given the respondent's national insurance number. The court will not disclose to the petitioner an address obtained from the DSS under this arrangement. A special form is available for these applications. See Practice Direction 26.4.88 at 1888 2 All E.R. p. 573.

Acknowledgment of service

The form of Notice of Proceedings will be found in its full form only in the Appendix to the Matrimonial Causes Rules (Form 5). The form issued to the respondent is adapted to the particular grounds of the pet-ition. A careful study of the form as printed in the Appendix shows what particulars are called for under each of the grounds for divorce as well as indicating the action to be taken if the grant of a decree is to be resisted, or, where the respondent consents to a decree, any arrangements for the parties or their children are disputed. The Acknowledgment of Service is also printed in the Appendix (Form 6) with alternatives and is adapted to the particular grounds alleged.

Provided the respondent answers "no" to the question. "Do you intend to defend the case?" it will proceed as undefended and any matters objected to, unless subsequently agreed, will be dealt with as the case proceeds at hearings before the district judge or the trial judge.

A respondent, on the other hand, who answers "yes" to that question has 29 days from the service of the petition to file an answer. If he has not already done so, the respondent should immediately consult a solicitor, because the answer has to be individually drafted to meet the allegations contained in the petition and indicate legal grounds on which the court could refuse to grant a decree. The matter will then proceed to trial in either the County Court or the High Court.

Where the petition is based on adultery and a co-respondent is joined, he has the same right to file an answer and defend the proceedings. A separate form of Acknowledgment is used for the co-respondent (Form D10(2)—"Party other than Spouse").

When an answer is filed, a copy is sent to the petitioner who may file a Reply within 14 days.

If a respondent fails to file his answer within 29 days, this does not prevent a later answer. However, at the expiry of the period for the answer, the petitioner is free to ask for the district judge's directions and if the answer is filed after she has taken this step, the leave of the court is required.

Special procedure

Although the procedure described in Mrs. Baker's case is called the "special procedure" it is in fact the usual procedure followed in almost all cases where the dissolution of the marriage is not opposed. It enables the divorce to proceed whilst consideration is being given also to the consequential matters; arrangements for the children, financial arrangements and the costs of the proceedings. Any of these matters on which the parties fail to agree can be settled by decisions of the judge or district judge. On the central issue of divorce, there is normally no trial before the judge and where there are no children the whole matter can effectively be dealt with by post. Of course, the district judge, when examining the filed documents and deciding on the "Directions for Trial" could order that there should be a formal hearing before the judge in open court, but this would be rare and would only occur, for example, where the petition and other documents raise a difficult point of law or the district judge has not been satisfied on reading them that the irretrievable breakdown of the marriage has been proved.

Under the special procedure the evidence will, therefore, normally be by affidavit. There is a different printed form of affidavit for swearing by the petitioner for each of the five grounds in section 1(2) of the Matrimonial Causes Act 1973 (M.C.R., r. 7(*a*)–(*e*)). In addition to the affidavit sworn by the petitioner, it may be necessary in some cases to obtain further evidence in the form of affidavits sworn by witnesses: for example, in a case based on the respondent's unreasonable behaviour an affidavit sworn by a doctor who has treated the petitioner for the injuries caused by the respondent's violence. Such affidavits would be filed at court at the same time as the petitioner's affidavit. If the petitioner has previously obtained an order in domestic proceedings in the magistrates' court (see p. 279), then this order will be included in the affidavit as an exhibit.

The decree

The certificate issued by the District Judge after he has considered the Request for Directions for Trial and the other documents in the case, is not a decree but merely a certificate to the effect that the district judge believes that a decree nisi should be pronounced and the case is suitable for the special procedure. The decree nisi must be pronounced by a district judge or a judge in open court but this is normally a pure formality if the district judge has issued a certificate.

The application for the decree nisi to be made absolute simply consists of the filing of a notice requesting this after the six-week period has elapsed. The decree absolute is not pronounced by a judge or district judge; as with the decree nisi, but is merely stamped with the court seal and posted to the petitioner or his solicitors. Before issuing the decree absolute the court staff must, however, verify certain matters; for example, that no appeal has been lodged against the decree nisi. This is dealt with more fully later. The court may direct that the decree nisi should not be made absolute until further order, if there are exceptional circumstances which make it desirable in the interests of any child of the family that such a direction should be made.

AN UNDEFENDED DIVORCE INVOLVING CHILDREN AND MAINTENANCE

Joan Butcher v. *James Butcher*

The assistant solicitor of Messrs. Makepiece, Phillip Friendly, has asked Mr. White to interview Mrs. Butcher about her marital difficulties, on which she has consulted him. As the interview proceeds he makes an attendance note:

MAKEPIECE & STREIFF

ATTENDANCE NOTE

INTERVIEW/~~TEL.CALL.~~		DATE:	1.9.93
WITH:	Mrs. J. Butcher	OF:	7 Westgate Avenue
TAKEN BY:	WW	TIME:	10.45–12.15

Full names: Joan Butcher. Married James Butcher on 1st May 1983. Occupation: Welder. Married at The Registry Office, Welbeck Street, Barset. Lived 7 Westgate Street throughout. Son Simon born 28th December, 1988. No other child born to Mrs. Butcher during the marriage. No other child of the marriage.

Marriage unhappy for last few years. Husband has frequently come home drunk. Several assaults on Mrs. Butcher. Constant verbal threats of physical violence. On or about 10th August 1993 Mr. Butcher left and returned to his parents' house, 88 Longsight Road. Mrs. Butcher has remained in the matrimonial home with her son. This is a council house on a weekly tenancy. Rent £22 per week. Mrs. Butcher has no job and receives no money from Mr.

Butcher. Has not paid her a penny since he left. In receipt of income support £62.40 per week, inclusive of rent allowance. No other income except child benefit. The Department of Social Security has arranged for Mrs. Butcher to be sent a maintenance application form with a view to obtaining support for Simon from James Butcher.

Mr. White explains that the firm can give advice and assistance under the Green Form scheme to bring proceedings for the decree, but that she will be acting in person with their help. If Mr. Butcher does not agree arrangements for the care of Simon or the maintenance payments, the firm will be prepared to apply for a full legal aid certificate so that Mrs. Butcher can be legally represented at any hearings that may be necessary (See Legal Aid, Vol. 1, p. 83).

Mr. White completes the Green Form (not reproduced, but *cf.* Vol. 1, p. 80). As Mrs. Butcher has no capital and no income other than the income support, he does not need to refer to the Key Card (Vol. 1, p. 81), which is kept on hand for ready reference in all cases in which the client may be eligible under the Advice and Assistance Regulations. In this case, there are no figures to insert and Mr. White obtains Mrs. Butcher's signature to the form.

Mr. White draws up the petition (D8—not here reproduced, but see petition in *Baker* v. *Baker* above, p. 215). The irretrievable breakdown of the marriage (standard para. (8)) is to be substantiated by proof of ground (*b*) of section 1(2) of the 1973 Act:

> "(10) The respondent has behaved in such a way that the petitioner cannot reasonably be expected to live with the respondent."
>
> The evidence in support of this is given in para. (11):
>
> "(11) PARTICULARS
> (i) From the beginning of 1991 the respondent has frequently drunk to excess and returned home intoxicated late at night. On such occasions he has frequently subjected the petitioner to abuse.
> (ii) In or about May 1991, the respondent returned home from work at 11.30 p.m. He was intoxicated by drink and vomited in the bedroom. He then assaulted the petitioner by beating her about the head with his fists, thereby causing bruising and lacerations.
> (iii) On February 28, 1992 the respondent returned home at 1.00 a.m. He complained to the petitioner that there was no hot meal ready for him to eat and then threw her down the stairs of the matrimonial home.
> (iv) On August 10, 1993 the respondent began to drink alcohol at home whilst watching television. Eventually he became intoxicated and threw a beer bottle at the television set. He then attacked the petitioner with the broken beer bottle causing lacerations to her face and arms. The respondent then left the matrimonial home and has not returned since."

In the prayer the petitioner asks that the marriage be dissolved. Paragraph 3, listing the various forms of ancillary relief, is left in with no deletions. Although not all possible kinds of relief are expected, this will make it possible to ask the court for whatever form of relief may be appropriate without filing a separate formal application. No application for costs is included in the petition.

Mr. White tells Mrs. Butcher that the court will send the petition to her husband with an explanatory notice (Notice of Proceedings, see p. 219 above) and a form on which he can acknowledge service (see p. 221 above). The court will send a copy of this to her with the Directions for Trial (Special Procedure) Form (D.84) which she should pass to the firm.

Mr. White also prepares the following forms:

Statement as to Arrangements for Children (D8A, (pp 240)) Application for Exemption of Fees (D.92, p. 248). It is required by rule 2–2 of the Family Proceedings Rules that the Statement of Arrangements for the Children be agreed with the Respondent. Mr. White, therefore, sends two copies of the Statement of Arrangements to Mr Butcher asking him to sign them in the appropriate section provided in the Forms (see page 247 below) and to return them to Makepiece and Streiff. Mr. Butcher does so.

Mrs. Butcher says she does not have the marriage certificate and agrees to call at the Welbeck Street Registrar's office to obtain one. She is asked to check the particulars carefully with the petition. Any discrepancy must be corrected in the petition. Mr. White hands her two copies of D8A and of the petition and one of D92, all of which she signs. She is asked to take them to the court office with the marriage certificate. There the chief clerk will assign a file number to her case and enter it on the documents. When she receives the respondent's Acknowledgment of Service she is asked to bring this to Mr. White.

On September 28th, Mrs. Butcher brings in the respondent's Acknowledgment of Service—Respondent Spouse (D10(3)) and Mr. White prepares the affidavit by petitioner in support of petition. Of this there are five versions set out in the appendix to the Matrimonial Causes Rules (M.C.R. 7(*a*)–(*e*)), corresponding to the five grounds of breakdown set out on p. 197 above. He uses D80B (not here reproduced, but compare the affidavit in *Baker* v. *Baker* p. 224 above). The only point of substance requiring notice here is the reply to question 4:

4. If you consider that the respondent's behaviour has affected your health, state the affect it has had	On the occasion referred to in paragraph 10(iv) of my petition I received medical treatment.

and the reply to questions 7 and 8

About the children of the family 7. Have you read the Statement of Arrangements filed in this case?	Yes
8. Do you wish to alter anything in the Statement of Arrangements or add to it? If so, state the alterations or additions.	No

Mr. White gives her two copies of the completed form together with the original and a photocopy of the Acknowledgment of Service, signed by her husband. She is asked to take these to the court office where the affidavit will be sworn—as this cannot be done by a solicitor of the firm acting in the case as we noted previously (see p. 223). The court officers will then accept the sworn affidavit for filing and for service on the respondent Mrs. Butcher tells Mr. White that she has received a maintenance application form from the Child Support Officer. This form is to be completed by her and will provide the Child Support Officer with various details he or she needs to obtain child maintenance from Mr. Butcher. She confirms that she has completed the form and has given details of Mr. Butcher's full name, address and age, together with other requested information, to the Child Support Officer. This form is a requirement of the Child Support Act 1991, which is explained more fully on page 270.

Statement of Arrangements for Children
(Form M4, Appendix 1 FPR 1991)

FAMILY PROCEEDINGS RULES
Rule 2.2(2)

In the	BARSET	County Court
Petitioner	JOAN BUTCHER	
Respondent	JAMES BUTCHER	
No. of Matter *(always quote this)*	93D219	

To the Petitioner

You must complete this form
if you or the respondent have any children   ● under 16

or ● over 16 but under 18 if they are at school
or college or are training for a trade,
profession or vocation.

Please use black ink.

Please complete Parts I, II and III.

Before you issue a petition for divorce try to reach agreement with your husband/wife over the proposals for the children's future. There is space for him/her to sign at the end of this form if agreement is reached.

If your husband/wife does not agree with the proposals he/she will have the opportunity at a later stage to state why he/she does not agree and will be able to make his/her own proposals.

You should take or send the completed form, signed by you (and, if agreement is reached, by your husband/wife) together with a copy to the Court when you issue your petition.

Please refer to the explanatory notes issued regarding completion of the prayer of the petition if you are asking the Court to make any order regarding the children.

The Court will only make an order if it considers that an order will be better for the child(ren) than no order.

If you wish to apply for any of the orders which may be available to you under Part I or II of the Children Act 1989 you are advised to see a solicitor.

You should obtain legal advice from a solicitor or, alternatively, from an advice agency. The Law Society administers a national panel of solicitors to represent children and other parties involved in proceedings relating to children. Addresses of solicitors (including panel members) and advice agencies can be obtained from the Yellow Pages and the Solicitors Regional Directory which can be found at Citizens Advice Bureaux, Law Centres and any local library.

To the Respondent

The petitioner has completed Parts I, II and III of this form
which will be sent to the Court at the same time that the divorce petition is filed.

Please read all parts of the form carefully.

If you agree with the arrangements and proposals for the children you should sign Part IV of the form.

Please use black ink. You should return the form to the petitioner, or his/her solicitor.

If you do not agree with all or some of the arrangements or proposals you will be given the opportunity of saying so when the divorce petition is served on you.

1

Part I — Details of the children

Please read the instructions for boxes 1, 2 and 3 before you complete this section

---

1. **Children of both parties**

(Give details only of any children born to you and the Respondent or adopted by you both)

	Forenames	Surname	Date of birth
(i)	SIMON	BUTCHER	28.12.88.
(ii)			
(iii)			
(iv)			
(v)			

---

2. **Other children of the family**

(Give details of any other children treated by both of you as children of the family: for example your own or the Respondent's)

	Forenames	Surname	Date of birth	Relationship to Yourself	Respondent
(i)	NONE				
(ii)					
(iii)					
(iv)					
(v)					

---

3. **Other children who are not children of the family**

(Give details of any children born to you or the Respondent that have not been treated as children of the family or adopted by you both)

	Forenames	Surname	Date of birth
(i)	NONE		
(ii)			
(iii)			
(iv)			
(v)			

2

Part II – Arrangements for the children of the family

This part of the form must be completed. Give details for each child if arrangements are different.
If necessary, continue on another sheet and attach it to this form

4.	Home details *(Please tick the appropriate boxes)*	
	(a) The addresses at which the children now live	7 Westgate Avenue Barset Barsetshire
	(b) Give details of the number of living rooms, bedrooms, etc. at the addresses in (a)	A 3 bedroomed semi detached council house with two reception rooms, a kitchen and separate bathroom and toilet. The child has his own bedroom.
	(c) Is the house rented or owned and by whom? Is the rent or any mortgage being regularly paid?	The house is owned by Barset Council of the Town Hall, Barset and rented by the petition from the council. ☐ No ☑ Yes
	(d) Give the names of all other persons living with the children including your husband/wife if he/she lives there. State their relationship to the children.	None.
	(e) Will there be any change in these arrangements?	☑ No ☐ Yes *(please give details)*

3

5.	**Education and training details** *(Please tick the appropriate boxes)*	
	(a) Give the names of the school, college or place of training attended by each child.	The child attends St Andrews Primary School, St Andrews Avenue, Barset.
	(b) Do the children have any special educational needs?	☑ No ☐ Yes *(please give details)*
	(c) Is the school, college or place of training, fee-paying?	☑ No ☐ Yes *(please give details of how much the fees are per term/year)*
	Are fees being regularly paid?	☐ No ☐ Yes *(please give details)*
	(d) Will there be any change in these arrangements?	☐ No ☑ Yes *(please give details)* It is intended that on reaching 11 years of age the child will attend Barset Comprehensive School.

6.	**Childcare details** *(Please tick the appropriate boxes)*	
	(a) Which parent looks after the children from day to day? If responsibility is shared, please give details.	The Petitioner.
	(b) Does that parent go out to work?	☑ No ☐ Yes *(please give details of his/her hours of work)*
	(c) Does someone look after the children when the parent is not there?	☐ No ☐ Yes *(please give details)* Not applicable
	(d) Who looks after the children during school holidays?	The Petitioner.
	(e) Will there be any change in these arrangements?	☑ No ☐ Yes *(please give details)*

7.	**Maintenance** *(Please tick the appropriate boxes)*	
	(a) Does your husband/wife pay towards the upkeep of the children? If there is another source of maintenance, please specify.	☑ No ☐ Yes *(please give details of how much)*
	(b) Is the payment made under a court order?	☑ No ☐ Yes *(please give details, including the name of the court and case number)*
	(c) Has maintenance for the children been agreed?	☑ No ☐ Yes
	If not, will you be applying for a maintenance order for the children?	☐ No ☑ Yes *(please give details)* The Petitioner has applied for a maintenance order under the Child Support Act 1991 through the Child Support Officer at the Department of Social Security Barset – matter ref no. BR/1679.

8.	**Details for contact with the children** *(Please tick the appropriate boxes)*

(a) Do the children see your husband/wife?	☑ No ☐ Yes *(please give details of how often and where)*

(b) Do the children ever stay with your husband/wife?	☑ No ☐ Yes *(please give details of how much)*

(c) Will there be any change to these arrangements? Please give details of the proposed arrangements for contact and residence.	☑ No ☐ Yes *(please give details of how much)* The Petitioner has no objection to the Respondent maintaining regular contact with the child.

9.	**Details of health** *(Please tick the appropriate boxes)*		
	(a) Are the children generally in good health?	☑ Yes	☐ No *(please give details of any serious disability or chronic illness)*
	(b) Do the children have any special health needs?	☑ No	☐ Yes *(please give details of the care needed and how it is to be provided)*

10.	**Details of care and other court proceedings** *(Please tick the appropriate boxes)*		
	(a) Are the children in the care of a local authority, or under the supervision of a social worker or probation officer?	☑ No	☐ Yes *(please give details including any court proceedings)*
	(b) Are any of the children on the Child Protection Register?	☑ No	☐ Yes *(please give details of the local authority and the date of registration)*
	(c) Are there or have there been any proceedings in any Court involving the children, for example adoption, custody/residence, access/contact wardship, care, supervision or maintenance?	☑ No	☐ Yes *(please give details and send a copy of any order to the Court)*

Part III – To the Petitioner

Conciliation

If you and your husband/wife do not agree about the arrangements for the child(ren), would you agree to discuss the matter with a Conciliator and your husband/wife?

☐ No   ☑ Yes

Declaration

I declare that the information I have given is correct and complete to the best of my knowledge.

Signed   *Joan Butcher*   (Petitioner)

Date: 8 September 1993

Part IV – To the Respondent

I agree with the arrangements and proposals contained in Part I and II of this form.

Signed   *James Butcher*   (Respondent)

Date: 6th September 1993

8

OYEZ The Solicitors' Law Stationery Society Ltd, Oyez House, 7 Spa Road, London SE16 3QQ

1991 Edition
6.92 F22621

Divorce 8

5046127

★ ★ ★ ★ ★

Application for exemption of fees in Matrimonial Proceedings

MATRIMONIAL CAUSES RULES

IN THE   BARSET   **COUNTY COURT***

~~**DIVORCE REGISTRY***~~

Delete and/or complete as appropriate

No. of matter   93D219

Between   JOAN BUTCHER   Petitioner

and   JAMES BUTCHER   Respondent

~~and~~   ~~Co-Respondent~~

I apply for exemption from any fee payable in these matrimonial proceedings on the following ground(s) ([1]):

([1]) Delete whichever is inappropriate

A. ~~that I am currently in receipt of Income Support/Family Credit ([1]). The address of the local office of the Department of Health and Social Security dealing with the matter is:~~

~~and the reference number is:~~

~~I agree that the court may ask that office to confirm that I am in receipt of Income Support/Family Credit ([1]).~~

B. that I am receiving legal advice and assistance from a solicitor under the Legal Aid Act 1988. The name, address and telephone number of his firm are:

    Makepiece & Streiff, Bank Chambers, Barset.
    Tel: Barset (00765) 4321

and his firm's reference number is: PF/WW/OBE

I agree that the court may ask my solicitor to confirm that I am receiving legal advice and assistance under the Legal Aid Act 1988.

Date: 8th September 1993   Signature: *Joan Butcher*

                                          Petitioner acting in person.

TO BE COMPLETED BY THE COURT

Signed:

Date:

                        (Senior officer not below the rank of Executive Officer.)

Mr. White later hears from the client:

MAKEPIECE & STREIFF
ATTENDANCE NOTE

~~INTERVIEW~~/TEL.CALL.		DATE:	14.10.93
WITH:	Mrs. J. Butcher	OF:	—
TAKEN BY:	WW	TIME:	2.35–2.50

Mrs. Butcher telephoned. She has Directions for District Judge's disposal on 27.10.93. Has letter from Rimes (ref.NW/O) Residence and Contact arrangements for Simon agreed. She has been informed by the Child Support Officer that a maintenance order in respect of Simon has been made by the Child Support Agency in the sum of £40 per week. The first payment is due to be made on October 25, 1992.

Appointment made for Friday 5th November at 11.30 re application for personal maintenance.

On November 5, Mrs. Butcher keeps her appointment bringing her papers, including the decree nisi (D29B), the certificate of satisfaction in respect of children of the Family (D84B p. 250) and the letter dated October 13 from Messrs. Rime (p. 251).

It is apparent from the letter that no offer of maintenance for Mrs. Butcher will be forthcoming without an application and that this will be likely to be resisted. Mrs. Butcher will, therefore, need to be legally represented and Mr. White makes out Legal Aid Form A2 (Matrimonial) and the accompanying CLA 4A Financial Application Form for submission to the appropriate Legal Aid Board Area Office. Mrs. Butcher signs both forms and Mr. White tells her that, when the certificate is issued by the Legal Aid Board, they will send a copy direct to her as well as sending the original certificate and one copy to Messrs. Makepiece. Mr. White says he will be in touch with her when the certificate is issued. This is received in due course, dated December 2, (p. 252) [Please note that the Legal Aid Board's Standard wording on the certificate regarding ancillary relief has now been amended following the implementation of the Child Support Act 1991] and Messrs. Makepiece write to their client the next day (p. 253). Note that if Mrs. Butcher were employed, the Legal Aid Board would also require a completed Form L17 (Statement of Earnings by Present Employer) signed by her employer, before deciding whether to grant her Legal Aid.

250

Family Practice

<table>
<tr><td>**In the**</td><td style="text-align:center">BARSET</td><td style="text-align:right">**County Court**</td></tr>
</table>

No of matter   93D219

Between   JOAN BUTCHER   Petitioner

and

                 JAMES BUTCHER   Respondent

and   Co-respondentXXXXXXXX

Certificate of satisfaction in respect of children of the family   *F.P. Rule 2.39(2)*

The Court certifies that it is satisfied that

[there are no children of the family to whom section 41 of the Matrimonial Causes Act 1973 applies]

[there are children of the family, namely

Simon Butcher

to whom section 41 of the Matrimonial Causes Act 1973 applies

but that the Court does not need to exercise its powers under the Children Act 1989

with respect to any of them

or give any direction under section 41(2) of the Matrimonial Causes Act 1973]

Date: 27th October 1993
           C Beckford
           District Judge.

If you write to the Court please address your letters to "The Chief Clerk"
and quote the **No of the matter** at the top of this form.

The Court office is at

and is open from 10am to 4pm on Monday to Friday.

Dd 8252454 117M 9/91 Ed(293116)

D84B

RIME & REASON, Solicitors

C. Reason	Invicta House	
N. Wisdom, BA.	Market Street	Tel. 00765 1234
R. E. Verse	BARSET	

Your Ref

Our Ref:　　NW/CFA/60　　　　　　　　　　　　　13th October 1993

Mrs. J. Butcher,
7 Westgate Avenue,
Barset.

Dear Madam,

Butcher v. Butcher

We have been instructed to act for the respondent, Mr. Butcher, in this matter. Our client has instructed us to confirm that he has no objection to Simon residing with you, neither does he object to any of the proposals made by you in your Statement of Arrangements.

However, our client would like contact with the child as suggested by you in the Statement of Arrangements. If you agree, our client would like to see Simon on Saturday afternoon each week from about 2.00pm to 6.00pm.

Our client instructs us that he has co-operated fully with the Child Support Officer at Barset DSS, and that a child maintenance order has been made in respect of Simon in the sum of £40 per week payable as from October 25, 1993.

Subject to your client's agreement for the contact arrangements, our client would like to commence seeing Simon on Saturday October 23.

We would be obliged if you would confirm your agreement with the above proposals regarding Simon.

Your faithfully,

(Signed)

Rime & Reason.

LEGAL AID ACT 1988
LEGAL AID CERTIFICATE

Reference 92/A/70/998   Solrs' A/C No. 349   Case Code 4

Assisted person

JOAN BUTCHER
7 WESTGATE AVENUE
BARSET
BARSETSHIRE

This certificate is financially connected with

Linked or
overlapped   Reference No. (This is not the reference number of this present certificate which appears on the top left hand corner of this form)

This is to certify that the above-named has been granted legal aid as specified below subject to the conditions and limitations (if any) specified below and the requirement as to contribution.

1. Description of legal aid

To be represented in divorce proceedings only as to ancillary relief (other than avoidance of disposition or variation unless the application is made before final decree) including the registration of an order in a magistrates court.

2. Conditions and limitations (if any)

Limited to securing one substantive order only.

Contribution to be paid. A determination of financial resources has been made as follows:-

Disposable Income £ Nil   Disposable Capital £ Nil   Maximum Contribution £ Nil

The Payable
Contribution is £   payable by   monthly instalments of   then   of £

4. The solicitor is   PHILIP FRIENDLY   Signed D. Reache
   Reference   NW/CPA/60   Address AREA 10 HOUSE
                                                            LUCREVILLE
                                                            BARSETSHIRE

MAKEPIECE & STREIFF
BANK CHAMBERS
BARSET

Authorised Signatory Legal Aid Area No. 20   10

Date 2nd December 1993

April 1989   'TO BE FILED WITH COURT'   Oyez Press Ltd

MAKEPIECE & STREIFF

<u>Solicitors</u>

Clement Amity
Anthony Adverse

Bank Chambers
Barset
Tel: 00765 4321

Ref: PF/WW/JHK/O

3rd   December
1993.

Mrs. J. Butcher,
7 Westgate Avenue,
Barset.

Dear Mrs. Butcher,

<u>Your Divorce</u>

I have no doubt that you have received a copy of the certificate granted by the Legal Aid Board for the proceedings against your husband to recover proper maintenance payments for yourself. I am now able to file the necessary application and serve it on your husband's solicitors. Following this, it will be for the respondent to give full information as to his means in an affidavit which his solicitors will file in court. When I have a copy of this, I will consult you about your reply, which will also be by an affidavit. There will be a hearing before the District Judge, when you and the respondent will have to attend and be prepared to answer questions about your position. I will write to you again about this.

May I remind you that application for the decree nisi to be made absolute may be made when the six weeks period expires on 8th December. I am enclosing the form you will need,* for your signature. Please send this to the Chief Clerk, Barset County Court, 20 River Street, on or after that date. You will then receive the Certificate making the decree nisi absolute and I would ask you to let me know when you have it.

Your faithfully,

(Signed)

MAKEPIECE & STREIFF

---

* Not reproduced, but *cf.* p. 230, above

The Legal Aid Board

LEGAL AID ACT 1988

NOTICE OF ISSUE OF CERTIFICATE

No.   93D219

In the   BARSET   COUNTY COURT

| ~~Division~~

Between   JOAN BUTCHER   ~~Plaintiff~~ |Petitioner|

and

JAMES BUTCHER   ~~Defendant~~ |Respondent|

TAKE notice that ~~an Emergency~~| |a legal Aid| Certificate No.   93/A/70/9298

dated the   2nd   day of   December   19 93 has been issued in Area No.   10

to   JOAN BUTCHER

in connection with the following proceedings:—

To be represented in divorce proceedings only as to ancillary relief
(other than avoidance of disposition or variation unless the
application is made before final decree) including the registration
of an order in a magistrates court.

TAKE further notice that, in consequence thereof, the

in these proceedings is and has been from that date an assisted person.

Dated this   3rd   day of   December   19~~9~~3.

(Signed) Makepiece & Streiff

of   MAKEPIECE & STREIFF   BANK CHAMBERS BARSET

Solicitor for   THE PETITIONER

To   The court and the Respondent.

Notice of Acting/Change

MATRIMONIAL CAUSES RULES
*Complete and/or delete as appropriate

IN THE   BARSET   COUNTY COURT

~~DIVORCE REGISTRY~~

No. of Matter   92D219

Between   JOAN BUTCHER   Petitioner

and

~~and~~   JAMES BUTCHER   Respondent

~~Co-respondent~~

TAKE NOTICE that I/we   MAKEPIECE & STREIFF

of   BANK CHAMBERS BARSET

(¹) have been appointed to act as the Solicitor of the above-named Petitioner

(¹) [limited for the following purposes:—

(¹) Delete whichever is not appropriate and if limited set out the limitations (as in the civil aid certificate).

    to be represented in divorce proceedings only as ancillary relief (other than avoidance of disposition or variation unless application is made before final decree) including the registration of an order in an magistrates court.

~~(¹) [generally in the place of~~

....

~~(¹) [intend to act in person in this cause.]~~ ---

My/Our address for service is   BANK CHAMBERS BARSET

Dated this   3rd   day of   December   19 93

To the above-named   Respondent   (Signed) *Makepiece & Streiff*

or h is   Solicitor

                    Solicitor for the   Petitioner

Address all communications to:
    THE DISTRICT JUDGE, THE COUNTY COURT 20 RIVER STREET BARSET.

~~for to the Divorce Registry, Somerset House, Strand, London WC2R 1LP)~~ quoting the number in the top right-hand corner of this form. The Court Office is open from 10 a.m. till 4 p.m. ~~(4.30 p.m. at the Divorce Registry)~~ on Mondays to Fridays only.

In the   BARSET   **County Court.**   No.   93D219   of 19

Between   JOAN BUTCHER   Petitioner

and   JAMES BUTCHER   Respondent

and   Co-Respondent XXXXXXXXXXXXXX

I   JAMES BUTCHER

of   80 LONGSIGHT ROAD BARSET IN THE COUNTY OF BARSETSHIRE

make oath and say that the answers to the questions below are true to the best of my knowledge information and belief and that they are a full and accurate statement of my means.
Save as set out in the said answers I have no capital or income.

1) What is your present occupation?   Welder
   If you are not now employed, give details of your last
   employment and any trade or professional qualifications.

2) What is your current gross income from:—

   a)   your employment, trade or profession

         (i)   normal   £175   per year (month) (week)

         (ii) overtime or other special receipts   per year (month) (week)

   b)   pension or annuities   )
)
   c)   interest on bank savings deposits   )
)
   d)   building society interest   )   None
)
   e)   dividends   )
)
   f)   any other source   )

   (So far as possible show all receipts in respect of the same
   period of time: i.e. give all weekly, all monthly or all annual
   amounts. Show all receipts as gross amounts before deduction
   of tax where possible: where not possible, indicate that the
   amount shown is the net amount received.)

   Do you receive any benefits in kind, such as free accommodation,   No
   use of car, etc? If so, give details

3) What National Insurance contributions are paid by you?   £14.20   per week

4) Are there any, and if so what, other expenses, which are
   necessary to enable you to earn the income set out above?
                                                               No

5) a)   What was your gross taxable income during the last complete
         tax year (6 April to 5 April) from your employment, trade   £8,800
         or profession including overtime or other special
         payments and taxable benefits?
   b)   What was your Income Tax liability during the   £ 240
         last complete tax year?

   (Where figures for the last complete tax year are not available, give them
   for the last year for which they are available. In the case of a fluctuating
   income give also the figures for two or more preceding years.)

D. 75 – Affidavit of Means.

1

6) What do you claim to be your necessary expenses of providing yourself with a place to live in, such as rent, rates, water rate, mortgage interest and re-payments, premium on endowment insurance used as a collateral, etc? £120

7) What maintenance payments (if any) do you make to or receive from your (former) wife/husband including any payments to or for any child and including school fees?

£40 per week to my child Simon Butcher as assessed by the Child Support Officer.

8) Are any payments to which question 7 refers made

   a) under a court order (give Court, date and details of order)

   b) under an enforceable agreement (give date and details)

   c) voluntarily?

   Under a Maintenance Assessment (as required by the Child Support Act 1991).

9) What payments (if any) do you receive from the Department of Health and Social Security by way of supplementary pension or supplementary allowance?

   None   per week

10) What family allowance (if any) do you receive for a child or children?

   None   per week

11) Was the former matrimonial home

   a) rented   Yes

   b) owned   (i) by you   No

               (ii) your (former) husband/wife

               (iii) jointly by you and your (former) husband/wife?

12) a) Is the former matrimonial home still occupied by you or your (former) wife/husband or by both of you?

   By my wife

   b) If it is owned by you or your (former) husband/wife or by you both jointly, at what do you estimate its present value?

   c) Is it subject to mortgage? If so, give details of the mortgage, including the rate of any re-payment, the amount outstanding and the date at which re-payment will be completed.

   If there is any collateral security in the form of an endowment assurance, state the surrender value of the policy.

13) Do you own any car(s)?   ~~Yes~~/No

If yes, what is its (their) make, model and year of manufacture
and what do you estimate its (their) present value?

14) What other assets do you have, such as cash at bank, savings bank accounts,   None
premium savings bonds, building society account, stock and shares,
reversionary interests, etc.? (give details and present value).

Include any house property owned or in which you have any interest,
jointly held property and articles of substantial value
such as jewellery or furniture.

15) a) Apart from any liability set out in the answers to questions 8 and 12   None
what other unpaid debts are at present due and payable by you
including hire purchase debts?

Also give particulars of any judgments against you.

b) Do you have any life or endowment assurance policy other than   £680
any set out in the answers to question 6? If so, give details
including amount of annual premium and date of maturity.   Annual premium £5

Date of maturity 2008

16) *(to be answered only by respondents to applicants for financial provision)*

If a decree absolute has been made, have you re-married?   No

If a decree has not been pronounced or made absolute, do you   Yes
intend to re-marry if one is made?

Do you provide for your wife/husband on re-marriage or will you   Yes
provide for your intended wife/husband by way of
accommodation, living expenses or otherwise?

Do you provide for any other person? If so, give particulars   No

In either case, has the wife/husband, intended wife/husband   No
or other person any means?
If so, state briefly what they are.

3

17) Are you a member of any pension or superannuation scheme
(other than State Insurance)?   Y̶e̶s̶/No

   a)   give details

   b)   would your (former) husband/wife have been entitled to any benefits
at your death in the absence of a decree absolute?   Y̶e̶s̶/No

18) Is, to your knowledge, your husband/wife a member of any
such scheme?   Y̶e̶s̶/No/D̶o̶n̶'̶t̶ ̶k̶n̶o̶w̶ x

If so, do you think you will lose any benefits by reason of
a decree absolute, and if so, what?

19) Is there any other reason which you wish to urge against paying
maintenance or are there any other matters which you wish
to raise in connection with this application?

If I am to remarry, I simply cannot afford to pay anything to my former wife.

Sworn at BARSET COUNTY COURT in the)

County of   BARSETSHIRE   )   *J. Bulcher*

this 12th day of January 1994   )

Before me

      Officer of a Court, appointed by the Judge to take Affidavits.

      This affidavit is filed on behalf of the Respondent.

Continue on next page if necessary

Mr. White prepares the Notice of Intention to Proceed with Application for Ancillary Relief made in Petition or Answer (D43, p. 261), the Notice of Acting/Change (D94, p. 255), notifying the court that Messrs. Makepiece are now acting for Mrs. Butcher, so that their name will be on the court record. He also prepares the Notice of Issue of Legal Aid Certificate (Legal Aid Act 1988, Form 1, p. 254), to be served on the respondent through their solicitors, Messrs. Rime, and a copy for the court.

Mr. White sends two copies of the application form D43, the court fee on the application, the D94, the Legal Aid Certificate and a copy of the Notice of Issue of Legal Aid Certificate to the court where the court clerk inserts January 26, 1994 as the date for the hearing of the application by the registrar. Having paid the fee and sent to the court D94, the Legal Aid Certificate and notice and the two copies of the D43, Mr. White receives back one copy of the latter, impressed with the court's seal for service on the respondent. Copies of all the forms are kept on the file.

Mr. White then posts the sealed D43 to Messrs. Rime with a copy of the Legal Aid Notice and a short covering letter. Mr. White writes to Mrs. Butcher to tell her that the hearing is on January 26, 1994 when she must attend, but that in the meantime he will be contacting her when Mr. Butcher' Affidavit of Means is received.

On December 14, 1993, Mr. White hears from Mrs. Butcher on the telephone that the Certificate making the Decree Nisi Absolute has arrived. On January 6, 1994, he receives from Messrs. Rime the respondent's Affidavit of Means (D.75, p. 256) and writes to arrange an interview and Mrs. Butcher on Tuesday, January 14th.

At this interview Mr. White takes Mrs. Butcher through the respondent's Affidavit of Means. She does not dispute his income figure, but asserts that the figure of £120 per week for his personal needs is high. She also queries his answer to question (19), as she thinks he has a duty to her and Simon. Mr. White confirms that this is so and asks if she knows whether he is living with another woman. Mrs. Butcher says that she believes he is living with someone else, but she does not know whom. Mr. White tells her that the court must have regard to what is practicable for him. There is little point in obtaining an order likely to lead to difficult enforcement problems. He thinks the answer to question (19) in his affidavit can safely be left to Mr. Friendly, who will appear for her on January 26th.

Mr. White prepares her affidavit in reply using the same form, D75 (not here reproduced) showing that her only income is from income support, now £16–55, the child maintenance order of £40, child benefit, £9–65 and one parent benefit £5–85 per week. He asks her to take the affidavit to the Court Offices and swear it before the officer appointed for this purpose, then to return it to him for filing at the court and service on the respondent's solicitors.

On this occasion, Mrs. Butcher has with her the Decree Absolute, to show to Mr. White and he asks her to keep this safely as she will need it if she should ever want to remarry.

No: 93D219

Between .... JOAN BUTCHER .... Petitioner

and .... JAMES BUTCHER .... Respondent

The Petitioner   JOAN BUTCHER   having applied in her
Petition for   Financial provision for herself

TAKE NOTICE that the application will be heard by the   District Judge in Chambers

at   The County Court 20 River Street Barset

on   Tuesday   the   26th day of   January   19 94 , at 10.00   o'clock.
on

TAKE NOTICE ALSO that you must send to the /District Judge so as to reach him within 28 days
after you receive this notice, an affidavit giving full particulars of your property and income. You must at the
same time send a copy of your affidavit to the Solicitor for the Petitioner
at the address below. A standard form of affidavit is available from the Court Office.

If you wish to allege that the Petitioner   JOAN BUTCHER   has property or income,
you should say so in your affidavit.

.... 30 .... minutes

Dated   3rd December   1993

Signed ...... *Natgerere & Steir* ....

Solicitors for Petitioner
of ....   BANK CHAMBERS BARSET ....

....

Address all communications to the Chief Clerk AND QUOTE THE ABOVE CASE NUMBER.

The Court Office at   THE COUNTY COURT 20 RIVER STREET BARSET

is open from 10 a.m. till 4 p.m. on Mondays to Fridays only.

Notice of intention to Proceed with Application for Ancilliary Relief made in Petition or Answer.

D43
MCR 361417/1/F24838 1m 11/85 TL

Butcher v. *Butcher* continued

Finally, he asks Mrs. Butcher to arrive at the court on January 26, at about 9.30 a.m. to allow half an hour in which Mr. Friendly can discuss any points on the two affidavits with her. It is possible, he suggests, that Mr. Friendly may be approached by the respondent's representative to see whether agreement can be reached on a figure of maintenance to be paid by him. Any such discussion would be "without prejudice," *i.e.* off the record so that, if agreement is not reached is not reached, the parties are free to proceed.

On January 26, Mrs. Butcher is met in the corridor outside the district judges' room by Mr. Friendly. Mr. Reason is also there and is joined shortly after by Mr. Butcher. After a while, the solicitors greet each other and stand apart for a discussion. No suggestion for an agreed settlement is put up by either, but it is made clear that the income figures are mutually accepted. Mr. Friendly, however, warns Mr. Reason of his intention to question the figure of £120 per week for the respondent's outgoings. Mr. Reason says he has the details and will be prepared to present them in court.

The case is called before district Judge Fairweather and is opened by Mr. Friendly.

Mr. Friendly: Sir, I represent the applicant and Mr. Reason is for the respondent. The applicant applies for periodical payments for herself. The Child Support Officer at Barset DSS has dealt with maintenance for the child Simon, and an order in the sum of £40 per week has been made and paid as from October 25, 1992. However, no agreement has been possible regarding maintenance for the applicant. There is no dispute regarding the respondent's income, as set out in his affidavit of means, but I must call on Mr. Reason to justify his figure of £120 per week as the respondent's personal needs.

District Judge: Before I deal with that point, will you give me a moment to read the affidavits?

After reading both affidavits, the district judge inquires of Mr. Reason whether he has the details of how the figure of £120 is made up.

Mr. Reason: I have Sir. Since leaving the applicant, the respondent has set up a new home for himself and the lady with whom he is living and whom he wishes to marry. His lady friend is unable to work as she has a child of her own, a boy of five years. She is divorced and has had social security benefits, but the DSS refuse to make any payments to her since she has lived with the respondent. The Child Support Agency has attempted to trace her former husband but so far, has failed to find him. Accordingly, no child maintenance is being paid. Once the respondent has paid the maintenance of £40 due for Simon, he only has £120 left out of his net income of £160 per week. This is all used on day to day living expenses.

District Judge: Give me the details of how the £120 figure is made up.

Mr. Reason: Yes, Sir.

He hands to the district judge a statement and passes a copy to Mr. Friendly:

Rent and council tax	£37.55
Household heat, light, etc.	14.00
Hire purchase of furniture for new home	23.55
Available for food and other living expenses	45.00
	£120.00

District Judge: Mr. Friendly, are you prepared to accept these figures as a true statement of the position?

Mr. Friendly, after briefly referring to his client sitting behind him: Yes, Sir. We have no reason to question them. I would only point out that the hire purchase commitment must be a recent one which the respondent must have undertaken with full knowledge of his liability to the applicant. Mr. Butcher's cohabitee will receive child benefit of £9.65 per week, which will add to the respondent's new family total income. I would also need to ask whether the respondent is due for a wage award in the near future.

District Judge, to Mr. Reason: Can you help on this?

Mr. Reason, after speaking to the respondent: I understand that a national agreement has been reached which will give the respondent an increase of 12 per cent. from January 1, next.

District Judge: If these figures are accepted Mr. Friendly and you have no other points to raise, I assume that it will not be necessary for me to hear oral evidence.

Mr. Friendly: The applicant does not dispute the figures you have been given and I have no other matters of evidence to submit, Sir.

District Judge: Very well. May I take it that the only dispute in this case concerns the amount of any order I may make?

Both solicitors: Yes Sir.

District Judge: Very well. Would you give me a moment to examine the new figures?

After examining the figures,

District Judge: Mr. Reason, your client's new income will be in the region of £200 per week.

Mr. Reason: Yes, Sir, but tax and national insurance will account for part of that, perhaps £35.

District Judge: Yes, but he will not suffer tax on the entire amount I award. (Tax relief up to a maximum of £1,720 is available to Mr. Butcher on maintenance payments to a former spouse.) Once he marries his cohabitee, he will again be able to claim a married persons tax allowance and this will reduce his tax bill.

Mr. Reason: Yes, Sir.

District Judge: Mr. Friendly, will you proceed?

Mr. Friendly: In the light of the figures which my friend has presented today, of which, of course, my client has had no previous intimation, I would ask you to make an order for £40, this being less than 1/3 of the joint gross incomes of the parties, but taking into account that the child maintenance order of £40 does contain an allowance for the applicant as carer of the child. My client has the utmost difficulty in making ends meet on the payments she is getting now from the Social Security Office and the only part of that she will retain is the Child Benefit and one parent benefit, totalling £15.50 per week. The respondent has somewhat rashly undertaken hire purchase and these payments will, in any case, come to an end in time. The fact that he is now supporting another family does not relieve him of the obligations he freely entered into to his former wife and son. That is all, Sir.

District Judge: Thank you, Mr. Reason.

Mr. Reason: An order of £40 would make it very hard for my client to cover the bare essentials of living of his new family. He would suffer considerable hardship. My friend has referred to the applicant's difficulties, but he did not take into account the rent and council tax rebates she can draw. Additionally, when the Child Support Officer made the assessment of £40 per week for Simon, she will, in using the formula laid down by the Child Support Act 1991, have included provision for Mrs. Butcher as the parent with care. Therefore, the £40 per week child maintenance being paid by my client, contains an element of maintenance for the applicant. The hire-purchase commitments are no more than the amount required for the basic requirements of the home and will continue for more than two years. Whilst my client's income is to go up, the increase no more than covers the increase in the cost of living in the last 12 months and he will be no better off. I ask you, Sir, to make an order of no more than £10 per week.

District Judge: If that is all?

Both solicitors: Yes, Sir.

District Judge: If as suggested by the Court of Appeal in *Wachtel* v. *Wachtel* and other cases, in arriving at a figure for the maintenance of the applicant, I were to take as a starting point one-third of the joint income of the parties, that would give a figure of about £60, since I am not permitted to take the applicant's income support into account. Having regard to the subsistence needs of the respondent and his new family, which I cannot ignore, however, and bearing in mind that the respondent's income is not a very high one, I consider than an order as high as this, as suggested by the applicant would be too high. A more appropriate figure would be £15. This will mean that the applicant will still be able to claim Income Support and qualify for passport benefits and free school meals. She will also qualify for full Housing Benefit and Council Tax rebate. There will therefore be an order for periodical payments to the applicant at the rate of £15 per week, payable weekly. Do you want leave to register the order in the magistrates' court, Mr. Friendly?

Mr. Friendly: If you please.

District Judge: Very well. Leave to register in the magistrates' court.

As he is speaking these words he is endorsing the papers to the effect of the orders he is making. Following the hearing, Mr. White receives the order in the post from the court (p. 265).

<u>MATRIMONIAL CAUSES RULES—ORDER</u>

In the   BARSET COUNTY COURT   No. 93D219

BETWEEN   JOAN BUTCHER   Petitioner

AND   JAMES BUTCHER   Respondent

ORDER

UPON HEARING the solicitors for the petition and the respondent and upon reading the affidavit of the petitioner sworn on the 17 day of January 1994 and the affidavit of the respondent sworn on the 12 January 1994.

IT IS ORDERED:—

1. That the abovenamed respondent to pay or cause to be paid to the above-named petition from the 31 January 1994 periodical payments for herself during their joint lives until the petitioner remarries or until further order at the rate of £15 per week payable weekly in advance.

2. That the prayer in the petition for a lump sum and property adjustment and all the applications in form 11 by the respondent shall stand dismissed.

3. Liberty to each party to apply.

4. That there be leave to register the order in the appropriate Magistrates' Court.

5. That there be a legal aid taxation of the petitioners costs.

Dated this 26 day of January 1994

Signed ....

Stuart Fairweather
District Judge.

All communications to the Chief Clerk, County Court, Barset,
20 River Street, Barset, Barsetshire.

Legal Aid

The difference between the full legal aid certificate (covering the whole costs of bringing or defending proceedings, including representation in court) on the one hand and the Green Form Scheme (covering legal advice and assistance given mainly in the solicitors' office) on the other is explained above (Vol. 1, Legal Aid, p. 76). As Mrs. Butcher's case illustrates, the legal aid certificate is not generally available in undefended divorce, but only where arrangements for the children or financial matters are in dispute. A certificate can be applied for on these matters or where the petition is defended or in any of the other matrimonial causes listed on page 2 of the Form A2 (Matrimonial).

Initially Mrs. Butcher is assisted under the Green Form Scheme, which enables the solicitor to give advice and assistance there and then, without reference to the Legal Aid Board. In her case there was no question about her eligibility because she was receiving income support. There was no need therefore, to make a calculation by reference to the Key Card. Mr. White was able to advise on what courses were open to

Mrs. Butcher and the legal consequences of a decree, to draft the documents for the petition and to guide her on the procedural steps. In effect, the client is expected to act as a litigant in person—the solicitor's name does not appear on the court record.

The solicitor acting will keep in mind the limit of costs that can be incurred in matrimonial matters under the Scheme and may write to the Area Director requesting the lifting of the limit where necessary, giving the reasons for the excess costs. When Mrs. Butcher's decree absolute is issued and Messrs. Makepiece have completed their work under the Scheme, they will make a claim for their fees on the reverse of the Green Form which, together with all other green forms claims for other clients will be sent to the Area Legal Aid Office at the end of the month.

In *Butcher* v. *Butcher*, the respondent's refusal to make any offer of maintenance payments for the petitioner made this a contentious issue for which a legal aid certificate could be granted. Messrs. Makepiece accordingly made application to the Area Legal Aid Office on Form A2. This includes, the Form L1, Applicants Statement of Circumstances, which, when the Form CLA 44 is received by the Legal Aid Board, is sent on to the Department of Social Security where an assessment officer determines the applicant's disposable capital, disposable income and maximum contribution. When, as here, the applicant is receiving income support, it is only necessary to check that this benefit is being received.

This being the case with Mrs. Butcher, the certificate was issued directly by the Legal Aid Board.

If the applicant's circumstances require that a contribution be made, the amount (up to the maximum assessed by the assessment officer) is fixed by the Legal Aid Board. A contribution from capital will usually be payable immediately. From income, it will be by instalments over up to 12 months.

As Mrs. Butcher was not asked to pay a contribution, the certificate (Form 2) was issued immediately. Had a contribution been payable, she would first have received Form 1(2) setting out an offer with particulars of the amount of the contribution and the method of payment. The applicant has 28 days in which to accept and give an undertaking to pay, or alternatively to refuse the certificate. On acceptance, the Legal Aid Board will issue the certificate on Form 1(1) which gives particulars of the agreed contribution.

Where the application for a certificate is refused the applicant has a right of appeal to the area committee.

When a certificate is issued, it is the responsibility of the assisted person's solicitor to serve a notice of the certificate on all other parties. He must also, as we saw, send a copy of the notice by prepaid post to the court office or registry.

Children

The Children Act 1989

Students should note that the law relating to children is now extremely complex, (particularly in relation to the powers of the local authority in relation to children) and is outside the scope of this book. However, the Act has had an important effect upon divorce procedure and the orders which can be made in respect of children upon divorce.

The Children Act 1989 bought in a concept which is known as "Non-intervention principle". Section 1(5) provides:—

"Where a court is considering whether or not to make one or more orders under this Act with respect to a child, it shall not make the order, or any of the orders, unless it considers that doing so would be better for the child than making no order at all."

In determining the child's interest, the court is required to bear in mind that the child's welfare is the court's paramount consideration. The Act makes it clear that the court should not interfere with unnecessary court orders where a child has a satisfactory relationship with its parents.

In a divorce where there are children, such as the case of Joan Butcher, when the District Judge is at the stage of entering the matter in the special procedure list and granting the certificate confirming the petitioner is entitled to a decree, he or she will also consider matters relating to any children concerned in the divorce. The District Judge will base his or her decision upon the contents of the Statement of Arrangements for the children in form M4. In the Joan Butcher divorce there are no applications pending for any order in relation to the child Simon Butcher (if there were, then the matter would be dealt with by a separate procedure which is outside the scope of this book).

In a case where there are no disputes or applications pending in relation to a child, the District Judge will consider the position regarding the children as is required by s.41 of the Matrimonial Causes Act 1973. The District Judge will take various steps:—

1. The District Judge will check whether there are any children of the family who are under 16 and also whether there are any children of 16 or over to whom he or she should direct that s.41 should apply. These latter children can be described as "special cases."
2. Where the District Judge is satisfied that there are no children of the family under 16 and no children of the family of 16 or over who are not "special cases," then the District Judge will certify that there are no children within s.41 of the Matrimonial Causes Act requiring the court's consideration.
3. Where there are children of the family who are under 16, or who are "special cases," the District Judge must then consider whether to exercise any of the powers under the Children Act 1989 or whether to give any directions under the Children Act with regard to them. If the District Judge is satisfied that neither of these courses of action are necessary, then the District Judge will give a certificate that he/she is satisfied that there is no need for the court to exercise its powers under the Children Act. Copies of this certificate will be sent to both the petitioner and the respondent.
4. If the District Judge is not prepared to give the certificate mentioned in paragraph 3 above, he/she may give the following directions:—

(a) Requiring further evidence with regard to the children.
(b) Require the preparation of a welfare report.
(c) Require the attendance of the parties at court.

Where the District Judge feels the court should exercise its powers with regard to any children of the family, this will not normally delay the granting of the decree absolute. However, the court does have power to direct that the decree absolute should not be made until further order, if there are exceptional circumstances which make it desirable in the interest of the child that such a direction should be made.

In the Joan Butcher divorce the District Judge will be likely to certify that he/she is satisfied that there is no need for the court to exercise its powers under the Children Act. Joan and James Butcher are not in dispute as to where the child Simon should live, nor are they in dispute over how much contact Simon should have with his father James. In line with the non-interventionist principle of the Children Act 1989, there would be no court order relating to Simon.

The Children Act attempted to replace the old fashioned idea of parental rights with a more up to date concept of Parental Responsibility. This is defined in s.3 of the Children Act as "all the rights, duties, powers, responsibilities and authority which by law a parent of a child has in relation to the child and his property." If the child's parents were married to each other at the time of that child's birth then each has parental responsibility for that child. Where the parents were not married when the child was born, then the mother has sole parental responsibility. Children whose parents marry after their birth are treated as though their parents were married at their birth. Parental responsibility can be acquired by an unmarried father, or by a non parent in various ways set out in the Act, which are outside the scope of this book. Additionally, a person with parental responsibility does not cease to have parental responsibility solely because another person subsequently acquires it. It should be noted that where more than one person has parental responsibility at the same time, he or she may act alone. A person with parental responsibility has the right to decide such matters as the child's education, any necessary medical treatment and all other aspects of the child's upbringing, provided that there is no order to the contrary.

Students should bear in mind the non-intervention principle and the welfare principle, as mentioned above. In addition, the courts are obliged to note that delay in resolving an issue may prejudice the child's welfare.

Section 8 of the Children Act defines the various orders which can be made in respect of a child. Section 8 orders are defined as orders making, varying or discharging:—

i) a residence order—this is "an order settling the arrangements to be made as to the person with whom the child is to live". This is wider than the old concept of "care and control", in that the court can now make a residence order in favour of both parents. It would usually specify closely the amount of time to be spent in each household. If, in the divorce of Andrew and Helen Smith a residence order is made in favour of Helen, this will not remove Andrew's parental responsibility in respect of their child, Simon. Both parents still have parental responsibility and can take decisions regarding the upbringing of the child without reference to the other party. Thus if Helen Smith wishes to send the child Simon to School X, she is entitled to do so and is under no obligation to consult Andrew about her decision. If Andrew objects to what she has done then he is obliged to apply to the court for a specific issue order. (See below).

ii) A contact order—this is defined as an order "requiring the person with whom the child lives, or is to live, to allow the child to visit, or stay with the person named in the order, or for that person and the child otherwise to have contact with each other."
This replaces the old concept of access. A contact order can be highly explicit and could cover an arrangement for contact by telephone call on a specific day of the week between specific times.

iii) A specific issue order—this is defined as "an order giving directions for the purpose of determining a specific question which has arisen, or which may arise, in connection any aspect of parental responsibility for a child."
This is meant to provide a parent with means to ask the court to resolve a particular problem. An example of the way this could be used is set out above, where Andrew wishes to dispute Helen's decision to send their child, Simon, to School X. If he would prefer School Y, and believes this would provide Simon with a better education, then Andrew could apply to court for a specific issue order whereupon the court would decide the matter.

(iv) A prohibited steps order—this is defined as "an order that no step which could be taken by a parent in meeting his parental responsibility for a child, and which is of a kind specified in the order, shall be taken by any person without the consent of the court."
The major use of this order is expected to be the prevention of children being removed from England and Wales. For example, if Susan and Armin separate and Susan commences divorce proceedings, she may well become concerned that Armin intends to take their son Omar to Saudi Arabia to live with his parents. To prevent this, it will be possible for Susan to obtain a prohibited steps order with a view to preventing this occurring.

Whenever the court is considering the making of, variation or discharge of a section 8 order it is obliged by the Children Act to have regard to a statutory check list which provides guidelines which are intended to help the court to apply the welfare principle. These are set out in s.1(3) of the Act. All of the above s.8 orders can be applied for by a parent or guardian or a person with a residence order. In addition, a limited number of persons will be entitled to apply for residence or contact orders only, these will be:—
(a) A spouse or ex spouse, in relation to whom the child is a child of the family or any person with whom the child has lived for at least 3 years. (A child of the family is defined as "a child of both parties and any other child, not being a child who has been boarded out with those parties by a local authority or voluntary organisation, who has been treated by both those parties as a child of their family". OR

(b) A person who has the consent of:—

i) Each person having a residence order; or
ii) the local authority, if the child is in care; or
iii) each person having parental responsibility.

It is possible for any person who is not entitled by virtue of being a number of one of the above categories, to apply to the court for leave to make an application for a s.8 order.

Child Support Act 1991

The Child Support Act 1991 deals with maintenance payments for the majority of children in the United Kingdom. Prior to the Act being passed, maintenance for children was dealt with via the courts. The Act applies to children who are under 16, and children who are under 19 and in receipt of full time education. There are limited categories of children who will be able to use the old system of obtaining maintenance through the courts. These include:—

(a) Children from wealthy families—the maximum order possible under the statutory rules set out in the Act should be obtained. A court order can then be obtained for a "top up" amount, appropriate to the substantial means available, in excess of the ceiling in the Act.
(b) Stepchildren.
(c) Children over the age of 19 who still need maintenance, (*e.g.* where the child is still in full time education).

The Act aims to reduce the demands being made upon the Social Security budget of the country by:—

(a) Single mothers with dependant children and
(b) Single parent families (resulting from marriage breakdown) with dependant children.

The Act limits the jurisdiction of the Court to award child maintenance to the exceptions listed above. As regards all other children, maintenance assessment, collection, and the enforcement of maintenance is the responsibility of the Secretary of State for Social Services who delegates the exercise of his/her functions to specially trained civil servants known as Child Support Officers (the CSO). The CSOs work through a division of the Department of Social Security (the DSS) known as the Child Support Agency. A full account of the Act and the duties of the CSO are outside the scope of this book. Briefly, the CSO will:—

(a) Deal with the tracing of absent parents.
(b) Deal with the assessment of child maintenance in accordance with the complex rules set out in the Act.
(c) Deal with the collection and enforcement of child maintenance payments.

The Act makes it clear that each parent of the qualifying child is responsible for maintaining him or her. An absent parent discharges his responsibility by paying child support maintenance in accordance with any assessment made by the CSO. The Act provides that the CSO only has jurisdiction to make an assessment for child maintenance with respect to a person who is:—

(a) A "Person with care"—defined as a person with whom the child has a home, *i.e.* with whom the child lives on a day to day basis. This person may or may not be a parent and could be a more remote relative such as a grandparent.

(b) An "Absent parent"—defined as a parent who is not living in the same household as the qualifying child (see below) who will have his or her home with the person with care.

(c) A "Qualifying Child"—defined as a child in relation to whom one or both parents are absent, (*i.e.* not living in the same household as the child).

The Act distinguishes between Persons with Care who are in receipt of state benefits, (*e.g.* income support or family credit) and those who are not. Where the Person with Care is in receipt of benefits, there is an element of compulsion in the Act requiring the Person with Care to authorise the recovery of child maintenance from the absent parent. Help must be given to trace the absent parent and there are various sanctions set out in the Act which can be used to persuade the Person with Care to assist the CSO. Where the Person with Care is not in receipt of state benefits, then there is no compulsion upon that person to pursue a claim for child maintenance.

The Butcher case study helps illustrate the workings of the Act. When Mr. Butcher leaves and Mrs. Butcher goes to the DSS to claim benefit, she will be required to authorise the Secretary of State to take action under the Act. She will be given a maintenance application form to complete and return to the child support agency. This form will ask for details of the name, date of birth and other information of use to the CSO about the absent parent. The CSO will then calculate the minimum sum considered (by reference to DSS allowance figures) to be necessary to maintain the qualifying child or children and their carer. This sum is known as the Maintenance Requirement. The Maintenance Requirement for Mrs. Butcher and Simon, based upon benefit rates as from 1992 will be as follows;

	April 1992 rates per week.
Child Allowance	£14.55
Family Premium	£ 9.30
Lone Parent Premium	£ 4.75
Adult Allowance	£42.45 +
sub total	£71.05
From this sum we now deduct Child benefit due Mrs. Butcher re Simon.	£ 9.65 −
Maintenance Requirement	£61.40

Having worked out the maintenance requirement, the CSO will calculate the assessable incomes for the absent parent and the person with care. Mrs. Butcher is on benefit, but Mr. Butcher is in employment. Once the CSO has obtained from Mr. Butcher details of his income and outgoings, the CSO will look at his gross weekly income and from this will deduct the tax he pays, his National Insurance contribution and one half of any pension payments he might make. This will give the CSO his net income. The next step is to calculate Mr. Butcher's exempt income. The regulations governing what is exempt income are extremely complex and outside the scope of this book, but, in simplified terms include the income support single persons allowance and Mr. Butcher's housing costs. Exempt income is deducted from his net income and the figure remaining would be Mr. Butcher's assessable income.

The assessable incomes of both of the parents of the child are then added together and the resulting total then divided by a figure which is at present 0.5. For example:—

Mr. Butcher—assessable income per week	£80.00
Mrs. Butcher—assessable income per week	£ 0.00
	£80.00
Divide by 0.5	=	£40.00 per week

This figure is checked against the maintenance requirement of Mrs. Butcher and Simon. If the figure is equal to, or less than, the maintenance requirement, then the assessment will be one half of the absent parents' assessable income—in the Butcher example it will be £40 per week, as explained above.

Where the CSO is dealing with low income families, a protected income calculation will be done as well, to ensure that the Absent parent is not depressed below a minimum level of income by the Maintenance Assessment Calculation. The allowances used in the calculation of protected income are more generous than the allowances available to calculate an Absent parent's assessable income. The protected income calculation should ensure that the absent parent will still have enough income (after paying maintenance) to meet their day to day needs and those of any second family they might have taken on. Day to day expenses are reflected. So if Mr. Butcher's income were found to be less than his protected level of income by for example £5.00, then the maintenance payments due in respect of Simon would be reduced from £40 by £5 to £35 per week. For the purposes of the Butcher case study, Mr. Butcher's income exceeds the protected level of income and so the maintenance assessment in respect of Simon will stand at the original figure of £40.00 per week.

Applications

The Matrimonial Causes Rules, although separate from the County Court Rules, follow a similar pattern. The main difference results from the approach to undefended divorce. Since the withdrawal of full legal aid, every effort has been made so to simplify forms and procedures so that in an uncomplicated case a petitioner can obtain a decree without legal representation. As we see, the petition and other basic forms are accompanied by explanatory material and the court staff will explain what has to be done and what forms to use. They cannot, of course, assist in form filling, but will encourage the use of solicitors' services under the Green Form Scheme for this purpose. A free booklet "Undefended Divorce" is published by H.M. Stationery Office and is handed out to petitioners who are acting in person. This can usefully be given to clients who consult a solicitor under the Green Form Scheme.

As in County Court proceedings, a great variety of applications may be made as the petition proceeds along its way to trial. The Matrimonial Causes Rules specify how each application is to be made and as in the County Court Rules there are two forms of application: *on notice* and *ex parte*. The rules specify which to use in each case and in some cases there is a prescribed form.

Applications *on notice* require the filing at the court office of two copies of the application. The court will make an appointment for a hearing, usually before the district judge, and will return one copy to the issuing party or solicitor with the appointment inserted. This then has to be served on the opposing party or parties, who can be represented or appear at the hearing. The application must be served at least two clear days before the hearing (compared with one clear day under C.C.R.) by leaving it at, or sending it to the address for service of the parties to be served or, if there is no address for service, the party's last known address. The court will need to be satisfied that the application has come to the notice of the party served and if necessary an affidavit of service must be filed.

Ex parte applications are those dealt with without involving the other parties. Most such applications must be supported by filing affidavit evidence with the application. This sets out the relevant facts and specifies the order applied for. The district judge, and in some cases the county court judge, will determine the application on the basis of the written submissions.

Whilst there is no simple rule to tell which applications are to be made on notice and which *ex parte*, it will be self-evident there are those—the great majority—in which any opposing party must be given the opportunity to be heard if he is to protect his interests in the proceedings. Such applications are, therefore, made on notice. Applications *ex parte* are appropriate, for instance, where the decision cannot adversely affect him or where it is impracticable to serve notice on him, or in cases of emergency.

Applications are, with few exceptions, heard in chambers, where counsel, solicitors and legal executives are all accorded the right of audience. Certain applications are reserved to the county court judge and some of these may have to be heard in open court where members of the Institute have the rights of audience given by the County Court (Rights of Audience) Direction 1977, but other unadmitted persons have no such rights.

Where a decision on an application is made by the district judge, any party may within five days appeal to the county court judge. Application for this purpose is made on notice and is usually heard in the judge's chambers.

All orders are drawn up and sent to the parties by the court.

Ancillary relief

The expression "ancillary relief" refers to all the orders which the court may make relating to the finances or property of the parties to a petition. The various types of long-term orders which the court may be asked to make can be seen from paragraph four of the prayer in Mrs. Butcher's petition. Broadly speaking, these orders may be summarised as follows:

(a) *Periodical payments orders*

These are orders for the payment of a weekly or monthly sum of money by one spouse to the other (or to a child who is not a qualifying child for the purposes of the Child Support Act 1991). Either party can apply subsequently at any time to vary the amount of such an order where there has been a material change in the financial circumstances of one or other of them. The right to apply for financial provision cannot be given up by any agreement between the parties and the application can be made before or after the decree absolute.

A periodical payment order for a spouse cannot take effect until decree absolute and then continues, generally speaking, until it is terminated by order of the court or by the death of one of the parties. The order automatically ceases on the remarriage of the one party in whose favour the order is made.

To obtain maintenance payments for the period between the filing of the petition and the decree absolute, application must be made for a separate order of maintenance pending suit. If granted, the order will automatically cease when the decree absolute is issued.

A secured payments order is one where the payment of the weekly or monthly amount is charged on some property of the payer, so that, if he defaults in making the payments, the payee may apply to obtain payment out of the property charged. In contrast to a straightforward order for periodical payments, a secured order can continue beyond the death of a paying spouse.

(b) *Lump sum orders*

These are orders requiring one spouse to pay to the other or to a child a lump sum of money. It is an essential feature of such orders that they can never be varied. The payer, therefore, cannot apply subsequently for repayment of any part of the lump sum. But neither can the payee apply for an increase. These are useful if a recipient has, *e.g.* an outstanding bill or debt to pay with reference to the formal matrimonial home.

(c) *Property adjustment orders*

These are orders which transfer the ownership of property (*e.g.* the matrimonial home) from one spouse or another or to a child. The court may also order that property to be held in trust for a spouse or a child. As with lump sum orders, such orders cannot subsequently be varied.

Not all these powers will be used by the court in each case. Thus, in Mrs. Butcher's case it would have been pointless for her to apply for a lump sum or property adjustment order when her husband had no capital or property that could be the subject of such an order. Nevertheless, a petitioner must be careful to ensure that she includes in the prayer in her petition a request for all the orders which she might conceivably require, since if any are omitted, the leave of the court is necessary to amend the prayer.

The question of how the court is prepared to use these powers and how it assesses the amounts of money to be paid is very complex and outside the scope of this note. An inkling as to how the amounts are assessed may, however, be gleaned from the decision of the district judge in Mrs. Butcher's case.

Decisions relating to financial and property matters are normally made by a district judge in chambers. A few weeks before the actual hearing at which the orders are made there may be in some courts a short hearing for directions before the district judge at which he gives directions as to the evidence and other matters in preparation for the subsequent hearing. In such cases, the date given by the Chief Clerk on the Notice of Intention to Proceed (Form D43) refers to the hearing at which the district judge will give directions. Once the directions given by the district judge have been complied with (*e.g.* filing further affidavits, or producing bank statements to the other party) either party may apply to the court for a further hearing date on which the court will make one or more of the ancillary relief orders. It should be noted that some County Courts prefer to issue Automatic Directions for trial at the same time as they issue the Notice of Intention to Proceed. The Automatic Directions should be served on the respondent along with the sealed copy of Form D43.

Unless the parties have agreed upon an order or there is no dispute as to the evidence, as in Mrs. Butcher's case, it is normal for the district judge to hear oral evidence from the parties and anyone else who has sworn an affidavit, so that they may be cross-examined by the other side. At the conclusion of the evidence the district judge will hear submissions about the facts or law from both parties and then will make his decision. It will be evident, therefore, that such hearing can occasionally last a considerable time especially as they involve the past and future financial position of both the spouses and the children.

The matrimonial home—occupation rights

Often, soon after the irretrievable breakdown, the respective rights of the parties in the matrimonial home assume vital importance. If the home is owner-occupied, as we have seen, the court, on granting a decree of divorce, can make a property adjustment order as to how the proprietary interests in the property, or the proceeds of sale, are to be allocated between the parties. However, for the wife it is often a basic issue of whether she can retain a roof over her head for herself and the children.

Where the house is owner-occupied (including the case where it is being bought with a mortgage advance) it may be in the name of both husband and wife or only one of them. Where as in the great majority of cases it is in the joint names, the proprietary interest of each will prevent the sale without the co-operation of the other. Where the house is in the name of one only, the Matrimonial Homes Act 1983 enables the spouse who has no estate or interest to resist eviction or exclusion from the house. If at the time of separation the party without estate or interest leaves the home the court may be prepared to make an order requiring the owner to give up possession in favour of the spouse. Where both continue in occupation pending divorce, the court will make such order as appears just with regard to the future use of the premises. Application under the Act is made to the county court (not necessarily a divorce county court). There is no limit of rateable value.

The Act also provides the means whereby the spouse who has no interest can be forewarned of any attempt by the owner to sell the property without either the agreement of that spouse or an order of the court. In the case of a house with unregistered title, this is done by registering a land charge Class F at the Land Charges Registry (see Conveyancing in Volume 1, p. 173). If the title to the property is registered, the same protection is afforded by entering a notice on the register of the property at the Land Registry. There is no need to lodge the Land or Charge Certificate.

Unfortunately these provisions will not normally prevent a mortgagee (*e.g.* a building society) from applying for an order for the sale of the house if there is default in making the mortgage payments. Where a wife is in occupation of a house being bought by her estranged husband, it may be necessary to try to persuade the building society to accept lesser payments, perhaps sufficient to cover interest only. However, the Act does provide that a spouse who has protected her statutory right of occupation by registration must be given notice of any possession proceedings.

In the case of a rented property, if there is no agreement between the parties to a divorce as to the occupation of the home, the court has power to make such order as appears to be most just for the parties and their children. If necessary a tenancy can be transferred from one party to the other, on granting the divorce.

Registration of orders in Family Proceedings (Magistrates') Court

In Mrs. Butcher's case, the district judge gave leave to register the order which he had made, in a magistrates' court. Only periodical payments orders may be registered, and the effect of registration is that the order is thereafter treated as though it had been made by the magistrates' court for the purpose of enforcing the order, varying it and collecting payments under it. Students should note that the magistrates' court, when dealing with Family matters, is now called the Family Proceedings Court.

The main advantage of this procedure is that once registered, payments under the order may be made to the magistrates' clerk who will keep a record of the payments and pay them over to the payee. If there is any default in payment the magistrates' clerk himself may take steps to enforce the order in the magistrates' court, which is obviously a great help to the payee. Moreover, where the payer has persistently defaulted, the payee may be able to "sign over" the order to the Department of Social Security who will take all payments, if any, under the order and in return will pay to the payee his or her full entitlement to benefit each week: this procedure known as the diversion procedure, is available only in respect of orders registered in, or made by, a magistrates' court.

Undefended Divorce Petition

Outline procedure—Solicitor acting

1. Instructions: including grounds; arrangements for children; ancillary relief; costs; marriage certificate.

2. Solicitor prepares and files
   · Petition (with copy for each party and the court)
   · (If children) Statement as to Arrangements for Children (MCR Form 4) with medical report (if any)
   · Certificate as to Reconciliation
   · Marriage certificate
   · Court Fee.

3. On receipt of Acknowledgment of Service (MCR 6) indicating Respondent's intention not to defend petition, solicitor prepares and files
   · Request for Directions for Trial (D84)
   · Affidavit In Support of Petition (MCR 7 (a)–(e))
   · Photocopy Acknowledgment of Service as exhibit to Affidavit.

4. A. Deputy Judge, satisfied with grounds for divorce enters matter in Special Procedure list
   · grants certificate petitioner is entitled to a decree and fixes date for pronouncement of decree nisi.

   (i) if no children, certifies that there are no children.
   (ii) if child(ren), considers whether the court needs to exercise any powers or give any directions with regard to them. If satisfied this is not necessary will issue a Certificate to that effect.
   (iii) where Petitioner has applied for costs:—
       (a) if Respondent does not object, certifies Petitioner entitled to order in terms applied for
       (b) if Respondent objects, refers application to judge to be dealt with when decree nisi granted.
   B. Deputy Judge, not satisfied
   · adjourns petition for hearing in open court by judge.

5. Arrangements for Children—Deputy Judge Certificate—as in 4(ii) OR
   · will call for
   (i) further evidence with regard to the children.
   (ii) the preparation of a welfare report.
   (iii) the attendance of the parties.
   (iv) in exceptional circumstances only the court may direct that the decree absolute is not to be granted.

6. On the day fixed in 4 above
   · pronounces decree nisi
   · (if required) makes order for costs.

7. Petitioner's solicitor gives Notice of Intention to Proceed with Application for Ancilliary Relief (MCR 13).

8. On or after 6 weeks from decree nisi
   · Solicitor makes application for decree absolute (D 36).

9. At appointment for hearing Application for Ancillary Relief
   · Deputy Judge makes order in terms considered appropriate.

MATRIMONIAL PROCEEDINGS BEFORE MAGISTRATES

The Family Proceedings courts' powers

Not all legal proceedings in relation to a marriage result in the termination of that marriage. The Family Proceedings court may make various orders in relation to a married couple and their children, but it does not have the power to end the marriage.

The court's jurisdiction in matrimonial matters is mainly to be found in the Domestic Proceedings and Magistrates' Court Act 1978. Broadly speaking, this Act empowers the court to make three types of order:

(a) *Personal protection and exclusion orders*

These are intended to deal with the consequences of matrimonial violence and enable the court to order one spouse not to molest the other or a child of the family. In addition, the court may order one spouse to leave the matrimonial home and allow the other to enter it. In each case certain conditions must be satisfied before the order may be made. Where the applicant can show imminent danger of physical injury, the court may make an expedited personal protection order (but not an exclusion order). In this case the order will have effect for up to 28 days, but in this period the applicant will have been able to apply for an ordinary protection order. An expedited order can be made even though the summons has not been served within a reasonable time before the hearing.

The power of the court to make an expedited order can be exercised by a single magistrate.

It may be noted that in the divorce court orders to the same effect as personal protection and exclusion orders are made by injunctions, which may be granted in the course of, or entirely separate from, divorce proceedings.

(b) *Orders for financial provision*

Magistrates do not have the same extensive powers in relation to the spouses' finance and property as does a divorce court. However, they can make periodical payments (*i.e.* maintenance) orders for a spouse. They also have power to order a spouse to pay the other a lump sum of up to £1000. Again, certain circumstances must be satisfied before the court may exercise these powers.

Procedure in the Family Proceedings' court

Matrimonial proceedings in a magistrates' court are commenced when a spouse or the spouse's solicitor makes an application to a magistrate or to a clerk to the justices. An example of such a complaint in which Mrs. Case, a client of Messrs. Makepiece, applies for a personal protection order and an exclusion order, as set out on p. 280. The form of application is usually signed at the court by the applicant and the court may then issue the application requiring the respondent to appear on a stated day before the court for the hearing at which the court will decide whether or not to make the order requested. The applicant takes two copies of the form to court. The top copy is kept by the court and the other copy is sealed and given or sent back to the applicant for service on the respondent. The hearing date must not be later than 14 days from receipt of the application. The application and notice of the courts powers are served on the respondent at least 1 day before the date fixed. At or before the hearing, the applicant must file a statement as to service. Before the hearing the parties must file and serve written statements of the oral evidence they intend to rely on. Examples of the application for a family protection order and notice are set out on pp. 280–281.

The hearing before the magistrates is, strictly speaking, a "domestic proceeding" and this has three main consequences:

(i) The public are not allowed into the court-room and press reporting is restricted;
(ii) The court must comprise not more than three magistrates who should include, if possible, both a man and a woman;
(iii) The proceedings should, so far as possible, be separated from any other business of the court.

The applicant may address the court and then call evidence. Normally, the respondent will then call evidence in rebuttal. At the conclusion of the evidence the respondent may then address the court, if he has not done so earlier. The magistrates, advised on questions of law by their clerk, will then make their decision.

Set out on p. 281–283 is a personal protection and exclusion order. It will be seen that in certain circumstances the court may attach a power of arrest to the order, authorising a police officer to arrest the respondent if he has reasonable cause to suspect a breach of the order. In order to attach such a power of arrest the magistrates must be satisfied that the respondent has physically injured the complainant and is likely to do so again. The final order must be served on the parties.

IN THE COUNTY OF BARSETSHIRE
DIVISION OF BARSET

APPLICATION FOR A FAMILY PROTECTION ORDER
(Domestic Proceedings and Magistrates Courts Act 1978, s.16)

BARSET FAMILY PROCEEDINGS COURT

Date	:	12 January 1994
Respondent	:	RICHARD CASE
of	:	19 WESTGATE AVE, BARSET BARSETSHIRE
The application of:		BRENDA CASE
of	:	(See note at bottom of this page)
		19 WESTGATE AVE, BARSET BARSETSHIRE
Tel	:	

Who being the spouse of the respondent, applies for a Family Protection Order under s.16 of the Domestic Proceedings and Magistrates' Courts Act 1978 on the grounds shown in PART A and/or PART B below.

PART A—Leave this part in if an order prohibiting violence or threats of violence is sought under s.16(2), otherwise delete it.

The respondent has used or threatened to use violence against the person of [*the applicant] [*and] [*a child(ren) of the family] and it is necessary for the protection of [*the applicant] [*and] [*a child(ren) of the family] that an order be made.

PART B—Leave this part in if an order requiring the respondent to leave the matrimonial home or prohibiting the respondent from entering it is sought under s.16(3), otherwise delete it. ALSO, delete any (1), (2), and (3) below which do not apply, but at least one must apply.

---

(1) The respondent has used violence against the person of [*the applicant] [*and] [*a child(ren) of the family].

(2) The respondent has threatened to use violence against the person of [*the applicant] [*and] [*a child(ren) of the family].

(3) The respondent has, in contravention of an order that he shall not use, or threaten to use violence against the person of [*the applicant] [*and] [*a child(ren) of the family] made under subsection (2) of the above-mentioned s.16, threatened to use violence against the person or [*the applicant] [*and] [*a child(ren) of the family].

AND [*the applicant] [*and] [*a child(ren) of the family] is/are in danger of being physically injured by the respondent (or would be in such danger if [*the applicant] [*and] [*child(ren) of the family] were to enter the matrimonial home.

*Delete those words in square brackets which do not apply.

NOTE: If you are concerned about giving your address, you may give an alternative address where papers can be served. However, you must notify the court of your actual address. You may give your telephone number if you wish to do so.

PART C—Leave this part in if you are applying for an expedited Family Protection Order of the type mentioned in PART A overleaf, otherwise delete it. An expedited order can in an urgent case be made ex parte (which in effect, means without giving notice to the respondent) where the court is satisfied that there is imminent danger of physical injury to the applicant or a child of the family. Such an order lasts until the full hearing of the application commences, up to a maximum of 28 days. There is no provision in s.16 allowing the court to make an expedited order of the type mentioned in PART B overleaf.

~~I apply in accordance with rule 3(4) of The Family Proceedings Courts (Matrimonial) Proceedings Rules 1991 for leave to make an ex parte application for an expedited order.~~

~~I apply for an expedited Family Protection Order under s.16(2) and (6) because there is imminent danger of physical injury to [*the applicant] [*and] [*a child(ren) of the family].~~

My solicitor's address for service (if applicable) is

Philip Friendly
Makepiece & Streiff
Bank Chambers
Barset
Barsetshire.

I declare that the information I have given is correct and complete to the best of my knowledge.

Signed **Brenda Case**   Date   12th January 1994

What you (the applicant) must do next:—

1. Fill in your name in the appropriate box on the Notice of (Hearing) (Directions Appointment).

2. Take or send this form to the court with an extra copy for the respondent to be served. The top copy will be kept by the court and the other copy given or sent back to you for service.

3. You must then serve that copy of the form on the respondent according to the rules.

COUNTY OF BARSETSHIRE

DIVISION OF BARSET

FAMILY PROTECTION ORDER

BARSET FAMILY PROCEEDINGS COURT

Date   : **28 January 1994**

Respondent   : RICHARD CASE

Address   : 19 WESTGATE AVE, BARSET BARSETSHIRE

Applicant   : BRENDA CASE

Address   : 19 WESTGATE AVENUE, BARSET BARSETSHIRE

Substance of Application	: That the Respondent has used, or threatened to use, violence against the person of the Applicant (~~or a child of the family~~).

(or)

~~That the Respondent has threatened to use violence against the person of the Applicant (or a child of the family) and has used violence against some other person.~~

(or)

~~That in contravention of an order made for the protection of the applicant (or a child of the family) the respondent has threatened to use violence against the person of the applicant (or a child of the family). (Section 16 of the Domestic Proceedings and Magistrates' Courts Act 1978).~~

Orders	: The application is granted and it is ordered that (delete where applicable)
Personal Protection Orders	(The Respondent shall not use, or threaten to use, violence against the person of the Applicant) ~~or against the Person of~~ .... ~~being a child/children of the Family~~ and that the respondent shall not incite or assist any other person to use, or threaten to use, violence against the person of the applicant (~~or against the person of the said child/children~~).
Exclusion Orders	(The Respondent shall leave (not enter) ....19 Westgate Avenue, Barset Barsetshire.... being the matrimonial home (and that the respondent shall permit the Applicant to enter and remain therein).
Where the Order is not an expedited order	(This Order shall take effect on **29 January 1974** and shall expire on **29 April 1994**).
Where the Order is an expedited Personal Protection Order	~~(This order shall take effect (on the date when (.... days after)~~ notice of the making of the Order is served on the Respondent and shall expire on the 10 February 1994 (being 28 days after the date on which this Order is made) or on the date of the commencement of the hearing, in accordance with the provisions of Part 11 of the Magistrates' Courts Act 1980, of the application ~~whichever occurs first.~~
Costs	~~And it is ordered that the Respondent pay costs of £..... to the Applicant forthwith (by weekly/monthly instalments of £.....) (not later than the .....day of .... 19.....).~~

BY ORDER OF THE COURT

Justices' Clerk   Justice of the Peace

(FOR POWER OF ARREST, IF GRANTED, SEE OVERLEAF)

IF YOU DISOBEY THIS ORDER YOU COULD BE SENT TO PRISON FOR UP TO TWO MONTHS OR ORDERED TO PAY UP TO £2,000.

~~When the order is an expedited Order.~~ This is a temporary order only and has been made because the Applicant has satisfied the court that there is imminent danger of physical injury to the Applicant or (a) child(ren) of the family. Before an ordinary non-expedited Order is made you will be able to be present in court and explain your side of the matter.

~~ENDORSEMENT OF EXPEDITED ORDER.~~

This Order was served on the Respondent on .... and (took effect on ~~that date) (will take effect on ....).~~

Clerk to the Court

(Power of Arrest
attached to
Family Protection
Order.

POWER OF ARREST ~~GRANTED~~* NOT GRANTED*
*delete where applicable

~~The court, having made an Order under Section 16 of the Domestic Proceedings~~
and Magistrates' Courts Act 1978, which provides that the Respondent:

a) shall not use violence against the person of the Applicant,
    or

b) shall not use violence against the person of ....   (delete any
    ....   provision
    .... being the child(ren)   which is
    of the family or,   inapplicable)

c) shall not enter ....
    .... being the matrimonial home.

and being satisfied that the Respondent had physically injured (the Applicant)
(a) child(ren) of the family and considering that he/she is likely to do so again, a
power of arrest is attached to the provision(s) mentioned at a)/b)/c) above.

A CONSTABLE MAY ARREST without Warrant a person whom he has
reasonable cause for suspecting or being in breach of any such provision as is
mentioned at a)/b)/c) above, by reason of that person's use of violence, or, as
the case may be, his/her entry into the matrimonial home.

(Justice of the Peace)

(ON AN EXPEDITED ORDER THE POWER OF ARREST SHALL NOT
TAKE EFFECT UNTIL THE FAMILY PROTECTION ORDER HAS
BEEN SERVED ON THE RESPONDENT. THE POWER OF ARREST
WILL EXPIRE IN ANY EVENT ON
~~THE ...... DAY OF .... 19.....~~

INDEX